"A typical English understatement.
It's wonderful."

Alma & David. Dec. 1996.

ENGLAND
AND
THE ENGLISH

Dmitri Kasterine

ENGLAND AND THE ENGLISH

WORLD'S WORK LTD

The Windmill Press   Kingswood   Tadworth   Surrey

For Cathy, Alexander and Caroline

Black and white prints made by Richard Dawkins

Text and photographs © 1981 by Dmitri Kasterine
Made and printed in Great Britain by William Clowes (Beccles) Limited, Beccles and London
SBN 437 08050 1

Contents

Introduction 7

Wherever 9

Jaunts 12

Assignments 15

Bathing 19

Weddings 23

Encounters 26

The photographs 33

Introduction

I wanted to show the beauty of the English countryside but without including too many popular spots. I wanted to find humour and tenderness in the photographs of people, and also oddness, and peculiarities. My photographic assignments have nearly always been of subjects that were political, fashionable or in some sense having an argumentative issue attached to them. I wanted to photograph more private subjects, those without controversy or cause, subjects where the mood or the shape or the expression was their most important aspect: non-essentials as television documentary producers call them.

The book was born, so to speak, in August 1978, when I drove down to Brighton to see a man who reads Tarot cards. He lives in a narrow street of shabby two-storey houses. I pressed the bell of number seventeen and after a very long wait a middle-aged man in grubby clothes and bedroom slippers asked me in.

He talked about my work. He said he thought it had mostly been done for other people; advertising agencies, and magazines that issued strong editorial directives, with the result that I had been led away from my true feelings of how I saw things. "Get back to these," he urged me.

This spurred me to remember the various ideas I had brooded on in the past, or had even begun to carry out only to put aside for fee-paying work. For a long time I had been photographing people and places that interested me as I travelled the country on my assignments. Why not, I thought, go on with this, but with a more concentrated and deliberate effort, by making special trips to parts of England that I like?

I could not, and actually did not want to cover all England. My preferences have always been for the North and for country and suburbs rather than towns. I found a lot of typical England on my doorstep in Putney. Occasionally, as I sat in the garden or whilst discussing the book with my children, I thought of some specific subject, but mostly *England and the English* is a personal look at the country, with scenes of life that I came across as I drove around and had a compulsion to photograph.

May 1981

Wherever

I made several special trips to various parts of England during the course of making this book. One of them was to the coast of Norfolk between Wells and Cromer. I'd already been there to do some stills for a film that the BBC were making about life in a Russian prison camp. I remember being struck then by the dullness of the landscape.

I drove up and down and around and couldn't see anything. It was exactly as I remembered it; a desolate place of miles of mud. It is a terribly long drive from London. No sooner are you there, than you are spoiling what little time there is left of the weekend by dreading the journey home.

Travelling further along the coast, I found two reed-cutters. Their cars were parked on a track leading from the main road towards the sea. The gate at the entrance to the track said 'BIRD SANCTUARY – KEEP OUT'. I parked my car behind the other two, grabbed my camera and walked the 3–400 yards to where I heard some dogs barking. Odd, I thought, for dogs to be anywhere near a bird sanctuary. I turned left and crossed a ditch with a plank over it. Two spaniels leaped about in the reeds howling and barking. I pushed through the reeds and came to a clearing where two men in white smocks were picking up bundles of reeds, tying them and stacking them.

Watching them was, of all people, a photographer. We greeted each other. I asked the reed-cutters if I could take some photographs of them, telling them that it was for a book about England. They said yes, certainly I could. The other photographer turned out to be a friend of theirs who was a keen amateur. Relief – I don't like working in front of other professionals.

But it was much worse than being with another professional. He stood a yard behind me and took everything that I did, using a camera with a very noisy shutter. I had to tell him it was a bit distracting; would he mind having his turn when I had gone?

He said, "No, of course, quite understand, sorry," and walked away to sit on a bundle of reeds and stare at me, which was as bad.

Fortunately he didn't affect the reed-cutters. They continued their work quite unselfconsciously. One of them is pictured on page 92. They were both fishermen by trade, but there was now so little to fish that they had decided to diversify. They had bought the plot of reeds two years ago and it was doing very well they said.

"Is it a bird sanctuary as well?" I asked.

"No, we put up that notice to keep people away."

I stopped three miles on along the coast, at Blakeney. It was a sunny, windless winter's morning. A few boats were lying at tipsy angles at their moorings in the low tide.

"The harbour's silting up," said a deeply-lined, middle-aged man leaning on his bike in the middle of the road. He paused, staring at the mud.

"Nobody bothers about it. There were seventy-five cars here last Sunday. Parked all along here. I counted them. People just looking. At what?"

Another pause. "And the seals have got all the fish. They lie out on the end of the point, hundreds of them. People want to see the damn things. I don't see any reason for them. As I say, they've eaten all the fish." I wandered away and headed back towards Norwich, leaving him still bemoaning life.

I reached Cromer. It was evening – the wind had got up. Shall I stay here, at the hotel, or should I go on down to Gillingham where I was expected by friends of friends? My friends had said something about babies everywhere, but then I remembered I had stayed at this hotel before and was unimpressed by the bed and breakfast. In the end I decided to go to Gillingham and risk the pile of nappies that might be in the bath.

I arrived at seven. There *were* babies; *and* cats, *and* dogs. But the babies were dealt with swiftly and I was left in peace in a comfortable armchair reading the *Norwich Evening News* with the dogs at my feet, while John and Patricia changed from their hunting clothes for dinner. (Hunting in Norfolk? Harriers, I discovered.)

Damn, why hadn't I bought this paper myself earlier in the day and seen what's on in Norwich? I read: Cromer Community Centre – Agoraphobics – Visiting Psychiatrists. I would have loved to have gone to that and seen how many people turned up. And if no one had, I could have gone on to the Ballroom and Latin American Dancing Classes (Intermediate) or to the club night for single over-25s at the Mischief Tavern.

Patricia's sister Beatrice joined us for dinner. She was married to a surgeon who was, as usual, working late. I mentioned how irritating I find it when people ask me what is the best camera, or what do I think is the matter with their camera, why doesn't so-and-so do it like that, and will it be very expensive to mend.

"Yes," Beatrice said. "Just the same with Michael. He is always being asked by people at cocktail parties what he thinks a recurring pain in the stomach is. Or they grasp Michael's hand and press it against a lump in their leg, asking 'what do you think this is?' "

Beatrice told me that Michael's patients shower him with bottles of whisky in gratitude for his services. (I suppose she means the successful services.) Neither Michael nor Beatrice like whisky. They had cases of it lying around in their flat. Although they could get rid of a lot to their friends, they still had a vast stock. Then they hit on the idea of taking it to the local off-licence. They sold it at a small discount and bought wine instead. Then everyone was happy.

Next morning I walked the length of the drive to collect the paper out of the short length of drainpipe. I was given superb scrambled eggs and coffee before starting my journey back to London by way of the Fens. Everywhere I looked there were straight lines. Lines of winter wheat showing vivid green against the jet black soil. Lines of poplars, of ditches and the line of the road itself. I looked for an interesting combination. I thought I had found one – it's reproduced on page 120 – but it wasn't until I looked at the transparency later that I realised I had been too absorbed with the patterns of lines to notice how dull was the sky.

I saw a man fishing grass out of a ditch with a sickle on the end of an eight-foot handle. He said that the machine had been along clearing the ditches, but it didn't do the job properly. It left bits everywhere which then fell back into the ditch and clogged it up. The council employed this man to finish the job. He was the last of six men originally employed by the council to look after the ditches. They all started with the council at the same time, thirty-seven years ago. The others were now dead or retired.

"They keep me on just to clear up after the machine."

I asked if I could take his picture.

"It's not for the press is it? This is classed as an offensive weapon," he said, waving his long-handled sickle about.

"When the machines came in, they thought there was no more use for these. But it's the only tool for the job. They want the place tidied up so they turn a blind eye."

"The photograph is for a book about England," I said.

"That's all right. I don't mind."

Page 93 shows the result.

Standing on the steep slope of the four-foot-wide ditch he cast his sickle at half submerged clumps of grass, bringing stuff out at every attempt. After working at several points up and down the ditch he looked at his watch. It was quarter past three and time to be going home for his tea, he said. He swung the sickle over his shoulder, together with his scythe, and set off on his bike, steering with one hand. A strong wind blew but he rode steadily. I noticed that he steered with his right hand, but the bell was fixed on the left handlebar.

I wondered if the council's public liability policy covered them if he was knocked by a car or wobbled in a strong gust of wind and sliced off the head of a passer-by.

Jaunts

Our destination was Yorkshire. For the picnic, I made tomato and watercress sandwiches from crusty new bread, thickly cut, with plenty of butter and salt and pepper. I also packed bits of roast chicken covered in home-made mayonnaise and rosemary, chocolate cake, fruit cake, cheddar cheese, a bottle of water, a thermos of tea and one of coffee – enough for myself and Caroline, my companion. The purpose of our visit was to take more photographs for this book and to see Caroline's father, the Brigadier, now retired from the army after long service and a man of immense good humour and gentleness.

I wondered what Caroline would be like on the trip. Would she sigh or yawn, hurry me or flinch when I drove fast?

No – she read her book, stretched her legs, soothed, spotted things and remained calm when I drove onto the verge or narrowly missed another car while looking at the passing landscape.

All the time I'm on the road I'm looking; not for anything in particular, just looking; alert and waiting; driving; heading for likely places. A picture can appear almost anywhere, so not too much planning. Just going along, awake, seeing – sometimes for a morning, or a whole day or even two. Nothing stands out so far, nothing I haven't seen before, nothing that sends a cold shiver down my back. Then, I see it! There it is . . . there! I swerve, brake, stop, burst out of the car, fling up the boot, haul out the gear and take it. Click, click, lots of clicks, different exposures, slightly different angle. Yes. The feeling. Without it, nothing; just a record. There, done it. No . . . . better from over there, maybe. Scramble, climb, jump. Yes. Terrific! Got it. The tension subsides – it's in the bag – rarely does anything go wrong in the processing, so I can count on a usable picture.

This is roughly what goes through my mind when I see a picture I want. The hurry to get it may be just excitement, or that the light is right and a cloud may come over at any moment and spoil it. The subject may not be a landscape of course, but the excitement is there, just the same – I may see someone leaning, sitting or walking in an odd fashion. Or they may be working at something quite normal, but doing it in an unusual way, or with great concentration. They may just have a marvellous face or peculiar clothes.

Caroline and I did several of these weekend photographic trips during the summer of 1979 and we tried to arrange places to stay before we left. On Monday evening, armed with *Farm Holiday Guide*, we would telephone the establishment with the most enticing description in the area we wanted to visit, and book for the following weekend. "Do you have cotton sheets?" was our only question if there was a vacancy. We had been caught with nylon sheets in Devon one night when we'd left our booking to the last minute.

Breakfast is normally served at eight forty-five at Bed and Breakfasts, and often we found we were the last down. We would enter the dining room, which becomes the landlady's front room between breakfast and the evening meal at six, to be greeted by a cheery "Good morning, did you sleep well?" from the landlady. The other guests nod as we pass by, and continue eating. Conversation, such as it is, is carried out at a volume only slightly above a whisper. Sometimes we would share a table with another couple who murmur good morning and push a colossal packet of cornflakes at us followed by an equally large bowl of granulated sugar and a jug of milk. We sit listening to ourselves pouring, sprinkling and crunching. And listening to the others clinking, scraping, tinkling, munching and whispering.

"Tea or coffee?" The landlady's voice booms across. It sounds so loud she might be on a parade ground yelling at recruits compared to our hushed tones.

"Both like a cooked breakfast would you?"

"Yes please," we say, barely audible.

Papers do not get delivered to Bed and Breakfasts so after the cereal bowls have been removed there is nothing to do before the egg, bacon, sausage and tomato arrive. Conversation can be tried.

"Is this your first time in these parts?"

"Oh no, we come every year. Is that your Citroen GS in the drive? Very heavy on petrol I hear."

And so on, listing places to see, hills to climb, routes to take and other makes of car that give you better mpg.

Our neighbours finish their cooked breakfast, go on to the toast, butter and golden shred and then excuse themselves. The room has emptied. We are still talking as if we are in church.

"Enjoy your meal?" the landlady asks, shattering the quiet.

One weekend we drove through the Dales, I remember. On a narrow road we saw a shop with the simple sign 'Grocer'. We stopped to have a look. The shop was reached through a rickety gate, up some steps, and through a door under a wooden porch. A tall man, who walked with a slow regular step came out of the shop. He was dressed in a black suit. A gold watch chain ran from one waistcoat pocket, through a button hole across his stomach, to the other pocket. He crossed the road to join his friend who was leaning over a wall looking into the river. His friend, also dressed in heavy clothes (it was a scorching June day) and thick leather boots, and pictured on page 47, grunted and shifted his position slightly as the other approached. They both stared into the river and smoked. I went over to them carrying my camera and tripod.

"I wonder if I could take a picture of you," I asked.

"If you want to – we don't mind," they replied, surprised, I thought, at being considered a suitable subject. They turned around and leant on the wall facing the road. I extended the legs of the tripod, loaded the camera and screwed in onto the base of the tripod. They remained leaning on the wall making an occasional remark to one another or to Caroline. I clicked away from this distance and that and occasionally they shifted their position to a more comfortable one. Mostly they stared ahead and looked into the camera totally unselfconsciously, observing the silence. When I stage-directed them, or told them how good they were looking, they reacted by becoming stiff and embarrased. But they soon settled back into their natural poses. It was best when I just looked at them and they looked back. They were shepherds having a day off they told us.

Assignments

During that same summer of 1979 Caroline and I made several trips to the tiny Oxfordshire village of Great Tew. I also went a number of times alone as I was doing an article about it for the American edition of the German magazine *Geo*. Thirty years ago Great Tew was a model village. Its sixteenth- and seventeenth-century cottages were well-maintained. The huge old yews were clipped and shaped. The gardens were perfectly tended and the village green was scythed every week of the summer. Great Tew won prizes as England's best-kept and most attractive village. About 1950, the village and the 3,000-acre estate and the house pictured on page 71 were inherited by a retired Major in the Coldstream Guards.

Over the years, the village changed completely. As fewer people were needed on the estate, some of the houses became vacant and were left to fall down. The major's policy was not to change the character of the village. He wanted no weekenders or well-off outsiders to buy the houses, restore and possibly alter them. Eventually about a quarter of the cottages fell into ruins. Roses, honeysuckle and meadow willowherbs swamped them. The council stepped in and insisted that repairs and rebuilding be carried out, in order to preserve the village from complete disintegration. Consequently a number of the houses were sold.

Arriving in the village knowing nobody, I knocked on the door of the vicarage. (The pub was being restored otherwise that might have been a good starting point.) The vicar, Father John, a tall handsome man with grey hair and a pipe, came to the door. I explained what I was doing and I asked if I could take his picture. He vaguely rejected me. I stood my ground like a good door-to-door salesman and described the quality of my wares. He led the way to his study, apologising for the mess. Then he did actually say, "Do take a pew". A television crew, he explained, had come down to photograph the village, but he had refused them permission to film in the church. Undeterred, they had put up their lights just before the service and started filming as Father John entered the church. He told them to stop. They could stay for the service if they liked and then film the congregation leaving. They agreed and switched off their lights. Half way through the sermon they switched them on again and began to film. Father John stopped in mid-sentence and with a great sweep of his arm cried "Get out!" As a result of this incident Father John was loath to have anything more to do with the press. However, he agreed to let me follow him round on his calls, and the picture on page 70 is one of the many I took of him.

The next morning we met at ten-thirty. He was dressed in his cassock and carried a shepherd's crook and had some calls to make in Little Tew. We drove the two miles. He told me on the way that he would rather not say that I was taking photographs for a magazine but to introduce me as a visiting friend of his. We stopped in the middle of Little Tew, also a very small place with just one shop, but no church. A dormobile was parked there with half a dozen pensioners sitting in it having coffee and biscuits provided by the council and run by some of the local ladies.

They obviously all adored Father John, who sat on the floor at the entrance to the dormobile, his crook tucked between his legs, making jokes, telling stories – and not paying too much attention to their complaints and troubles. When we left he stooped at the door of the vehicle, stretched his long arm out over them and said, "Bless you my dears."

Next we went to see a young mother with four children who was troubled about having missed church the previous Sunday through being too tired and too busy. After that we saw an old lady living alone who complained a very great deal about her physical ailments. Father John sat on her bed with her and listened affably and said prayers with her. This was followed by a visit to a very ancient but spry lady living with her daugher in a large house. There we drank sherry.

The following day we met again. He suggested we drop in on a couple called Peter and Rosemary, also living in Little Tew. He is a writer, left wing and Jewish and something of a wag. She was born and brought up in Switzerland and is now a literary agent. Rosemary gave us coffee made from beans ground there and then and chocolate cake she'd made herself. Father John loved being in their company. I saw them on several occasions afterwards when they gave me delicious meals.

I asked Father John why he didn't go into Great Tew itself much. He replied, "There are too many of *them* there." *Them* are the worshippers of Pan and closely connected with black magic. During his nine years at Great Tew Father John believes that on several occasions black magic services were held in his church. He felt it would weaken their effect if he blessed black magic symbols and hung them in the church. He called it "applying our own positive force".

There was one occasion, however, when it didn't work. Two tough young men from the village volunteered one night to guard an exhibition of tapestries being held in the church. They took their sleeping bags and Father John locked them in. He returned at midnight with a thermos of coffee and some sandwiches for them. As he approached the church he heard a tremendous battering. As he got closer he realised it was the young men hammering on the door of the church. He quickly unlocked the door and to his astonishment found the two men, on their knees, cowering and whimpering. They had been terrified out of their wits by an inexplicable bad feeling in the church.

The reason given by the villagers for Father John not going into Great Tew very much is that soon after he arrived in the parish he entered the pub one Sunday morning armed with a dozen hymn books, handed them around to the villagers and asked them to join him in some hymn singing!

Wherever I went in the village I used to meet Rita. She had most to say and the most time to spare. Her reaction to almost anything I said was to shake with delight, accompanied by a high pitched, drawn out 'oooh'. She always carried her gall stones in a jar with her and almost every time we met she asked me if I wanted to have a look at them. One day she could bear my refusals no longer. She whipped them out of her bag and, with eyes gleaming, rattled them in front of my face before I knew what had happened. They sounded like marbles. Sadly, in the end Rita and I fell out. Her husband refused to let me photograph them having their Sunday lunch because I had been caught lying in wait in the Major's shrubbery, hoping to snatch a picture of the Major on his return from his walk. (The magazine had insisted that I should get one and I felt I had to try.)

Rita had seen me hiding there on her way down to the shop. She had been unable to restrain herself and it was around the village in a flash that I was lurking in the Major's grounds. Before I knew it I was flushed out by a posse of his men, armed with pitchforks, and slung out. Actually I wanted the photograph of Rita and her husband much more than one of the Major, but the truth was that I was enjoying the hunt and I would have shot my prey had I not let Rita see me.

During my various visits to Great Tew I spent a good deal of time at a farmhouse, wandering in for cups of tea or to watch the children help their father on the farm. Jack one of the estate's tenant farmers, and Shirley, have thirteen children and fourteen grandchildren, the eldest of which is older than their youngest child. From the age of eight each child takes it in turn to help their father with the milking. Jack's father was tenant before him. He bred champion herds. Every beam in the cow shed is covered by faded red, blue and yellow certificates for prizes won in shows. The writing is no longer legible on most, but they go back to the early thirties.

I suppose I must have met nearly every one of the seventy-five or so inhabitants of Great Tew and photographed a good number of those. One of them was the handsome young butcher with flashing blue eyes. He wears black shirts off duty and has a sense of the macabre.

"Someone has just paid £30,000 for that wreck next door," he said. "I wonder if they know that the last two owners hung themselves there!"

Then I spent a day out in the fields with Jack the hedger. He still has his gloves made from sealskin (very much in evidence in his photograph on page 36), because they are the toughest. Jack is also the village grave-digger. He lives with his brother Tom. They say that Tom was a brilliant schoolboy, but that his early promise vanished, and he never worked. He stays at home all day, except to go once in the morning and once in the evening to draw his water from the village tap on the green.

Most people enjoyed having their picture taken and nearly always asked for copies, which I gave them. Margaret, the shepherd's wife, posed for a photograph sitting at a table in her front room making corn dollies. A side of home-cured bacon hung on the wall behind her. She said that it is getting very hard to find the long straws needed for corn dollies because so few farmers have a reaper and binder working now.

"I usually manage to pinch a little straw from the thatcher when he comes."

There was one working at Great Tew during one of my visits. He was a very young man who had qualified under a government training scheme.

The village shop is owned by a man and his wife from Birmingham. One day I asked him where the builders were who had erected the scaffolding around the school-house chimney. I told him I thought I could get a good picture of the village from the top of it. But he made it pretty clear that he didn't care for me or my photographs. I discovered from the people who were living in the school-house for the holidays that the builders had come two weeks before, put up the scaffolding and hadn't been seen since.

I climbed the scaffolding, without permission, and saw what a good picture of the village could be taken from the top – if it weren't for the cars in the street. Everybody moved their cars except for the shop keeper. However, some weeks later when I went back to the village he allowed me to take a picture of the shop. I wondered why he had changed his tune. Perhaps someone had shown him the pictures I had done of them and he had thought he'd like one too.

Bathing

I drove all the way to Northumberland to photograph dramatic winter landscapes, but came back with only the picture of nude male bathers on page 57 and of reflections of the bare branches of trees in a pool on pages 34–5. The drama was hidden in mist and cloud.

I stayed at a hotel in Bamburgh. There was a chill to the place as you walked in. The proprietor led me down an icy corridor and unlocked the door at the end of it. The room was degrees colder than the corridor.

The proprietor told me that it wouldn't take a minute to warm up, as he bent down to switch on a small convector heater. This gave a lurid orange light, but hardly any heat. I thought that perhaps by after dinner the heater would have taken the chill off the room. I raced down to dinner not bothering to unpack. It was cold in the dining room too, and I shocked the waitress by asking her to warm up the wine by putting it in a bucket of lukewarm water. The bottle was as cold as everything else in the hotel.

The heater had not taken the chill off the room by the time dinner was over. The temperature in the room was now about the same as in the corridor. Nor had the room got any warmer an hour later as I lay shivering in bed. The heater was just not up to it. It was fighting a losing battle. Action had to be taken. I got out of bed and dressed in vest, long pants and pyjamas. Then I lay my anorak on the bottom sheet and got back into bed. I slept quite well.

In the morning, as I stood at the basin, I looked back at the bed and noticed a white cord running down from the mattress to the skirtingboard. A 13 amp plug was attached to the end of the cord. I hadn't thought to look, and the proprietor hadn't told me.

Two girls in their late twenties, one tall and the other square arrived at breakfast. They were teachers from a school for backward children in the Lake District. It was their half term and they were trying to "get away from it all". They loved the miles of empty beaches and the fishing villages where you saw nobody at this time of year except the locals.

We drove out to the beach in our separate cars and walked along the white sand against the biting wind. The girls had a Jack Russell terrier that had spent the night in the car. I took a photograph of the two girls dressed in their identical and matching knitted hats and scarves. The ragged edge of the sand dunes ran on for miles.

They walked on along the beach while I scrambled up into the sand dunes. From the top I saw two orange tents lurking in a hollow. Three girls and four men stood around drinking coffee and eating cornflakes. This was one of their reunions, they said. They had been at Newcastle University together and twice a year they went camping.

"Only in the winter?" I asked.

"Sometimes in the summer," they replied, laughing.

The tents seemed very small. They must have been warmer than I was last night. One of the men was despatched to fetch sea water for the washing up. This included last night's spaghetti bolognese which had hardened on the saucepans and plates.

"You should have been here earlier. Mike and Dave went for a swim, naked!"

I said, "Would you go in again so I can take a picture of you?"

"No," they shivered. Then one of them said: "Come back in the morning about nine. We might go in again then."

I said I probably would.

The teachers and their dog were making their way back along the sand and we returned to our cars together. I liked their company and asked them where they were going to spend that night, but it was somewhere too far away for me to be back at the beach for the morning swim.

We said goodbye and I walked towards my car fishing in my pockets for my keys. I couldn't find them. I plunged my hands into each pocket in turn, scrabbling about trying to feel the long thin shape of the keys among the roundness of lenses, and film canisters. I searched through every pocket three or four times not believing that they weren't somewhere there. But they weren't. I must have locked them in the car. To make matters worse, it began to snow.

The most likely explanation I could think of was that I had locked the front door with the key, reached into the back to find something in my camera bag and dropped my keys in the process. Then I locked the back door from the inside and slammed the door shut.

This, I thought was where I spend the weekend; until the Citroen garage in Newcastle 56 miles away opens on Monday. I wondered what the AA would suggest. The two girls gave me a lift back to the hotel. "You need Robert. He can get into anything," the proprietor said, drawing a map of the way to Robert's house. It wasn't far, but Robert was out. Robert's wife stood on the doorstep, with snow billowing into the house, telling me that Robert was out on a job but should be back at lunchtime.

"But I'm not sure he can get into Citroens. Fords yes. Any model of Ford he can get into."

I felt very angry that Citroens weren't his speciality, and after telling his wife that I would wait for him at the hotel, I trudged back through the snow.

Robert wasn't long. He turned up in a perfectly kept ten-year-old Ford Escort. The interior was as spotless as a hospital ward, with fitted patterned carpets in the floor of the front seats. Robert was bald and unsmiling. He explained that Fords always had a gap somewhere, where you could slide through a piece of wire with an eye on the end of it. You hooked the eye over the plunger door lock and raised it.

"Don't know about Citroens though."

I thought: No, blast them, the doors and windows fit far too well.

As we were setting off from the hotel I saw a car similar to mine drawing up. I went across to the driver. "Do you think, by any chance at all, your key will fit my car?" I asked, explaining that I had locked my keys in my car.

"I doubt it," the driver said cheerfully, "but we'll go and try if you like." His keys didn't fit my locks, which was in a way rather reassuring. Neither was there a space for Robert to push his wire through. "Boot locked?" asked the Citroen owner, whose name was Steve.

"Of course, I've got most of my photographic equipment in it."

"Pity, might have been able to take out the bulkhead between the boot and the back seat, and reach for the keys through a gap in the arm-rest."

He seemed to know all about it.

We wandered around the car hoping that an idea would come to us. I put my thumb on the bootlock and pressed, just in case. The lock yielded and I flung up the door of the boot with a grin. The equipment was in its place. We removed it all and undid the screws holding the bulkhead between the boot and back seat. Then Steve, who had taken charge, borrowed Robert's wire, climbed into the boot and pushed down the arm-rest. He slid his hand through the gap, but could not quite reach into the bag. He groped around for the keys on the back seat but drew a blank.

I began to think; supposing the keys aren't there at all. What then? However, with Robert's wire Steve could reach the handle of the back door, using the same means of entry – through the gap between the arm-rest and the back seat. It was only a second or two before he had hooked the handle and there was a delicious and familiar click as the catch went.

I delved into the bag as soon as I had pulled open the door, and felt for the keys. I heard them clink as I moved a lens. How marvellous – there they were. I held them up triumphantly.

Robert charged me £1 for the hire of the wire; Steve was very happy to have been of such help and accepted some coffee with his family back at the hotel.

I did return to the campers at nine the following morning, after spending another night at the same hotel, (the only one open in the district) but in a different room.

"This one's over the bar, so it's basically warmer anyway," the proprietor said. The room also had a larger heater, an electric fire in the bathroom and, I noticed straight away, an electric blanket. I put them all on and kept them on. There were no other guests in the hotel that evening. I was served dinner sitting in an armchair beside a blazing coal fire.

There were no signs of life at all when I arrived at the campers the following morning. I spoke a gentle good morning at the tents but received no response. I tried again some minutes later – but still nothing.

Then a male hand appeared undoing the flap of one of the tents. A sleepy face appeared in the gap.

"I don't think you'll get them out there this morning. Too cold." Too jolly snug in their tents, I thought. Then the whole figure emerged from the tent. He looked around him and stretched.

"No, it's too cold for them," he shivered.

I presumed that Mike and Dave were probably awake and listening, so I went on: "No, no it's not, it's lovely. And there's the sun."

The faint outline of the sun glimmered through the clouds.

"We'd catch a cold if we went in today," said Mike from inside the tent.

I sat down in the dunes and waited. There was a stirring at the entrance to the tent and Mike crawled out.

"Come on, you'll love it once you're in. And I've brought you some wine."

Mike shook his head. Then Dave appeared.

"What's this about wine? Come on Mike, I'll go if you will."

"Two bottles if you go nude."

Mike thought for a moment.

"OK then," he said.

They stripped fifty yards from the edge of the sea, and without a moment's hesitation ran across the sand and plunged into the icy water. They didn't stay in long. When they reappeared from the waves they were blue with cold.

"I've sold my body to the press," yelled Dave as he tore up the beach back to the protection of the sand dunes. I handed over the wine and drank some coffee with them before leaving.

Weddings

When I was fourteen I worked during my school holidays as apprentice assistant to a photographer in Sevenoaks called George King. He had a thriving business. In the week I assisted him when he photographed houses for the local estate agent and helped him in the dark room with the developing and printing.

On Saturdays we did weddings. After a few times with him Mr King gave me a camera and said I could do the bridesmaids. He never allowed me to do the bride or groom. We rehearsed taking the picture very carefully in the shop before we left for the church. I was to call together the bridesmaids politely but firmly as they arrived outside the church, line them up in a row with the sun over my right shoulder, set my camera at F16 if the sun was out and F8 if it was cloudy, put the focus on 15 foot then, most important, remove the dark slide from the back of the camera, thus allowing the light to hit the plate when the shutter was released. I was then to step back to fill the frame with the figures, place one foot behind the other, bend the knees slightly and, saying, "Not too seriously please", squeeze the shutter.

We arrived at the church ten minutes early. I was very nervous. The heavy camera wobbled in my hands as we went through the drill again. At last the wedding party arrived. Mr King arranged the bride's dress confidently and smoothly and stood her father beside her. I was so nervous at the sight of the bridesmaids that they became a sort of wandering pink blur. Somehow I managed to get them into a line and set the camera. As I was about to say my piece about not being too serious, Mr King's voice snapped "Dark slide!" I had forgotten to remove it from the plate holder, but Mr King had been watching me out of the corner of his eye and had spotted the omission. The picture was fine, if a little unsharp due to camera shake. By the time I'd done two or three more weddings, I'd got the hang of it. I began to enjoy steering people into line and actually seeing them clearly.

I still photograph weddings; apart from many that I've done in London, I've photographed them all over England as well as in Paris and Vienna. I would like to do one in Russia, also in Midwestern America. I still line up the bridesmaids though now I use my Leica. The bride and groom posed with their parents must be done too, but the most interesting pictures are of the guests, the way they hold their cigarettes and drinks; the funny attitudes they strike, their expressions of boredom, seriousness, sadness, exuberance or preoccupation, such as those on pages 86 and 87. Country weddings are always lovely. If it rains you get pictures of people scurrying about under umbrellas. If it's fine the men's dark morning clothes and the ladies' hats stand out clearly against mown lawns.

Although the Church and State still presume we intend to marry for life, and the services and ceremonies are appropriately worded, our attitudes to love and relationships have changed. I clearly remember one bride who set very little store by the marriage service!

The bride, who had been living with her fiancé for some time, was on her way to her grand wedding. I was travelling in the front of the car with the chauffeur, having been at the house to photograph the bride getting ready. We got caught in a big traffic jam. It became obvious that we were going to be very late for the church. The bride became extremely agitated at the thought of this and told the chauffeur to turn off and go straight to London Airport.

"I'll telephone David at the church and tell him to meet me in the departure lounge. Never mind about the wedding."

The father remained calm during his daughter's outburst and ordered the chauffeur to continue towards the church. Three quarters of an hour later, they arrived at the church and the service went ahead.

Many people groan at the thought of a wedding: what to wear, who they will bump into and not want to see (or who you must ask and don't what to, if it's your wedding), the dreadful champagne and, above all, the crowds and interminable standing and waiting to get into the reception. Much of this delay is caused by the conventional formal group photograph at the reception as soon as the bride and groom, bridesmaids and their families arrive from church. People get lost or stuck in traffic, the photographer is interrupted by waiters serving drinks, friends standing about catching the eyes of the sitters making them giggle, and nannies fussing about the appearance of their charges.

My preference is for the guests to be received straight away and the group photographs taken in a side room away from the guests, when the receiving is finished. But then, what are you to do when there is a beautiful staircase in a country house, with flowers from the garden entwined in the bannisters and more flowers in huge arrangements at the side of the stairs, and this is where the guests will be received and this is where they will be milling around after they have been received, and you must group the family on the staircase because, well, there are all these lovely flowers and it would be so nice to have them in the picture. Then you do the shot before the receiving of the guests – and make them wait.

Sometimes I feel I never want to photograph another wedding. They have to be planned as closely as a bank raid, but there's far less time once inside! There are feuds to be dealt with – you can't help it – you are in the thick of it – people ask you to mend their cameras or worse, ask you to get out of the way because they want to take a photograph. I've been elbowed by many a fierce woman with instamatic and flashes.

"I've known the bride since she was born," they say with a vicious backward jab of their elbows. Or, as I am busy trying to be inconspicuous, waiting for a good moment to photograph someone, I hear a loud voice boom behind me at the subject, "I say, Catherine, chap wants to take your picture". Of course, Catherine immediately becomes selfconscious and the picture is lost. But there are, in spite of the difficulties, always some marvellous moments; weddings produce feelings in people that range widely, showing expressions that would be almost impossible to find elsewhere.

Encounters

I wanted to know what was happening in Wokingham that might be worth photographing so I called at the offices of the *Wokingham Times* to see what their reporter was going to cover that day.

I thought ladies modelling clothes they had designed and made themselves sounded interesting. The session was being held at a branch of the Bracknell College of Adult Education. Excited female voices echoed from the first floor as I entered the building. I followed the voices and found myself in a room with seven or eight ladies ranging in age from thirty to sixty. They were standing around between long desks strewn with dress-making equipment, plastic bags and cloth, adjusting each other's clothes and looking at themselves in the glass.

"Can I help you?" asked a lady in a brown-check woollen dress. I told her that I was a freelance photographer. "The teacher has gone to the shop to try and sort out a problem with her flash. She won't be a minute. But I'm sure it will be all right."

The teacher arrived back almost straight away, clutching a camera and flash. She said of course I could take some pictures of them. In any case, she went on, they could do with some publicity for next year's course. Her name was Hilary. She had short dark hair, expertly applied black eye make-up and blushed cheeks, and a trim figure. She would have looked good in a WRAC's uniform. She certainly had the voice. "Come along girls. Out on the stairs!" she bawled.

They obeyed at once, lining up against the bannisters one behind the other, like chorus girls, except they didn't know what to do with their hands: they flapped them in the air as though hoping they would vanish.

They made adjustments to collars and belts and giggled. As soon as Hilary was in position at the bottom of the stairs, they stopped giggling and looked self-conscious, suspicious. Hilary aimed her camera up at them. The flash fired.

"That was lovely. Now, I'd like to take one of you, Maggie, alone in your lovely floaty dress."

Maggie went off to change. Hilary lined her up on the stairs; her hands hung loosely by her side. The camera clicked, but no flash.

"Oh, not again!"

Hilary fiddled with the camera.

"Damn, I forgot to switch the flash on. My husband will kill me if I waste any more."

Next time there was a click and a flash.

"Now I want you all out here again, this time in your nighties."

There was murmuring from the girls.

"We didn't bring them," said one. "We thought we shouldn't."

No doubt because the local paper had promised to take some photographs, and was bound to have wanted one of them in their nightdresses.

"You chickened out, didn't you?" accused Hilary.

Then turning to me she said, "What a pity, the girls have made some really sleezy nightdresses."

But one of the girls, Jessie, had brought hers. Jessie was a forty-year-old mother of four with a happy round face. Having changed, she went out onto the landing to be positioned by Hilary.

"Put your feet apart more so we can see the slit."

The slit came up to her knee. Jessie said, "You should see Jane's, her slit comes up to here," pointing to one inch below her waist.

With that, Hilary's photography was over. The girls returned to their cutting, pinning, fitting, sewing and gossiping with what was left of the morning.

There was much disappointment that the photographer from the local newspaper hadn't turned up. Then, leaping up the stairs two at a time he arrived.

"Thank you ladies, if you wouldn't mind – yes – just change back into your frocks."

They were out on the stairs again.

"Thank you ladies, oh, that's beautiful – oh – yes – yes – big smile – yes – thank you! Just one more – yes – that lovely big smile again."

*   *   *

My father died when I was four, but it was not until about fifteen years ago that I discovered where he was buried. My parents divorced when I was two and my mother, who never spoke much about my father, died when I was fifteen. It was the aunt of my assistant who told me that my father was buried in the cemetery at Binfield in Berkshire. She had known my father quite well and also knew the circumstances of his death.

I found the cemetery tucked away off a tree-lined lane, half a mile from the church. I parked the car and pushed open the large wooden doors of the lich-gate. In front of me lay a tarmacadamized path with graves either side of it. A clump of cypress stood near the middle of the cemetery.

I walked across to a man digging a grave. "Good afternoon. I wonder if you can help me. I'm looking for my father's grave. I believe he was buried here."

The man straightened up and looked at me. He wore a trilby with a wide band and a tattered old tweed jacket. I noticed how well cut it was. The grave-digger had a kind face with one eye that went off in the wrong direction.

"His name was Kasterine," I went on. "He died in 1936."

At this point I was expecting him either to say that if I came back when he had finished work, we could go and look at the parish records, or possibly refer me to someone else. But he said: "Wait a moment," and there was a short pause while he thought. "Yes, a very tall gentleman. Six foot two. He was Russian." Then he pointed to his left. "Over there, at the top, one row down from the fence."

The grave-digger climbed out of the grave and together we walked across the cemetery towards the top fence. He stopped at an unmarked grave, its outline barely visible, the earth having sunk in over the years.

"This is it here. It had a wooden cross of the Orthodox Church, but that rotted a long time ago." He went on. "We had a lot of trouble with your father. He was killed in a motor accident in the north, near Newcastle I think, and being a foreigner nobody wanted him. But a friend of his – Mrs Roper up at Court House – arranged through the Red Cross for him to be brought here."

I felt sad. Only a wooden cross. Had he died with no friends, except this one woman, who through her position in a charitable organisation had found him a place to be buried? I stared at the grave and wondered what his life had been like.

The grave-digger's name was Charles Fisher. We went back to his house where his wife made us a cup of tea and we looked up the records. I ordered a headstone for the grave and asked to take his picture, shown on page 97.

Charles Fisher was sixty-five years old. After the First World War he had lived in The Hague for six years where he was clerk and verger to the vicar of the Anglican church.

"Very busy time it was; weddings galore; Dutch girls marrying Tommies." The vicar died suddenly, so Mr Fisher returned to England where he became butler to the headmaster of Wellington College.

"We had all kinds of distinguished visitors. The Duke of Connaught often came. He called one day when I was out and the kitchen maid answered the door. The Duke asked her if the headmaster was in. She replied, 'Dunno love. I'll go and see.' The Duke never called again. I left Wellington after a few years. I never liked the headmaster. I can't bear forgetfulness. He couldn't remember anything."

It wouldn't be easy to match Mr Fisher's memory, I thought.

"There's always pencil and paper!" Mr Fisher concluded.

Mr Fisher told me he then became clerk and verger here in Binfield, where he also played the organ and rang bells.

"I started a chimney sweep business, too – first man around here to use the vacuum. Then, when people stopped going to church, they didn't need a clerk and a verger. I told the vicar that I'd look after the cemetery. I'd finance it by subscription. I've now got over three hundred people to subscribe."

A handsome, much decorated Victorian piano stood against the wall behind me in the house. I asked Mr Fisher if he played.

"Used to, until I pulled my arms out. Almost paralysed my fingers when I pulled my arms out."

I asked him what he meant – how did he pull his arms out?

"Picking pears. I was up the tree and slipped. To save myself I grabbed the branch. But the weight of the basket of pears on my back, added to my own, was too much for my arms and I pulled them out."

He held his arms high above his head, then lowered them and demonstrated how they had been pulled out of their sockets in the shoulder, while swinging from the branch.

Finally, I asked him how long it took him to dig a grave.

"Two days," he replied. "The young men these days do it in one, but when the coffin descends it goes bump, bump, bump. I plane the sides." ·

*   *   *

In 1968 I was commissioned by the *Daily Telegraph* supplement to photograph pollution. The article covered many aspects of the subject. It included pollution of our coastlines by tankers flushing oil from their tanks, factories polluting rivers with dyes and toxic wastes, local authorities emptying raw sewage into rivers and sea and other pollutants from steel works, traffic, brick works, etc. The article also included a feature on the visual pollution of the countryside – caravan sites, a farmer who litters ten acres of land in Kent with old strawberry boxes, and a car breaker's yard in Northamptonshire positioned in full view of a large number of people living on an estate on the opposite side of the road.

Car breakers are among those people who do not welcome photographers. Whether it is because their business attracts men with records, or whether it is simply that all breaker's yards are unsightly and cause bad relations with the council, I don't know.

The proprietors of this particular yard had earlier told the *Telegraph* writer to remove himself from their premises before he had asked a single question so I knew it would be fruitless to try and persuade the proprietors to stand in front of their yard, with their wives, children and dogs to have their picture taken.

Instead I drove three hundred yards past the site down a hill. From this point the yard stood out well, and showed also its nearness to the housing estate.

I parked in a gateway another hundred yards farther on, took my gear out of the car, walked back up the road and set up the tripod and camera. I selected a lens. Its focal length was too short – everything looked too far away. I changed it for a lens with a longer focal length. As I peered into the view finder I saw two large men run out of the yard and down the road towards me. There was no doubt in my mind about their intentions. They were heading this way to smash my camera, and me too.

If I had been set up near my car, I could have chucked my equipment into it and vanished. As it was I had a hundred yards to go to the car and by the time I had worked out what to do, the men were only a hundred yards from me. I carried on looking through the view finder pretending that the fact that they were running this way couldn't possibly have anything to do with me. The steel tips to their boots clicked on the asphalt. As I adjusted the camera, I heard the sound of their panting. They slowed and stopped in front of me.

I looked up. "Hello, good morning," I said in a friendly voice. I was terrified. I had heard of photographers being beaten up. What will these two do to me. Kick, slash with razors, punch? And where? The smell of oil and sweat coming from their clothes and bodies was strong. I began to undo my camera from the tripod.

Then the thinner of the two men spoke.

"We don't like photos being taken of the yard. Let's have the film in that camera. Come on."

He put out his enormous hand, black, glistening with grease. I tipped the tripod and camera away from him. His friend moved around behind me.

"I really don't see why I should give it to you," I said rather primly. "There's no law against taking photographs of people's property from the Queen's highway."

I realised as I was talking that we were not in dispute over a point of law.

"Give us that - - - camera, quick," repeated the thin one.

His friend from behind me said: "Do as the man says," and after a pause, "for your own good." I didn't like the sound of that remark at all. I thought: don't be silly, give them the film. You can always come back later.

"I'm getting impatient," said the thin one. His hand moved nearer to me. His fingers twitched.

Instead of giving it to him as he asked, which, I imagined, would result in his throwing the camera into the road as many times as it was necessary to cause the back to fall open and the film to roll out, I quickly opened the back and pulled out the film exposing it all to the light. "There," I said, "now I'll be off."

I thought that would be an end to the matter, but the man behind me grabbed the film as I held it up and yanked it out of my grasp. I said "There won't be anything on it; you can see its all exposed to the light."

"How do I know," he replied. "I'm not taking any - - - chances. Now clear off and if we catch you here again your friends won't recognise you." With that he turned and stumped off up the road, with handfuls of exposed film dangling at his side. His friend followed.

I returned later that day and got my picture. As I was taking it, I had the door of the car open and the engine running for a quick getaway. I imagined a rifle being trained on me, but no bullet came, nor was there a sign of life.

I have never photographed wars or riots or demonstrations. The car breaker's yard and the episode of Great Tew were the only occasions when I have run into trouble trying to take a photograph.

*   *   *

A fair amount of my work are portraits for magazines. Often I photograph the people in their homes. A few have been difficult and some have been easy, in that they have accepted my suggestion for a picture and have let me see whether it worked by using a Polaroid. I seldom actually have a pre-conceived idea. I prefer to wait to see what people are like, what they have to wear and what the choice of backgrounds are.

Not infrequently, however, I am greeted at the front door, led into a small cluttered room and asked in a peremptory tone: "What do you want to do then"; or "where do you want me?" Writers are often the culprits. Surely they must think before they write, or look at the subject before they describe it. So I reply that I don't know and I would like to look around.

I like to have time, but not too much, and I like to look around alone, set up my camera and lights and then ask the sitter to come and be taken. Only when I am immediately at ease with someone can I walk around the house with them. Otherwise, when I am looking, I am inattentive to what they say, so they might as well not be there.

What an odd relationship I have now with the few hundred people that I have photographed in this way. Taking their picture hardly constitutes an introduction to them; I can't think of my subjects as acquaintances, but a closeness existed for a period of time that most of their acquaintances or even some friends have not felt. When I meet somebody after taking their picture, I experience the same strange intimacy, and if the photograph worked, if they revealed something to the camera, it remains.

The expressions that are the hallmark of the finest portraits have always come from the sitters themselves. The photographer can arrange the shape and the lighting but he must allow the subjects to express themselves through face and gesture. It is the mark of the photographer's expertise to coax and capture the expression to the full and at the right moment.

Meadow in Yorkshire 1979
Old-fashioned permanent pastures full of self-seeded grasses and plants are still
very good for grazing lambs, but no good for cattle these days. Cattle need the
nourishing richness of rye grass or timothy to give high milk yields.

Reflections of trees, Northumberland 1981
This was taken looking into a stream which moves through the lower slopes of
the Cheviots.

Hedge layer at Great Tew, Oxfordshire 1979
Jack the hedger, about whom there is more in *Assignments*, protects his hands
from being torn to pieces in the hedges he maintains by wearing an old pair of
sealskin gloves.

Gateway in Somerset 1979
It was taken in May, in damp, misty weather that gives the heavy saturation of
colour.

ABOVE
Richmond Park, Surrey 1981
Willows, taken in the late afternoon on a still, mild day in February.
    Earlier I had seen two nuns strolling across the park. You seldom see nuns stroll,
more often they are hurrying from place to place.

OPPOSITE
Spectators at a cricket match, Oxfordshire 1979
In his day, Jack the shepherd, on the right, was one of the finest cricketers the
village has known. Now, each Saturday when the village team play at home
Jack and his friend Alf watch the match from this gate.

Farmer in Oxfordshire 1978
The farmer, more concerned at the time with his daughter who had just fallen over, left his six-year-old son to look after the sheep. This the boy did most competently with the help of two dogs and a large stick.

1958 Massey Ferguson tractor near Askrigg, Yorkshire 1979
At first glance I thought this tractor had been abandoned, but on closer inspection I saw that it was
in working order. The farmer had just gone to tea.

Wheat fields in the Lincolnshire Wolds, 1979
Poppies in themselves don't do much harm. Farmers don't like them because they can't show a nice
clean field when showing the crop to the Ministry man.

Scarecrow, Suffolk 1979
A rural terrorist. He even had a black glove. My only criticism of his performance as a pigeon-scarer is that his gun was not visible to the pigeons.

Thwaite, Yorkshire 1979
I went to Yorkshire in May 1979 to photograph a car in beautiful spring
countryside for an advertisement. I got there and found leafless trees and
snow on the moor. I stayed in this village.

OPPOSITE
Yorkshire shepherd 1979
There is more about him in *Jaunts*. BUT, did you know that in olden days farmers
often sewed a cut-throat razor into the peak of their cap? On seeing a rat, they
whipped off their cap and slashed at it.

Yes, of course you knew.

ABOVE *Christina, aged nine, from Berkshire 1980*
I met this girl while staying with some friends in Berkshire. As soon as I saw her I was struck by something extraordinary in her face. At first she was selfconscious and put on faces in front of the camera. I grew disheartened. But I had seen how marvellous she could look when the camera was not pointing at her. I moved her from place to place; I praised her; I flattered her; still the wrong face. Finally, as she stood in light from the garage door, I scolded her.

   She responded openly and directly and I had my picture.

LEFT *Prep school boy, London 1975*
One afternoon a friend came to see me with her son. They had just been to Harrods to buy his first school uniform.

ABOVE
Athletics day at Kings House School, Richmond, Surrey 1979
The firm but gentle hand of father leads his son away from the field. Why the tears? Perhaps he had been enjoying himself and it was now time to leave.

LEFT
Junior school, Queen's Gate, London 1980
As I drove up Queen's Gate in London I noticed this Victorian-looking school mistress. She was trying to organise her pupils into a crocodile for their morning walk. It was taking quite a time as she insisted on inspecting each little girl's state of dress before moving off and being seen by the wide world.

ABOVE
Sixth-form English class, Radley College, Oxfordshire 1981
I was at Radley from 1945 to 1950 – a period of bad food, no heat, intense
heartiness and much bullying. When I returned in 1981 for the first time since I
had left, I felt nervous. I looked to see if my shoes were clean, rubbed my sticky
hand on my trouser leg and straightened my hair.

    The place had of course changed enormously – much more like a Hilton Hotel.

OPPOSITE
Head Girl of Cheltenham Ladies College, Gloucestershire 1980
I was asked by *Harper's & Queen* magazine to photograph and talk to head girls of
prominent schools. I asked each of them why they thought they had been chosen
as head girl.

    "A bit loud-mouthed in the prefects' lobby, I should think," said Caroline, head
girl of Cheltenham.

OVERLEAF
Ludlow Town Band, Shropshire 1974
Esso Petroleum asked me to photograph the finals of the schools hockey
championship. The Ludlow Town Band played during the warming-up
preliminaries. The euphonium player took the opportunity between
numbers to blow the spit out of his mouthpiece.

Three boys in Kent 1974
I was immediately attracted by the faces of these boys and the manner in which they were standing around when
I arrived at the house where they were staying. I didn't have a camera with me, but fortunately one of the people
living in the house was a photographer and she lent me hers.

ABOVE *Low tide at Scarborough, Yorkshire 1979*
It was a dull overcast day. Everyone was indoors somewhere, either in the amusement arcades or eating. A perfect time for a man and his dog to enjoy the space.

RIGHT *Northumberland 1981*
I spent a cold winter weekend in Northumberland looking for photographs. My hotel was freezing and I had to sleep on my anorak for warmth. I went for a walk along the beach and met these two. The whole extraordinary weekend is recounted in *Bathing*.

ABOVE
Barrow boy in Chelsea, 1968
I saw this boy running with his barrow when he was halfway down the street. I had to race after him to ask him if he would run past me several times so that I could take shots at varying shutter speeds. Later I selected the one that had given the best effect. I think it was 1/15th second.

LEFT
Clapham Junction 1981
The three boys came up from Reading for the day, with sandwiches and thermos flasks. They had travelled on specially reduced fares for members of train-spotters' clubs.

By standing at the end of Platform 4, they could get a clear view of the trains arriving at all the platforms. When I talked to them during a lull in arrivals, they wore anxious expressions and their eyes flicked from me to the tracks over my shoulder in case they missed a number – though if one of them did miss one the others would give it to him.

At the rush hour they were going up the line to Victoria.

The Girls' Brigade, London 1981
I'd been to photograph students at the Royal College of Music and had drawn a blank. As I left the college I saw hundreds of black-clad figures spilling out of coaches parked round the Albert Hall. I walked over and watched the girls being gathered together and led into the hall for their annual rally.

Stall in Portobello Road, London 1964
Amid the muddle and confusion in London's best known antique market, I found this ten-year-old calmly waiting for customers. She is the third generation to hold this stall.

Coloured boy in Victoria Park, London 1976
"When you are feeling lonely, be lonely. Or go somewhere different, somewhere you don't know," a friend said, so that lonely Sunday afternoon I drove to Victoria Park in the East End of London. I'd never been there, it was just a large green patch on the A–Z which attracted me.

   The picture shows how misleading photographs can be. If the background had been included in the photograph the mood would have been quite different. He was in fact one of several boys playing a peaceful game of cricket. They happened not to have any bats, only stumps.

Primary school class, Gloucestershire 1979
I remember feeling very excited when the teacher turned her attention to the boy and he took one foot in his hand, so coyly. The scene had been too dull to make a good photograph when he was just standing on two feet.

Eastbourne beach, Sussex 1976
Obviously not their child. The responsibility was a huge strain. Possibly the little girl was their grandchild.

Grandmother, her head protected from the sun by the child's dress, was so heavily sunk into the deck chair that she had no hope of reaching the little girl. Grandad, in his new sandals, grabbed the child just in time before she was on her feet and off to the sea.

OPPOSITE   *Break at Great Tew Primary School, Oxfordshire 1979*
Almost everything about this boy's stance suggests he will never make a batsman.
However, his lack of natural ability did nothing to prevent his enjoyment of the
game.

Bell ringer, London 1979
This ten-year-old boy, watched by his proud parents, is ringing for the first time
in his life the treble bell at St Paul's Cathedral.

Father John, Vicar of Great Tew, Oxfordshire, 1981
Father John is a tremendous character, with whom I spent quite a
lot of my time in Great Tew. *Assignments* tells you more about
him.

70

Great Tew, Oxfordshire 1979
The large gaunt house overlooking the village is owned by owner of the village (described in more detail in *Assignments*). So that the original look of the village wouldn't be spoilt, he insisted that no new houses were to be built and no alterations undertaken.

The result is a village crowded with the cars of sightseers marvelling at how unspoilt it is.

ABOVE
Coverdale, Yorkshire 1979
A bitterly cold, howling wind blew across the valley as I took this photograph on a May evening.
To keep the camera steady I slung two gallon-size plastic water containers over the tripod.

OPPOSITE
Stall on the village green at Great Tew, Oxfordshire 1979
This stall operates every Saturday afternoon in the summer, selling the most mouth-watering
home-made jam, fudge and cakes. The proceeds go to the upkeep of the church. Everything these
ladies have time to make during the week is sold by Saturday evening. I bought a delicious coffee
and walnut sponge cake.

OVERLEAF (74–5)
Devon 1979
A serene patchwork landscape near Exmoor. If I had turned the camera through 180° I would have
taken a road jammed with Whitsun holiday traffic, disgruntled and fuming.

OVERLEAF (76–7)
Near Hatch Beauchamp, Somerset 1979
Approached from the east, this tor stands out from three or four miles away. As I got closer I could
make out the family playing under the tree; by the time I reached the foot of the hill, they were
half way down on their way home for tea. I asked them if they would go back up the hill and play
around again.

Page boy, 1961
I can't remember who was at the other end of the train, but I do remember being impressed at the time by this boy's direct look.

Glastonbury Tor, Somerset 1981
I left my camera, set up in a field, to get a filter from the car. When I returned to take this photograph the tripod was surrounded by cows licking the camera bag and nudging the tripod. I walked very slowly through them, trying to talk soothingly, until my hand was on the camera.

It was the canvas camera bag, slung over the tripod handle to steady it, that attracted the cows, and it was drenched by their continual licking.

PRECEDING PAGE *Village wedding, Suffolk 1979*
The photographer was having a hard time trying to take the group photograph. The smallest bridesmaid kept crawling away from her position each time she was returned to it.

All attempts to get the page into the group were given up. He had discovered that it was more fun leaping on and off headstones. If anyone tried to stop him he burst into tears.

ABOVE *Wedding at the Ritz, London 1975*
Just a small party of eight for lunch overlooking Green Park on a clear sunny
February day. The couple had been married at the Queen's Chapel, St James's
Palace.

RIGHT *Wedding guest, London 1960*
He was standing there waiting. I lived in a flat that I shared with my sister overlooking the street. She spotted him as she watered her window-boxes. I just had time to fetch my camera and take one frame before a taxi stopped and carried him off. He did not have to remove his top hat; cabs are still designed to allow enough headroom for persons to sit in their top hats.

BELOW *Wedding at Claridge's Hotel, London 1962*
I wondered what the woman with her back to me had said to cause such astonishment on the faces of the other two. Were they discussing Telstar or the Cuban missile crisis or any of the other events that made the news in 1962? It was probably something much more intimate – and prosaic – but it made a good picture.

OPPOSITE *Country wedding, Hampshire 1974*
Undeniably, it is lovely to take the weight off one's feet. Weddings are exhausting occasions especially on piping-hot July days. Why not lie down and feel the cool grass underneath?

Bride's and groom's luggage leaving, Hampshire 1976
I was waiting to photograph the bride and groom leaving for their honeymoon when out of the front door charged the chauffeur with their luggage.

This was a small wedding in the country. The couple had been married in a private chapel in the house. After the service the couple walked through a door of the chapel into the garden where, on a perfect June day, they drank champagne before a sit-down lunch. I like photographing country weddings best, which I mention in *Weddings*, because there is so much more activity. At this one, the children were racing back and forth across the lawn, tumbling and rolling on the grass; neither their parents nor their nannies seemed to mind the state of their clothes.

OPPOSITE
Northumberland shepherd, near Anwick 1963
Derek Scott, amateur steeplechase jockey and full-time farmer,
keeps his horses fit shepherding his sheep.

ABOVE
Shepherd in Arkendale, Yorkshire 1979
Although friendly and pleasant enough to talk to, this man was
only at ease when communicating with his dog.

ABOVE
Cambridgeshire ditcher, 1981
Modern technology is not always as efficient as is made
out to be. This man is employed by the council to
follow in the wake of the machine that is supposed to
clear the ditches but in practice clogs them up. I have
written more about him in *Wherever*.

LEFT
Reed cutter in Norfolk 1981
A plot of reeds to cut and sell is more profitable
to this Norfolk man than his previous occupation as
a fisherman. I write about him and his partner in
Wherever. To keep people off the plot there is a large
notice marked BIRD SANCTUARY – KEEP OUT.

ABOVE *Sea-front café, Weymouth, Dorset 1980*
It was November. I was sitting in a brightly lit, orange-coloured café on the sea front. It was almost deserted. A rush of bitterly cold air surrounded me as a customer pushed through the door. She collected her cup of tea and very sensibly sat well away from the door.

I noticed how self-absorbed she looked, and how lonely and distressed. I got up and moved to a table next to her. Her stare didn't alter. But in case her eye caught the movement of my camera as I raised it, I took her picture with it resting on the table.

OPPOSITE *Old lady in slippers, Putney, London 1978*
You don't often see people in England sitting in their doorways or front gardens – the weather doesn't allow it. This wonderful old lady was simply a sight that made me want to stop and record. She and her cat have great dignity.

ABOVE
Gentleman with cigar, Putney, London 1965
A misty day on the river at Putney Reach.

Figures stand out so beautifully in the mist. I crept up to this
man. His thoughts obviously far away, he never even noticed me.

OPPOSITE
Mr Fisher, gravedigger, Oxfordshire 1965
Mr Fisher is the gravedigger and caretaker of Binfield cemetery.
After thirty years he remembered where he had buried my father.

"Yes," he said, "a very tall gentleman wasn't he? He's over there
by the fence."

In *Encounters* I have recounted more of Mr Fisher's life.

ABOVE
Kensington Gardens, London 1975
Was it just the fun of lancing the milk bottle
with his stick, or does this man, I wonder, collect
litter of all kinds that lies in his path?

RIGHT
*Bracknell station, 8.30 am on a weekday, Berkshire
1981*
Overcoats and burberrys waiting on the up line,
anoraks and raincoats arriving on the down line.
I was surprised at the number of arrivals at the
rush hour, most being met by luxury coaches
that whisked them off to their giant office blocks
in the new town.

   And the man in the bowler? Looks like a
military man – Ministry of Defence, perhaps?
Or could he be working for a firm that hires
out men's formal attire?

OPPOSITE   *Brokers in the City, 1979*
I waited outside the Stock Exchange at closing
time, to catch people leaving. I tried to look as
much like a stockbroker as I could, dressed in a
dark suit and carrying a bundle of papers.

ABOVE *Kutchinsky's, Knightsbridge 1979*
This photograph, taken at half past eight one summer morning, would have been less effective if
the three assistants hadn't seen me. As it is, they all seem to have a guilty look. As for the one in the
window, he really looks as if caught in the act.

ABOVE
Buffet at Charing Cross station 1981
I walked into the buffet at about three o'clock one afternoon. The couple in the photograph were really enjoying each other's company and were too absorbed to notice me.

I sat opposite a man with a cup of tea and a Bath bun in front of him. Both were untouched. I noticed that he had one good hand, with fingers and thumb intact, whilst on his other hand he only had one finger and some stumps on the end of his knuckles. He chain-smoked with this hand.

ABOVE RIGHT   *World's End Public House, Chelsea 1968*
I have noticed that groups of people leaving a pub together don't part immediately. They stand about for a final goodbye or to get their bearings.

ABOVE   *Couple in the sea at Margate, Kent 1976*
This couple, who live in the North of England, have come to Margate for their holidays every year for the past twenty-five years.

OPPOSITE   *Donkey rides on the beach at Scarborough, Yorkshire 1979*
This man's father started giving donkey rides as a sideline to his coal-merchant business. During the summer months, when coal deliveries were slack, the horses were put out to grass and the stables used for the donkeys. The business petered out as less and less coal was delivered to private houses.

Now there are just the donkeys – and nothing in the winter.

PREVIOUS PAGE   *Front garden, Suffolk 1979*
I took this in one of those pink-washed, overkept villages in Suffolk that live almost entirely off coach- and car-loads of tourists.

These two, waiting in the sun for the onslaught, run the antique shop next door.

ABOVE   *Croquet at Hurlingham Club, London 1979*
Light but steady drizzle that later turned to a downpour did not in the least deter this man from playing his regular game of croquet. He was in fact the only player on the six croquet lawns at Hurlingham during the annual one day pre-Wimbledon tennis tournament.

OPPOSITE   *Alterations shop, Putney, London 1978*
This is a most useful establishment, where they put a new lining in your favourite jacket or alter hand-me-downs for your children. The man was a shirt-cutter in Jermyn Street, but turned his hand to tailoring after retirement, helped by two local housewives.

106

Bingo at Clapham Junction 1981
This club was founded twenty-one years ago and is one of the very few remaining independent clubs.

"We love it here," a lady member said. "It's more of a family place. You should go to the Tooting Granada. That's real plush. But it's not safe to walk home from there alone."

Three men in a pub, London docks 1965
One Sunday morning I went to the London docks to find a location for an advertising picture. At lunch time I went into a pub and saw these three men.

By coincidence I had been commissioned for a beer advertisement, but my brief was nothing to do with pubs, just for a moody dockland picture shot at the end of the day.

TOP *Putney cricket club, London 1978*
The pavilion is on wheels. After each match it is trundled across the ground to the secretary's front garden.

BELOW *Putney Horse Show, London 1980*
The clothes-horse, winner of the fancy dress competition.

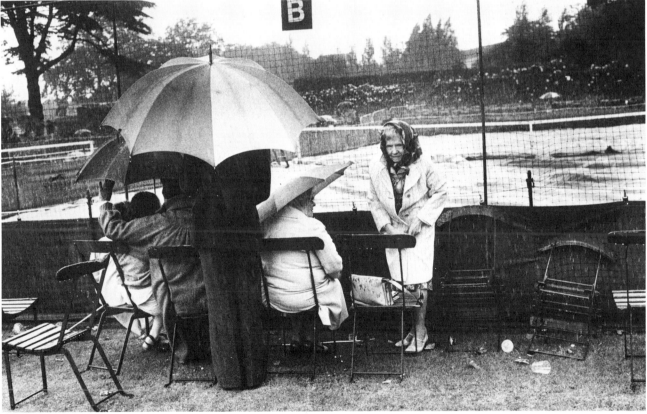

TOP   *Pheasant shooting at Beaulieu, Hampshire 1976*
The safest and best position to photograph this action is squatting about five feet in front of the guns.

BELOW   *Hurlingham annual pre-Wimbledon tournament, London 1979*
In the pouring rain my Leica was soaked although it was tucked into my shirt, but it still works beautifully.

OPPOSITE
Stewards at the Ludlow Hunt Point to Point 1981
Point to points are a market place for the exchange of gossip and business. The
young discuss tonight's or last night's party. Farmers nudge each other, heads
down, asking if they've seen so and so's top field which is in a mess.

ABOVE
Garage in Devon 1981
The trend for large garages to sell anything from bicycles to garden furniture is
spreading to smaller establishments.

OVERLEAF
Stonehenge, Wiltshire 1971
I like the contrast between the chunks of stone and the finely carved figures of the
family. Had the people not been there I would certainly have taken this
photograph on the merits of the light alone, but the people show you how large
the stones are.

What fascinated me about this scene were the zigzag formations of the sand lying
between two stretches of water.

I had been looking for a dramatic winter landscape, as I mention in *Bathing*, but
found it elusive.

ABOVE
Stagnant pond, Hartley Witney, Hampshire 1978
A green skating rink in the evening sun.

LEFT
Dead elm, Oxfordshire 1979
They stand out in the English countryside like rows of pylons because many
farmers find it too expensive to have the dead elm trees cut down and carted
away.

OVERLEAF
The Fens, Cambridgeshire 1981
I had a memorable trip to the east coast, which is related in *Wherever*.
 I looked at this photograph with my assistant, whose father is a farmer.
 "Nobody who works on the land would notice the patterns in the countryside,"
he said.
 "It's all around them, but they are too busy looking at the state of the crops."
 "And the wildlife," I added.
 "Yes, they shoot it," came the reply, sharply.

*Charlie, Anderton Lift operator
Cheshire 1970*
The Anderton Lift connects the
Weaver Navigation with the
Trent & Mersey Canal in
Cheshire.

"Very unhealthy, living on
canals. Had pneumonia several
times," said Charlie, who was
born on a coal barge drawn by
horses.

A lane in Buckinghamshire 1980
An irresistible combination of bold line and single colour.

Cumbria 1979
This was a bit of luck. I had seen nothing all day that I wanted to photograph, but at eight o'clock in the evening, on the way from our B & B to dinner in Kendal, we passed this scene. The sun stayed on the hillside just long enough for me to get out my camera and tripod and take the picture.

PREVIOUS PAGE
Farmhouse near Newbiggin, Durham 1981
I was racing back across the moor to Barnard
Castle for dinner. My headlamps were perfectly
focused and I was enjoying the empty, well-
surfaced roads.

I had already stopped once to take a similar
twilight scene, but I knew, as soon as I saw it, that
this one was better.

"Damn it, work again. Certainly late for
dinner now."

But it didn't take long – it couldn't; daylight
was fading and would only be balanced with the
light in the window for another five minutes.

...ive village." [6] In 1840 he had
...Concord, but with every inten-
...ls) of gathering material for a
...Juan. On February 8, 1841, he
...counting-room of the gods, "and
...ount from day-book to ledger."
...ivine ledger as something shut up
...by the riverside; it is vellum in
...nt on the hills." [7] The crow, the
...his quill, but it matters not if his
...even if it gropes in slime and mud,
...eed." In the ecstasy of this time he
...hinder him; his scrawls, he all but
...cidents as cosmic as earthquake or
...owland, forest and field have been

...urances, however, there were already
...strange and unaccountable things this
...gest," he mused on January 29, 1841. [8]
...d if he cluttered his counter with home-
...delighted to find, on looking over his
...wrote better than he knew: "and what
...oon of dried apple or pumpkin will prove
...diamonds, or pearls from Coromandel."
...eason why he never ripped these volumes
...he wanted to discover what they would
...had more experience with writing. They
...to him, beyond even the richest pages of
...use — sparse, even crabbed as they are —
...By 1856 he would berate himself that too
...*urnal* become (as he held Emerson wantonly
...come) a preserve of things well done or said
...rd of experiences and growth. "The charm
...he then pleaded with himself, "must consist

3

The Method

It is remarkable what a curse seems to attach to any place which has long been inhabited by man. Vermin of various kinds abide with him. (September 22, 1859; *J*, XII, 340)

SINCE VOLUME 3 is an integral part of the initial six, it can hardly be discussed separately. With the complete record (to the extent Thoreau was pleased to make it) of 1837 to 1842 reunited, we can for the first time think coherently about the literary apprenticeship of Henry Thoreau.

However, we must note that Thoreau did not abruptly cease "journalizing" on April 3, 1842, with the end of volume 6. Torrey and Allen had a fragmentary notebook for 1845–1846, probably kept while Thoreau was at the Pond (they print this as pages 361–402 of *Journal*, Volume I). They also had a mutilated collection of items, mostly undated, which they ascribed to 1845–1847 (pp. 403–437) and a "commonplace book," presumably filled before 1847, from which Thoreau obviously drew in composing the *Week* (pp. 438–488). [1]

After the Walden Edition, collectors, libraries, scholarly sleuths nosed about for Thoreau material. We are now assured that he kept at least one systematic journal in 1842 and 1843 (pieces of this are in the Houghton Library, Harvard University), and another from September 24, 1843, to January 7, 1844 (fragments of this are now in the Huntington Library, HM 13182). The latter has annotations by Sanborn, and in part is printed in his *The First and Last Journeys of Thoreau* (Boston, 1905). Sanborn says that Thoreau himself

tore up the volume, and we can assume that he likewis[e]
wrecked his other manuscripts between 1842 and 1850.

This volume, of the autumn of 1843, was evidently begun
on Staten Island. An early page, another of his many efforts
to define the function of the poet, concludes:

> He records a moment of pure life. Who can see these
> cities and say that there is any life in them? I walked
> through New York yesterday — and met no real or
> living person.[2]

There endures also a cover for another notebook which
Thoreau probably wrote at the Pond, the index of which shows
that it once held matter incorporated into both books. While
generally the narrative of *Walden* is put in the past tense, there
are striking shifts to the present, often in the middle of a
paragraph. For sixteen days Thoreau "saw" the workmen
harvesting ice from the pond: "now they are all gone, and in
thirty days more, probably, I shall look from the same window
on the pure sea-green Walden water there. . . ."[3] These
alternations appear studied; we detect behind them the
existence of a notebook composed mainly in the present tense.

Still, whatever the kind or kinds of journals Thoreau kept
between April 3, 1842, and the spring of 1850, they all went
into the hopper of his creative operation. They were disem-
boweled and cannibalized. Odds and ends of work-sheets also
remain — enough to show either that he did his revisions on
pages of an eviscerated journal or upon pages copied from a
journal manuscript. We see that this process went on
ferociously, that many portions have been subjected to a dozen
recastings.

However, though he later made use of about half the entries
in the first six volumes, these books he never physically pulled
apart. Sometimes, as our passages show, he worked over a
paragraph, revising his original ink with a pencil, but whatever

in a certain greenness, though freshness, and not in maturity." [9]
These six volumes are green, but they sprouted out of Henry
Thoreau's freshness. So in 1861, when life was failing him,
when there was no more freshness, he made a box to hold
his masterpiece, and took care to fit into it these six fragments
of his youth.

Wherefore the recognition dawns upon us that these manuscripts — volume 3 well illustrates the point — are not journals
in the sense of being diaries about daily occurrences, nor are
they receptacles of sudden inspirations and rough inventions.
The entries are already products of revision, they are anything
but spontaneous. They are extracted out of a previous manuscript, have already been gone over, been rigidified. He knew
precisely what he was doing: he subtitled volume 1 "Gleanings
or What Time Has Not Reaped of My Journal," and he was
entirely disposed to let time reap what it might if only he could
hang on to the gleanings. They are Henry's selection of
nuggets which best stood the test of filing, that proved in his
judgment *not* to be "the meanest homemade stuffs." They
are precious stones, meticulously selected and exquisitely
colored, by one who even this early found himself committed
to working entirely in the method of mosaic.

On page 73 of volume 2[10] Thoreau writes across the bottom,
and underscores, "End of my Journal of 546 pages." This
follows an entry of June 11, 1840, which dwells on the epic
river voyage of the previous September, and later is reproduced
in the *Week* as though it had been a thought of that time.
Yet it is obvious that volume 1 plus 73 pages of volume 2
come to many fewer pages than 546. Sanborn, notoriously
unreliable, is for once circumstantially convincing about there
having been still another journal in these years (he calls it
"the long Red Book"), which he says went to 596 pages.
Furthermore, on page 33 of volume 4 an entry runs, "End of
my Journal of 396 pages"; this we must suppose was the early,

or an earlier, draft of the volume before us and of the first 33 pages of what is now volume 4.[11] So even these mementoes of young dedication are transferred from some field notebook, or from what I may call an "Ur-journal," to become "expensive" sentences, to lie like boulders on the page, to "contain the seed of other sentences, not mere repetition." [12] Bradford Torrey quickly perceived, at least with the first years of the *Journal*, that he was not dealing with a firsthand text. Yet, when he found in volume 6, for March 21, 1842, opposite the question, "Who is old enough to have learned from experience?" a penciled memorandum, "Set the red hen," Torrey argued that by then he must have come "to the original Journal." [13] But volume 6, all the way through, is precisely like the preceding five. Marginal comments, such as the hen, are indications that Thoreau not only extracted bits and pieces from the working notebooks or from the "long Red Book," but, once he had transfixed them, read them over. It is safe, therefore — or rather, dangerous to do otherwise — to acknowledge that in these volumes, down to April 3, 1842, we have no factual record of Thoreau's life, must hazard no biographical guesses out of them. We have merely an anthology of what he deemed his best sentiments. These bear only a distant relation to the entries initially put down, and a still more distant relation to anything that was happening to him. In the delight of posturing as an enigma to himself, on June 18, 1840, he marveled, "I am startled when I consider how little I am *actually* concerned about the things I write in my journal." [14] Time has a way of wreaking vengeance upon such presumption, but then those who most thrive under the chastisement are those who most ardently, even while quivering before the lash, invite it.

In other words, different though the orientation of the early volumes may be from the later, they are a prophecy of how the great *Journal* would come into being, and also of how the two books would be fabricated. Long before March 27, 1857, the method had become an unbreakable habit, but on that day, as on a few others, he could momentarily gain the illusion of freedom by presenting his vice as a virtue:

> I would fain make two reports in my Journal, first the incidents and observations of to-day; and by to-morrow I review the same and record what was omitted before, which will often be the most significant and poetic part. I do not know at first what it is that charms me. The men and things of to-day are wont to lie fairer and truer in to-morrow's memory.[15]

On November 8, 1851, Thoreau tells how William Ellery Channing (nephew of the great Channing, the poet who exalted the Transcendental imperative into a long life of irresponsible whim), while walking with him, "takes out his note-book sometimes and tries to write, as I do," but, getting bored (as he easily and frequently did), puts it away, announces himself a devotee of pure ideal who must leave grubbing with "facts" to Henry. Thoreau's narrative works off on Ellery some of that bile which perfumed this, as it did most, Transcendental friendships. Channing sounds ridiculous, as Thoreau intends he should, while orating, "I am universal; I have nothing to do with the particular and definite." But for us, what is valuable in the episode is Thoreau's confession of the way he worked, and of the problem this method was making for him: he can't help chiding himself that he too wished to encompass something more than mere facts, so that these "should be material to the mythology I am writing." [16] This is breath-taking. It thrusts us directly into the secret of the *Journal*. The immense work is, from the beginning, a self-conscious effort to create a "mythology" out of the village Apollo, Henry Thoreau.

This is one among many inadvertent — designedly inadvertent? — hints that the *Journal* is really a work not of the fields but of the study. "Do not," he exhorts himself in July 1851, "tread on the heels of your experience. Be impressed without making a minute of it. Poetry puts an interval between the impression and the expression." [17] After a while, though we smile at his transparent deceptions, we learn caution about hailing in him the reporter of unhandseled Nature. He was indeed a marvelously acute observer, but his *Journal* is artifice. And for that reason it hovers on the edge of a tragic precipice. Channing's exasperation had a point. In April 1852, he mounted to a rage and cursed Henry for committing thoughts to a diary instead of sharing them generously with his friend. The blow was cleverly direct:

> Awful as it is to contemplate, I pray that, if I am the cold intellectual skeptic whom he rebukes, his curse may take effect, and wither and dry up those sources of my life, and my journal no longer yield me pleasure nor life. [18]

Thoreau did indeed go into the woods, in every weather, until he wrecked his health and hastened his death; in that sense, he had his eye on the object. But never for the object's sake. The dogged composition of the *Journal*, particularly where it seems most artless, resulted in a narration as contrived as any in the language.

When we come, therefore, to one of those superbly dramatic passages, told in the present tense, which purport to be a tonal reproduction of the moment, we must learn how to hear it. Take, for instance, that amazing moonlight walk starting at 1:30 A.M. on Tuesday, August 12, 1851,[19] which chronicles sensations minute by minute, makes the struggle of moon against clouds a gasping for breath, which fluctuates from joy to despair and back to the ecstasy of the dawn, all the while centering upon the "traveller." It is as near to some romantic piano prelude or Beethovian moonlight sonata as words can come. But this we know: whatever telegraphic or abbreviated "minutes" he made by the light of that moon, these were whittled, polished, tested and sifted before Thoreau entered into the *Journal* what presents itself as an on-the-spot impression of the experience. With this clue firmly grasped, we can then comprehend that *Walden* is not the transcript of an adventure in primitive living, but a highly schematized pattern of words, product of a hundred revisions, designed not so much to make a sociological point as to become a thing of beauty, to translate facts into form. It is the song Apollo sang even while in terrestrial enslavement to King Admetus.

4

Consciousness

I find that I can criticise my composition best when I
stand at a little distance from it, — when I do not see it,
for instance. I make a little chapter of contents which
enables me to recall it page by page to my mind, and judge
it more impartially when my manuscript is out of the way.
The distraction of surveying enables me rapidly to take new
points of view. A day or two surveying is equal to a
journey. (*J*, VI, 190)

STUDENTS OF LITERATURE know that writers keep
journals. Perhaps even Shakespeare did, though somehow we
doubt it. Certainly with the early nineteenth century and the
Romantic cult of "Genius," the Western World developed
what often seems an interest in the processes of creation
greater than in the creation itself. Thoreau's volume 1 is
studded with extracts from Goethe's *Italienische Reise*, which
the master Genius of the age lent to the public as one might
lend a private diary to an intimate. An assumption was abroad
that if an artist were truly artistic — fecund in mind and
fancy, curious, observant — he was bound in passing to notice
in his "journaux intimes" more than he could express in poem
or novel. This interest still leads us to the notebooks of the
Goncourts, Baudelaire, Flaubert, Hawthorne, Henry James,
André Gide. In the American setting, Emerson's *Journals* are
much more valuable to us than their having served him as a
"savings bank" because he deposited a vastly larger capital than
he ever withdrew.

More than almost any other comparable journal, Thoreau's

has to be read as a whole. He was peculiarly impelled after 1850 to concentrate his entire being upon it. He had no other outlet: even the composition of *Walden* could not drain his reservoir. Editors of Emerson's *Journals* leave out sections later incorporated in printed essays, but Bradford Torrey rightly perceived that to omit anything from Thoreau's *Journal* because it supplied a paragraph, a sentence, even a phrase, in the *Writings* would be to violate an integrity. Had Thoreau ever become a "successful" writer, to even such an extent as Emerson became in 1841 with the first *Essays*, he might then have journalized with the public in mind. But the failure of the *Week* in 1849, the seemingly hopeless fate of *Walden* thereafter, and then the dull thud with which the book did fall in 1854 — these circumstances decreed that for him the *Journal* would become not a means to an end, not a storage room for items subsequently to be displayed, but an end in itself. It became *the* work.

The final accomplishment — the fourteen volumes of the Walden Edition, with this splinter now replaced — offers many incidental charms. There is, for example, the character of George Minott, or that of John Goodwin, "the one-eyed Ajax." By the end of the narrative they have become as much creations of literature as Queequeg. And there are innumerable side glances at the town which, taken by themselves, amount to a sort of hilarious gazette. And of course, at the end there is the passionate material about John Brown. But in general Thoreau's *Journal*, as compared with Emerson's *Journals*, is of little use as a historical record, social or intellectual. (One would never know from our volume that in November was concluded the most raucous and violent presidential campaign the republic had yet suffered!) Measured against such a voluminous account, personal and public, as the *Diary* of George Templeton Strong, Thoreau's is a meager "source book" for the historian. It has fundamentally only one quality, and such relevancies as may here or there adhere to it are adventitious: it is perpetually, consumedly preoccupied with Henry Thoreau. He had not time to note anything so insignificant as the boisterous election of Tippecanoe and Tyler Too; he was too busy reporting himself.

Yet, while this statement is true, it is at the same time a little unfair to Thoreau. (To be fair to Thoreau, even at this remove, is as hazardous as it was to try to deal fairly with him in his lifetime; part of his peculiar genius consists in a strategy for putting his friends, and so his literary partisans, in the wrong.) What is more accurate and more just to say is that from the beginning, even while trying to gather material for an "author," Thoreau cherished a sneaking love for the activity itself, without regard to consequences or utility. Indeed, he worked on his two books and on his essays in good faith, and he went through the motions of seeking a market. Yet (the correspondence with Horace Greeley proves that anyone who presumed to act as Thoreau's agent excited a hornet's nest of ingratitude), the *Journal* shows that he could derive so much gratification from failure, so relish the assurance that he was the better for it, as to cause us to wonder whether in inner fact he simply courted it. The real impetus of the *Journal* assuredly, even in these first years, is something quite other than the young writer's ambition to become someday as famous as his patron. It is, as a James Joyce might have recognized, not a preparation but a portrait — a self-portrait.

Though at first sight the linkage may seem absurd, the personality created in the *Journal* has striking similarities to Stephen Dedalus. They would have understood each other. Even at the beginning, though more so after 1850, the *Journal* is a mode for expressing the self, using for defense of that self only the arms Joyce permitted himself to use — "silence, exile and cunning." With this difference, that Thoreau enacted his exile within his native town instead of going to Trieste; but geography is irrelevant, and one can be as irrevocably exiled in Concord as in Ravenna. In any case, the important element is the cunning.

On January 27, 1852 — when there seemed no chance of publishing *Walden* — in what for him was a mood of dejection, he toyed with the idea that "thoughts written down thus in a journal might be printed in the same form with greater advantage than if the related ones were brought together into separate essays." [1] Might they not thus be more related to life, more simple, less artful? "Is the scholastic air any advantage?" We are tempted, even understanding the anguish, to note here, as almost everywhere, Henry was crying "sour grapes" about something he desperately wanted but could not get. On the other hand, the tone to notice is the alacrity with which he was accommodating himself to defeat.

Still, this entry of January 27 has to be read in relation to one made a week before, January 22, 1852, in which he takes a farewell — a long farewell — to the greatness he dreamed of, to the prestige which is, in America, the reward of success:

> To set down such choice experiences that my own writings may inspire me and at last I may make wholes of parts. Certainly it is a distinct profession to rescue from oblivion and to fix the sentiments and thoughts which visit all men more or less generally, that the contemplation of the unfinished picture may suggest its harmonious completion. Associate reverently and as much as you can with your loftiest thoughts. Each thought that is welcomed and recorded is a nest egg, by the side of which more will be laid. Thoughts accidentally thrown together become a frame in which more may be developed and exhibited. Perhaps this is the main value of a habit of writing, of keeping a journal, — that so we remember our best hours and stimulate ourselves. My thoughts are my company.

Introduction

> They have a certain individuality and separate existence,
> aye, personality. Having by chance recorded a few dis-
> connected thoughts and then brought them into juxta-
> position, they suggest a whole new field in which it was
> possible to labor and to think. Thought begat thought.[2]

Surely, he would practice a great "profession," distinct in
all men's estimation, who could rescue from oblivion sentiments which do visit all men more or less generally. But
suppose the sentiments which visit this recorder, multitudi-
nously, happen not to be shared by the generality of men? The
answer to the doubt is yoked to the bravado, as always in
Thoreau: an unfinished picture may be the more valuable
for what it suggests about harmonious completion than any
simpering completeness. Henry Thoreau was never able,
with the best will he could muster, to put his mind to the task
of writing books or essays — though he did his manly duty in
that area of King Admetus's estate. The best he could do in
the *Week* was a compilation; that he ever again could have
achieved such a mastery of form as *Walden* may be doubted.
What the *Journal* demonstrates, and the books try to prove,
is that bare juxtaposition does beget the thought. Which
is to say that consciousness clips the coupons of the universe:
if a writer is adroit enough, he may shove onto some theo-
retical cosmic economy the responsibility for coherence, and
demand back from it a coherence of the parts. The investor
may of course blame the universe if it fails to pay such interest; that is why Emerson called his notebooks his bank,
and was pleased that they lived up to their obligations.
Thoreau was willing to let it transact the whole business for
him, which is the fatal limitation upon his artistry; though he
ought to have cared, he did not, for meanwhile, "My thoughts
are my company."

Harrison Blake did the reputation of Thoreau immense

harm by issuing four volumes from the *Journal* under seasonal titles. Thoreau thus became stereotyped as a "naturalist." Bradford Torrey was a professional ornithologist, and discovered himself shocked at Thoreau's inaccuracies and amateurism. Out of Transcendental scorn of the artificial, for instance, Thoreau would not stoop until 1854 to looking at his birds through a glass! Later students — scientists with literary curiosity — occasionally argue that he was perceptive about ecology or some branch of botany,[3] but if he was, the praise should go to the general Transcendental sense of "discipline," not to Thoreau's primary intent. This lover of Nature was not a lover of nature itself: as he said, he ever sought the "raw materials of tropes and figures." For him these metaphors — or, as he sometimes called them, "types" — were the rewards of an exploitation of natural resources, as self-centered, as profit-seeking, as that of any railroad-builder or lumber-baron, as that of any John Jacob Astor. Emerson has been laughed at for casting Henry, among the village equivalents of his *Representative Men,* for a "Napoleon." But Emerson was more shrewd in this case than when he insisted upon Thoreau's "Stoicism." Every student of the *Journal* becomes aware of a thrust in this emperor of the soul's hamlet (see below, p. 143) which invites the adjective Napoleonic. Even when serving Admetus, Thoreau was never gathering grains from the threshing floor. He strove to transcend not only experience but all potential experience; had he achieved what he intended, he would have become pure act, and his beloved Nature could then have been consigned to oblivion.

"My life, my life! why will you linger?" he exclaims, even in the selectivity of a *Journal* out of which spontaneity has been squeezed, on March 11, 1842, after he has come through the "sympathetic" lockjaw attendant on John's demise. Reviving to face the ordeal he could not escape, he dares ask

Introduction

God if He can afford that Henry should forget Him! Recognizing what he has, and all that he has, to work with, Thoreau makes his first venture — what was to become unfortunately a somewhat tiresome habit — into blasphemy:

> Why, God, did you include me in your great scheme?
> Will you not make me a partner at last? Did it need
> there should be a conscious material? [4]

The true "mythology" of the *Journal* is that Henry Thoreau, by the royal right of consciousness, identified himself with the Absolute, not even using Emerson's palliating circumlocution, "Over-Soul." So he fought for what remained of "my life" to be partner with the Almighty. Obviously he who strives to play the drama of such arrogance on the solid soil of Massachusetts is heading as recklessly as Tamburlane or Faust toward catastrophe.

The Christian centuries record many who aspired to be conterminous with the Godhead; the standard judgment is that they invite the destruction which invariably consumes them. The literature of Thoreau's youth was populated by Titans, Enceladuses, Prometheuses, Manfreds, Don Juans, all of whom plunged, from one pinnacle or another, into the debacle of selfhood. Concord — the very name imposed a social check upon the ego — was an American community, wherein no fancied Faust could gratify delusions of grandeur by seducing a rustic Margaret. Still, as Mr. Emerson was explaining, in the Transcendental philosophy circumstances do *not* alter cases. Mere maidens, let them be Margarets or Ellens, are small game. Nature, feminine counterpart of the Almighty, is a creature the ravishment of whom would be a conquest more resounding than any in Don Giovanni's inventory. To transcend the self would be a small price to pay, if only because such a victory would free the self from its

34

loathed identity. But in daily behavior, this aspiration called for anything but self-abnegation. The townsmen of Concord may not have apprehended much about the Romantic Agony; however, when Thoreau confronted them with his rustic caricature of the Byronic egotist, they, remembering their Puritan heritage, could recognize a limb of Satan when they saw one.

In volume 1, Henry was trying out, extracting from the Ur-journal, whatever seemed promising. He gave headings to his thoughts — "Heroism," "Suspicion," "Truth," or even "The Loss of a Tooth." On August 13, 1838, he hit upon "Consciousness." Could he close his ears and eyes, could he live with nothing but consciousness, then all walls and barriers would be dissipated, earth roll from under him, and he would float, "a subjective, heavily laden thought, in the midst of an unknown and infinite sea." He would come from no beginning, know no end, no aim. He could say, "I am a restful kernel in the magazine of the universe." [5]

Those who knew, and those who then were denouncing, the "German disease" would have had no difficulty diagnosing the symptoms Thoreau displayed. They would see in his madness one more example of the contagion Mr. Emerson was innocently spreading broadcast. Emerson might be insane only when the wind blew in one or two directions, but assuredly such an imitator as young Henry was exposing himself to gusts from every point of the compass, in the delusion that pure consciousness solved all riddles — "all straight lines making there their two ends to meet, eternity and space gambolling familiarly through my depths."

To James Russell Lowell, as to other guardians of sanity in the period, it seemed obvious that Thoreau mouthed the more extravagant solipsism of his master. Emerson did indeed, in his earlier utterances, speaking out of the Neo-Platonic side of his face, extol Romantic egoism; but even then, and increas-

ingly as the years went on, from the Montaigne-side he incul-
cated the prudence which knows that every man, instead of
being a kernel of the universe, is just one among others —
especially in America.

A slight illustration, out of a thousand, of the contrasting
(and essentially antagonistic) temperaments of Emerson and
Thoreau appears in their post-graduate dealings with the
Harvard College Library. Emerson summoned the young men
of America, and those of Harvard, to become "scholars." By
this he did not mean professional researchers, but persons who
could both read and dispense with books. His admonition
required that they have access to bookshelves, if only to refuse
to go near them. The best repository in the vicinity of Boston
(or perhaps next-best to the Boston Athenaeum) was Harvard
College. By a custom that came down from the seventeenth
century, the only graduates still entitled to take books out
of the Library were the occupants of pulpits in Cambridge
and adjoining towns. On June 25, 1846, Emerson requested
the Corporation that he be allowed to borrow, on the grounds
that, engaged in literary pursuits, he had need of the volumes;
furthermore, that his residence was "conveniently situated
for easy access to Cambridge." [6] The story is that he reinforced
his last argument by pointing out how the railroad had in
effect made Concord contiguous to Cambridge.

Somehow, the legend arose (Emerson accepted it) that
Thoreau then went to Cambridge, argued face-to-face with
the President, and that he also adduced the railroad. Contemporaries held this to be one more act of the monkey doing
what monkey had seen. The fact is, though Emerson may
have set the precedent, that not until 1849, the year of his
crisis, did Thoreau take action, and then by submitting a letter
to President Jared Sparks (which has not, I believe, before
been printed):

Consciousness

Concord Mass. Sep 17 — '49

Sir,

Will you allow me to trouble you with my affairs?
I wish to get permission to take books from the
College library to Concord where I reside. I am encouraged to ask this, not merely because I am an
alumnus of Harvard, residing within a moderate distance of her halls, but *because I have chosen letters for
my profession,* and so am one of the clergy embraced
by the spirit at least of her rule. Moreover, though
books are to some extent my stock and tools, I have not
the usual means with which to purchase them. I therefore regard myself as one whom especially the library
was created to serve. If I should change my pursuit or
move further off, I should no longer be entitled to this
privilege. — I would fain consider myself an *alumnus*
in more than a merely historical sense, and I ask only
that the University may help to finish the education,
whose foundation she has helped to lay. I was not then
ripe for her higher courses, and now that I am riper I
trust that I am not too far away to be instructed by her.
Indeed I see not how her children can more properly
or effectually keep up a living connexion with their
Alma Mater than by continuing to draw from her intellectual nutriment in some such way as this.

If you will interest yourself to obtain the above
privilege for me, I shall be truly obliged to you.

Yrs respectly
HENRY D. THOREAU[7]

President Everett acceded graciously to Emerson's petition,
since Emerson was discussing Carlyle with him; also, in 1846
many were appreciating that Emerson was, even though hereti-
cal, an ornament to the College's reputation. On the margin
of Thoreau's letter President Sparks gruffly wrote "one year."

37

Since there is no record of further action, we assume that Thoreau, being Thoreau, went on using Harvard's books with as few qualms of conscience as when he borrowed Alcott's axe. "It is difficult to begin without borrowing." [8] As for the axe, though Alcott called it the apple of his eye, Thoreau says he returned it sharper than he received it. He would similarly hone the volumes borrowed from Harvard, on the stone of his intelligence.

What is, inevitably, striking about his letter is the disguised truculence. He who italicizes *"because I have chosen letters for my profession"* is he who for years has been making a parade of having no profession. This was no time for meeching. He begged no favor from Harvard College, he permitted it to do him one. The letter flows from sublime arrogance: in the town he had no occupation except, as far as most could see, loafing and wasting time among such of its reprobates as John Goodwin; but to President Sparks he spoke as though the cultivation of his own consciousness were the ultimate profession. Nine years after Henry Thoreau, class of 1837, composed our volume of his *Journal*, he demanded permission from the College to continue his education; we can appreciate the spirit in which he set down even these tentative notes in 1840 only if we appreciate that he had already dedicated his entire consciousness to "letters."

5

Consciousness at Harvard

If Paris is much in your mind, if it is more and more to you, Concord is less and less, and yet it would be a wretched bargain to accept the proudest Paris in exchange for my native village. At best, Paris could only be a school in which to learn to live here, a stepping-stone to Concord, a school in which to fit for this university. I wish so to live ever as to derive my satisfactions and inspirations from the commonest events, every-day phenomena, so that what my senses hourly perceive, my daily walk, the conversation of my neighbors, may inspire me, and I may dream of no heaven but that which lies about me. A man may acquire a taste for wine or brandy, and so lose his love for water, but should we not pity him? (March 11, 1856; *J*, VIII, 204: "Thermometer at 7 A.M. 6°")

BEFORE THOREAU, whether or not at Emerson's magisterial hint, commenced the *Journal*, he already had undergone a sort of literary apprenticeship. Not so severe, perhaps, as that which Emerson and Margaret Fuller administered, but still moderately rigorous: he attended Harvard College. In those Spartan days, students were obliged to write a staggering number of themes. Under the direction — one may even say the dictatorship — of the Boylston Professor, Edward Tyrrell Channing (brother of the great divine, another uncle of Thoreau's off-again-on-again friend, the younger William Ellery), Henry did his stint of what, in the terminology of Professor Channing, were called "forensics." (Possibly nothing could have prevented Thoreau from writing in a forensic vein, but I think we must attribute much, for better or worse, to this argumentative training!) The Professor set the topic:

39

for example, "Whether the Cultivation of the Imagination Conduces to the Happiness of the Individual," or such a banality as whether the titles of books are pertinent to their contents or merely ingenious.

Though President Quincy complained that Henry slighted his studies (we can hardly imagine how "parietal" were the regulations of 1837), and Emerson pleaded on his behalf that Henry's health was poor, still a sufficient number of his college exercises remain to show that he trotted along with Professor Channing's assignments. Had these themes been composed by any other undergraduate — one who had no sister Sophia to worship his genius — they would long since have started some kitchen fire. Sanborn salvaged twenty-seven of them, marveling that they were preserved, which he printed (inaccurately) in his 1917 *The Life of Henry David Thoreau* (which is such a very different book from his 1882 *Henry D. Thoreau* in the "American Men of Letters" series). Since 1917 others of these exercises have been disinterred and treated to reverent annotation in scholarly journals.

They reveal much about Professor Channing's ideal of the student, and more about genteel standards of education in America, but they tell precious little about Thoreau — other than that these standards were imposed upon him, and that he would clearly have to work his way out from under them. Even the positions which seem prophetic of the later Thoreau were, I am certain, the sort of approved dissent from received precepts which in Channing's classes had become a new orthodoxy. Even that Commencement Part — the "Conference with Henry Vose" — would not for a moment offend President Quincy or the Boston businessmen who assembled on August 16, 1837, to despatch these young men into commercial America. Those who took the day off from pursuit of gain, in the depths of the Panic, would ceremonially applaud these sentiments:

> We are to look chiefly for the origin of the commercial
> spirit, and the power that still cherishes and sustains it,
> in a blind and unmanly love of wealth. Wherever this
> exists, it is too sure to become the ruling spirit; and as a
> natural consequence, it infuses into all our thoughts
> and affections a degree of its own selfishness; we become
> selfish in our patriotism, selfish in our domestic rela-
> tions, selfish in our religion.[1]

If that seemed like taking too literally injunctions of the New
Testament, the candidate recovered himself by noting that
"The Commercial Spirit" should not be categorically repro-
bated: it is an indication "of the entire and universal freedom
of the age in which we live." (One thinks ahead to Emerson's
"Napoleon" in *Representative Men*.) It is an advance in an
infinite series of progressions by which man casts off "earth-
born desires" on his predestined march toward becoming
"the Lord of Creation." [2]

Not by the most orthodox Whigs on the Harvard Corporation would the youth's declamation have been received as
anything but what pious, high-minded youths were expected
to say. And similarly applauded would have been his college
forensics. These do show, it is true, that he had ventured into
modern as well as classical literature, and had learned a few
terms of which Professor Channing was suspicious. From
whatever source, he grasped the distinction, emanating from
Germany, between the "classical" as being southern and
Christian, against the "romantic" as northern and pagan. He
could discriminate between the fancy and the "Imagination,"
and spell the latter with a capital.[3] In 1836, between his junior
and senior years, Orestes Brownson, William Henry Furness,
George Ripley and Bronson Alcott published books or articles
disturbing to the liberal Unitarianism which governed Harvard
College — and Emerson added to the affront by issuing on
September 9 a small book, *Nature*, which to that mentality

was plain obscurantism. Still, every Overseer would nod in complacent agreement at hearing Thoreau satisfy Professor Channing's query about the values of a literary life by declaiming, "Happy the man who is furnished with all the advantages to relish solitude! he is never alone, and yet may be retired in the midst of a crowd." [4]

This was what was left — which is to say that a great deal was left — of the clerical spirit in which the College had been founded. More and more graduates might be going into secular professions rather than to the ministry, and some even plunging into business, but that Harvard College existed for any other purpose than to prepare a man — even if not a "literary" man — to occupy his solitude with profit had never been questioned. As Thoreau concluded, those who relish literature can entertain sentiments of the sublime which lead them through Nature to Nature's God.

Likewise we follow Harvard's tuition in the youth's praise of simplicity in style,[5] his exhortation to follow "Truth," and even in his argument that certain forms of politeness, though they be insincere, permit a judicious resort to lying.[6] His preceptors so decorously paid their respects to the pastoral verse of eighteenth-century Britain that they could not be disturbed when, rising to Channing's bait of "Barbarities of Civilized States," Thoreau showed that he got the point:

> Wisdom is the result of education, and education being the bringing-out or development of that which is in man, by contact with the Not-me, — that is by Life, — is far safer in the hands of Nature than of Art.[7]

The only twinge of apprehension Professor Channing might, in 1837, have felt would be over this use of "Not-me" to signify the realm of outer existence: Emerson had given the phrase a peculiar stress in *Nature*. This youth appeared to be saying that education of the "me" should be assigned to a Nature which was not human — though he was not saying it with sufficient emphasis to alarm.

Nothing quite so fantastic was yet said. Actually, what Sanborn notes about several of these disquisitions may be said of all: they are so little practical that they must have fatigued Professor Channing as they still do the reader.[8] Nor did Thoreau achieve anything revolutionary when he answered Channing's inquiries about a native, original American literature.

Ever since the Revolution, spokesmen for American nationality had been proclaiming, or pleading for, the emergence of a distinctively American expression. For a brief moment in the 1820's Americans took satisfaction in the belief that Irving, Bryant, Cooper had proved the proposition in the affirmative. Yes, the Americans had done *something*, they had written what the world would read — even though, within a few years, Irving did seem to be derived from Goldsmith, Bryant from Wordsworth, Cooper from Scott.

After what Americans conceived to be a military triumph in 1815, proclamations that this nation was a new — exempt from the curses of any old — civilization were issued at every Commencement and Phi Beta Kappa ceremonial. C. J. Ingersoll pronounced from Philadelphia in 1823, "The Influence of America on the Mind." In 1824 Edward Everett told the Harvard Phi Beta Kappa of "The Circumstances Favorable to the Progress of Literature in America." But, though young Emerson listened, nobody (in New England) seemed to do anything about the summons. By 1837, when Thoreau was graduated, hundreds of orators had chanted upon native genius, but not one — not, for all his greatness, even the Reverend William Ellery Channing — had produced an original sentence. Except, that if any seemed to have done it, there was Emerson. As Henry Adams remarked about the Harvard Class of 1857 — which came of age in the same climate as that

43

of 1837 — Harvard College existed in order to impart calm. Hence Thoreau could write about the chances of American genius with a calmness of which, for the rest of his life, he would grow progressively ashamed. To find a way out of this complacency would become — by 1840 it has already become — a necessity. Then he would be constrained to salvage exquisite sentences in his *Journal*, trusting that ultimately these would become a vindication of American literary talents.

In March 1836, Professor Channing put to his juniors what already was a tired topic, "Advantages and Disadvantages of Foreign Influences on American Literature." Henry answered, once more, according to form. We of New England, said he — as all New England took pride in saying — are devoted to utility: "We are a nation of speculators, stockholders and money-changers." We do things by steam, and our only question about a book is whether it will sell. Politically we are independent, but still we read (when we have time to read) Milton and Shakespeare, Cowper and Dr. Johnson. Who, the boy asks — and stays for an answer — "will say that the influence they have exerted has been prejudicial to our literary interests?" [9]

At Harvard the question was rhetorical: no answer was forthcoming and no answer was needed. Men such as Everett, Professor Channing, Jared Sparks called upon the College to give the nation intellectual leadership, but muted their bugle-like notes by explaining that we need not go to such violent lengths as casting off the heritage of Europe and civilized manners. By 1836 many preceptors were becoming uncomfortable as to whether they had not overdone their vaunts of self-sufficiency, had not thus encouraged dangerous and disruptive proclivities. Therefore we wonder, when Henry composed, for March 20, 1836, a review of William Howitt, *The Book of the Seasons: or the Calendar of Nature*, just how much Professor Channing would have comprehended his further thoughts on native literature — or if Channing simply checked these off as the sort of rhetoric Everett had stimulated. Germany, Thoreau reports Howitt as saying, has by main force created a national literature; how infinitely mightier then should be the American utterance: America, "with her beautiful and stupendous scenes of nature; her immense lakes; her broad and sweeping rivers; her clime melting into all the varieties of the globe; her cataracts shaking the earth; her mountains kissing the heavens; her solitudes and forests, yet hushed in primeval silence." [10]

I have made a long digression, but the point has to be emphasized: you can hardly read this volume 3 of 1840, or the entire *Journal*, or indeed anything of Thoreau's at all, unless you understand that at the heart of him he was the most "nationalistic" of all our writers, beyond even Melville and Whitman, though his New England inhibitions prevented him from becoming as strident as Whitman. In the end, he would be envious of Whitman's open bragging.

In 1836, at Harvard, to allow a boy of nineteen to ride this rhetorical charger would not seem to the Harvard Faculty encouraging him to hurt himself, since nobody took such boasting seriously enough to let it run amock. But within a year or two, this august body was jolted into a realization that the rhetoric had broken the checkrein, that it was indeed galloping madly through the imaginations of the more promising youth, was riding roughshod over everything for which Harvard College stood in the way of decorum and good manners. From professors at Harvard, Longfellow and Lowell, with assists from such a model of urbanity as Dr. Oliver Wendell Holmes, came an increasingly ill-tempered sneer at the basic idea that there should be any proportion between the sublimity of American expression and the vastness of her mountains, that her poets must roar like Niagara or sound as stupendous as the Mississippi. These gentlemen mounted their counterattack chiefly against a group of literary patriots in New York calling themselves "Young America," who emitted reams of grandiose exhortation, and who offended Bostonian critics as much by merely being New Yorkers as by being blatant. But these Bostonians had also to deplore manifestation of nativist frenzy closer to home. They soon appreciated that Mr. Emerson was fundamentally sane, and that he could be admitted to the Saturday Club. Still, they did regret that a few of his more extravagant remarks were taken too literally by impressionable youths. By 1849, we have seen, the damage done to Thoreau was permanent. He was then demanding the privilege of using Harvard College Library on the grounds that, having chosen the profession of letters, he was self-elected to the Brahmin caste of New England. However, when Emerson suggested that he might for once unbend and visit the Saturday Club in the Parker House, Thoreau's answer showed what really followed from a Transcendental hostility to civilization: "The only room in Boston which I visit with alacrity is the Gentlemen's Room at the Fitchburg Depot, where I wait for cars, sometimes for two hours, in order to get out of town." [11]

In the tradition of New England it was respectable — nay, even imperative — that youths compose diaries. Several influences converged on this responsibility. Puritans kept diaries to record the fluctuation of grace and desolation, and so improved them as means for their own salvation. At nineteenth-century Harvard, the agony of regeneration was not quite so pressing, but the habit of introspection, and of making a record of introspection, was pervasive. Furthermore, there had grown up in the society, as a corollary of the first concern, a persuasion that everybody should preserve an account of his own tribulations in order to edify his children. And then, in the Revolutionary and subsequent decades, participants in events had so vivid a sense of living through history that they felt a tremendous need for getting history recorded. John Quincy

Adams would as soon have thought of going to bed with face and hands unwashed as to retire before he brought his diary up to date. Thus when Professor Channing propounded as a topic in 1835 the keeping of journals, he assumed that every boy would commend the practice, as — had the question ever been proposed — each would have endorsed chastity. Thoreau did not disappoint him.

If the subjects Professor Channing lined out week after week seem to us unexciting, we should not blame him; after all, teaching composition to boys who care nothing about writing is a tiresome business. Whatsoever his methods, Channing is still known to posterity as having "turned out" more writers than any other instructor in the history of the Ivy League. In this instance we may especially condone his platitudinous choice of subject.

Henry, as I say, approved of journals. He spurred his imagination to the inventive fancy of a machine capable of instantaneously arranging on paper each idea as it occurs, without any exertion on the writer's part. Then he went off on what may have struck Channing as a curious tack: after all, said the young Thoreau, the preservation of our scattered thoughts is the least value of a journal. Most men can think, but few can express what they feel. If each would make a reckoning to himself at the end of the day, then "he may be able to detect what false coins have crept into his coffers." [12] In this pursuit, he would cease to dwell upon the past, would every day turn over a new leaf, prepared to distinguish it from the preceding. Not quite said, though by implication conveyed, is an objection to being deceived by counterfeit banknotes; but the pressing question is why one should be obliged to undertake these revisions:

> Most of us are apt to neglect the study of our own characters, thoughts and feelings, and for the purpose of forming their own minds, look to others; who should

merely be considered as different editions of the same great work. To be sure, it would be well for us to examine the various copies, that we might detect any errors; but yet it would be foolish for one to borrow a work which he possessed himself, but had not perused.[13]

One may read this quite simply as another instance of that introspective disposition which the youth of New England retained; if it speaks a bit too strongly a fascination with the self, it regains perspective by confessing, in the Harvard manner, that the diarist should not lose all sense of proportion. Surely nothing here suggests that this retiring young man would, by the act of keeping a *Journal*, become so identified with his journalistic self as to cast himself in the abrasive role of a chanticleer waking up his neighbors. Or, is this a prefiguration of a writer who later would unrepentantly announce that whereas in most books the "I" is omitted, "in this it will be retained; that, in respect to egotism, is the main difference"?[14]

While Frank Sanborn is never to be trusted, he did know his man; he notes that this piece about journal-keeping is the most "significant" of the college essays. What Professor Channing could not have known in 1836, his nephew Ellery, along with several others, informed him and the Faculty between 1840 and 1844 when he and they wrote the (financially) unsuccessful *Dial*. In the last year of that heady publication — conceived, as its title implies, not so much to be a magazine as a "journal" — Ellery projected a visionary hero-ideal of himself in "Edward Ashford" — who virtually screams out his cousinship with Roderick Usher. For once the most eccentric of eccentrics delineated the whole group:

He is one of a class of young persons, who have lately sprung into existence, as distinct from the youth of the last generation, as Italians from Icelanders, — the children of the new birth of the century, whose places have not yet been found. This mania for what is natural and this distaste for conventionalism, is exhibited as the popular idea, yet inaccessible to the class in which he was born, and which is the last to feel the auroral influences of reform. But not in our day will this new idea of civilization complete itself, and hence these unconscious reformers will be the last to discover their true position. They cannot unite themselves with sects or associations, for the centre of their creed consists in the disavowal of congregations, and they wander solitary and alone, the true madmen of this nineteenth century.[15]

Forty or more years after *The Dial* went into limbo, Emerson remembered, albeit faintly, the spirit of that time. "The young men," he recollected, "were born with knives in their brain, a tendency to introspection, self-dissection, anatomizing of motives." In the manifesto which he composed for the first number of *The Dial* (by revising Margaret Fuller's draft), in July 1840, he tried not to set his sights too high: Emerson wagered that the new influence in America would manifest itself more in a higher tone of criticism than in creative works. Even so, his plan embraced more than criticism. He aspired to give expression to a fresh spirit which might lift men to a higher platform, which, raising them to the level of Nature, might take "away its melancholy from the the landscape, and reconcile the practical with the speculative powers."

We do not know just what Thoreau thought of Emerson's formula for reconciling the practical and speculative by removing melancholy from the landscape. *The Dial* does, however, exhibit the literary and philosophical knives which by 1840 were flashing through the brains of the young men. These were all of foreign manufacture: Wordsworth, Coleridge, Carlyle, and shining blades of German steel. Volume 1 of Thoreau's *Journal*, even when reduced from the original 546 pages, is full of quotations from Goethe, some of which he used in the *Week*. Without too much effort these English and German writers were harmonized into a system of doctrine which could raise its acolytes to the highest platform of "religious sentiment." But there was one liberator of the early nineteenth century in whose presence the most liberated of New England Puritans found themselves acutely uncomfortable — Lord Byron.

If they were to be fair — Transcendentalists strove to be fair, even when it hurt — they had to confess that, more than Wordsworth, Byron prepared the way for them. His fabulous popularity among Americans in the 1820's raised the specter of some American "Edward Ashford" that could not, even by the Commercial Spirit, be disregarded. Unitarian and Orthodox clergymen vied with each other in denouncing him, but if one were to say, as with Emerson in *The Dial* for October 1840, that "subjectiveness" was the keynote of the age, then he had to reckon with Byron. Emerson got around the problem in "Thoughts on Modern Literature" by accounting for the "consciousness" that was everywhere present in the new criticism as signifying that men were now conscious of the one mind in which they all participate. Thus they hunger for unity; this love of the vast can be seen in Madame de Staël and in Wordsworth, it is absent from Crabbe and Scott — in Byron it is pre-eminent, but "in Byron it is blind, it sees not its true end." The will of Byron is perverted, and for all his power he ends by worshiping the accidents of society: "his praise of Nature is thieving and selfish." The high seriousness of the Transcendentalists, along with their incurable predilection for "ideas" (the Puritan heritage they could denounce but not outgrow), made Byron to them a figure more enticing but as morally repellent as he was to the Reverend Andrews Norton.

In what Thoreau preserves of his journalizing, Byron figures rarely. Yet in volume 1, on December 8, 1838, not quite two years before Emerson's judgment, there is a curious paragraph, with a heading:

BYRON

Nothing in nature is sneaking or chapfallen, as somewhat maltreated and slighted, but each is satisfied with its being, and so is as lavender and balm. If skunk-cabbage is offensive to the nostrils of men, still has it not drooped in consequence, but trustfully unfolded its leaf of two hands' breadth. What was it to Lord Byron whether England owned or disowned him, whether he smelled sour and was skunk-cabbage to the English nostril or violet-like, the pride of the land and ornament of every lady's boudoir? Let not the oyster grieve that he has lost the race; he has gained as an oyster.[16]

On the surface, this seems an odd way of vindicating, even partially, the author of *Manfred* and *Don Juan* — by equating him with the skunk-cabbage. But on second thought, why should a Harvard graduate, returned to Concord in order to keep a *Journal*, and thus to perfect his own private edition of the "great work," strengthen his courage by aligning himself with both Lord Byron and the skunk-cabbage? Why seek a model in the oyster?[17]

What a reading of Byron did to young sensitivities throughout this republic was to make them painfully aware of the parochial limitations of their experience. They might have knives in their brains, and violet-likenesses which no less than Byron's panted for selfhood, but in not many parts of a country ruled by "The Commercial Spirit" — least of all in Concord — were there boudoirs in which to practice becoming Childe Harold.

This is what the six early volumes of Thoreau's *Journal*

are: efforts to discover how to be conscious of the self in a commonplace, prosperous American town. As the second paragraph of *Walden* confesses, after flinging down the gauntlet of "egotism": "Unfortunately, I am confined to this theme by the narrowness of my experience." [18] Margaret Fuller understood the dilemma, and teased Emerson about it (with slightly more pressure her pleasantry could become a taunt):

> It is a fine day for composition, were it not in Concord. But I trow the fates which gave this place Concord, took away the animating influences of Discord. Life here slumbers and steals on like the river. A very good place for a sage, but not for the lyrist or the orator.[19]

Thoreau was culling out of his notebooks poems and passages which could temporarily be put in the *Journal,* on their way toward becoming compelling orations. But would Concord provide enough subject matter? The answer emerges slowly: where Byron refined and cultivated the supple consciousness that plays through *Don Juan* by flinging himself into the wildest range of experience, a Concordian Byron had of necessity to narrow the limits of his experience, and then as wantonly exhaust them.[20] So when *The Dial* is about to offer him a chance to explain himself, Thoreau undertakes two sustained compositions, a trumpeting of rural libertinism under the guise of the heroic in "The Service" and a hymn to that paragon of self-infatuation, titanic (at least as young Henry sees him) beyond Byron and Goethe, "Sir Walter Raleigh." He has just finished the "Persius" when this volume begins, and is hard at work on these two pieces, by which he expects to become as famous as Emerson was predicting; before it ends, Margaret has loftily rejected them both.

But there would need to be more than the formidable Miss Fuller to stop him. The central passage among the entries designed for "The Service" is that on page 143, below, about the silent hamlet of the soul.[21] If he could not get his thought published there, then he would try again in "Sir Walter Raleigh." [22] The way to become a Byron in Concord was not to improvise stanzas in the early morning after a night's debauch, but to lose no shred of elegance. At the end of "Monday" in the *Week* the travelers blissfully sleep to the sound of some tyro's beating a drum in preparation for a country muster, and this least spontaneous of consciousnesses enacts his masquerade:

> Still the drum rolled on, and stirred our blood to fresh extravagance that night. The clarion sound and clang of corselet and buckler were heard from many a hamlet of the soul, and many a knight was arming for the fight behind the encamped stars.[23]

A masquerade indeed it is, for the memory of the drum beating on the banks of the Merrimack is not entered in volume 2 until June 18, 1840, ten months after Thoreau may have heard it,[24] which is to say, ten months after he probably made a note in the Ur-journal. Yet in the *Week* it is woven, with the utmost nonchalance, into the twice rejected moral of volume 3, composed in July or August 1840. The Byronic skunk-cabbages could hardly be more persistent, or less chapfallen.

But then, compared with Byron's boudoirs, what has consciousness to work with in America? In January of 1852 Thoreau would again, as he had done before and frequently would afterwards, examine his pretensions to being a "traveller." Compared with Plutarch or Montaigne, how much of the world had he seen? "Perhaps no man's daily life has been rich enough to be journalized." [25]

Still, the question posed by Concord, as Margaret Fuller slyly put it before she fled to New York, Paris and Rome, was how to create the necessary discord. While Thoreau was putting together volume 3, he was still respectable: he was teaching a school. So he was keeping his diary as an adjunct to a quite other profession, trusting to achieve the eminence he had hailed in his forensics. By July 1851, the configuration of distinction in an American town had become clarified; it was not attained by the *Week* and it seemed unlikely to be achieved by *Walden*. There was left only this way for the graduate of Harvard College to become unique:

> There is some advantage in being the humblest, cheapest, least dignified man in the village, so that the very stable boys shall damn you. Methinks I enjoy that advantage to an unusual extent. There is many a coarsely well-meaning fellow, who knows only the skin of me, who addresses me familiarly by my Christian name. I get the whole good of him and lose nothing myself.[26]

Here, though not visible to the casual eye, is the link between Concord and London; in either setting the Byronic assertion could be so recognizable that an American provincial need not hesitate to equate himself with the noble Lord. If out of rejection by the community come both *Don Juan* and the *Journal*, who is to say which is the more authentic voice of exiled Apollo?

The only anxiety which then pesters both *Don Juan* and Thoreau's *Journal*, for all their remarkably similar determinations to compel the world to accept the authors on their own terms, is this: How did divine Apollo become enslaved in the first place?

6

The Stratagems of Consciousness—Death

It was strange that only the funeral bell was in harmony with that scene, while other sounds were too frivolous and trivial, as if only through the gate of death would man come to appreciate his opportunities and the beauty of the world he has abused. In proportion as death is more earnest than life, it is better than life. (October 7, 1857; *J*, X, 76)

WHEN MAN STRIVES to become conscious of himself, standing alone in the universe, without divine support and distrusting any promise of immortality, history remarks that he is promptly overcome with a sense of finitude. This is quickly followed, in standard lamentations, by the realization that he dies. He may glory in his power of thought, but he is reminded that he is only a reed which happens to think.

If Emerson's call to self-reliance and the deliriums of subjectivity had an invigorating effect upon the Edward Ashfords of Massachusetts, it also struck terror into many who could not resist his spell. He seemed to ask scholars to become madmen, to dispense with the historic consolations of Christianity. For many, his optimistic rhetoric only half concealed the bleached skull. Could the impersonal Over-Soul compensate for a loss of the hope of — the very concern for — personal survival?

Isaiah Thornton Williams came to Concord to teach school in 1840; in the Berkshires of his boyhood, the old orthodoxy still reigned, undisturbed by Unitarianism, let alone by Transcendentalism, but he was an impulsive youth, and soon found himself reeling from the fumes of Concord grapes. He was, said Emerson, "very handsome very intelligent." Emerson urged Margaret Fuller to call on him in 1843; if the good man was matchmaking, he ought to have known that nothing would come of it.[1] By the autumn of 1841 Williams was studying law in Buffalo, New York, which, viewed from the Concord perspective, was far in the West. Homesick for what had seemed to him the wonders of conversation with the two Thoreaus, Alcott, and Emerson, he conveyed his yearnings to Henry on September 24. His dithyrambic epistle is too verbose to quote entire, but since it has never hitherto been printed, I select those portions which illustrate, more ingenuously than any I know, just what several would-be Ashfords had to resolve with themselves:

Buffalo, N. Y. Sept. 24, 1841 —

When I left Concord I felt a strong desire to continue the conversation I had so fortunately commenced with some of those whom the Public call Transcendentalists. Their sentiments seemed to me to possess a peculiar fitness. Though full of doubt I felt I was fed & refreshed by those interviews. The doctrines I then heard have ever since, been uppermost in my mind — and like balmy sleep over the weary limbs, have they stolen over me quite unawares. I have not embraced them — but they have embraced me — I am led, their willing captive. Yet I feel I have but yet taken the first step. I would know more of this matter. I would be taken by the hand and led up from this darkness and torpidity where I have so long groveled like an earth-worm. I know what it is to be a slave to what I thought a Christian faith — and with what rapture do greet the hand that breaks my chains — & the voice that bids me live.

Most of the books you recommended to me I was not able to obtain. — "Nature" I found — and language can not express my admiration of it. When gloom like a thick cloud comes over me, in that I find an amulet that dissipates the darkness and kindles anew my highest hopes. Few copies of Mr Emerson's Essays have found their way to this place. I have read part of them and am very much delighted with them. Mr Parker's Sermon I have also found — and as much as I should have shrunk from such sentiments a year ago — half, as I already receive them. I have also obtained "Hero Worship" — which of course I read with great interest, and as I read I blush for my former bigotry and wonder that I had not known it all before [—] wonder what there is in chains that I should have loved them so much — Mr. E's Lecture before the Theological Class at Cambridge I very much want. If you have it in your possession, allow me to beg you to foreward it to me & I will return it by mail after perusing it. Also Mr. Alcott's "Human Culture" — I will offer no apology for asking this favor — for I know you will not require it.

I find I am not alone here, your principals are working their way even in Buffalo, this emporium of wickedness and sensuality. We look to the east for our guiding star for there our sun did rise. Our motto is that of the Grecian Hero — "Give but to see — and Ajax asks no more." . . .

My sheet is nearly full & I must draw to a close — I feel I have already wearied your patience. Please remember me to those of your friends whose acquaintance I had pleasure to form while in Concord. I engaged to write your brother. Mr Alcott also gave me the same privelege — which I hope soon to avail myself of. I hope sometime to visit your town again which I remember with so much satisfaction — yet with so much regret — regret that I did not entire[ly] avail myself of the acquaintances, it was my high privelege to make while there and that the lucubrations of earlier years did not better fit me to appreciate & enjoy. I cheer myself with fanning the fading embers of a hope that I shall yet retrieve my fault — that such an opportunity will again be extended to me — and that I may once more look upon that man whose name I never speak without reverence — whom of all I most admire — almost adore — Mr Emerson. I shall wait with impatience to hear from you.

Believe me
ever yours —
ISAIAH T. WILLIAMS.

Williams gives us an authentic illustration of just what the Transcendental ferment signified in the year of our volume 3. Above all, he shows what the younger men beheld in the regal bearing of Emerson, the glorious impact upon them of *Nature* and "The Divinity School Address." "Mr Parker's Sermon" is A *Discourse of the Transient and Permanent in Christianity*, delivered at the South Boston Church on May 19, 1841 — to which, and the tremendous furor about which, there is in Thoreau's *Journal* no slightest reference! What Williams calls Alcott's "Human Culture" is his *The Doctrine and Discipline of Human Culture* (1836), which today not even those most admiring of Transcendentalism can read. Williams's "Hero Worship" is, of course, Carlyle's *On Heroes, Hero-Worship, and the Heroic in History*, published early in 1841. (Thoreau, unwittingly, had tried to anticipate Carlyle with "The Service.")

In other words, we get in Isaiah Williams's frenetic letter the swirl of ideas, to the point of convulsion, which the Transcendental barrage was evoking. By implication, he was asking where did Henry stand?

Our text of Thoreau's reply is dated September 8. However, this is a copy, in the Berg Collection of the New York Public Library, presumably in Blake's hand. Since Blake was always slipshod, and since this is clearly an answer to Williams, we assume that Blake meant October 8. In any case, the important fact is that Thoreau, in the autumn of 1841, being still the personality of our volume 3, elected to read this bumbling puppy a lecture (a temptation to which, with most of his correspondents, Thoreau was always ready to yield).

In order to appreciate just how pontifical Thoreau waxed, we must first note another strain which Isaiah was so indiscreet — or so naïve — as to sound. He came from rural New England, and now was seeking his fortune, having sought it in vain through northern Ohio, in the metropolis of the West. After 1815, thousands of New Englanders moved westward, eager to grow up with the country, never to give another thought to the barren hills of Massachusetts and Connecticut. But a few cherished a sense of exile. Isaiah Williams, when he wrote his pathetic letter of September 24, 1841, was not yet acclimatized to Buffalo; he suspended his struggle against Christianity to voice this wail:

> For myself my attention is much engrossed in my Studies. Entering upon them as I do without a Public Education — I feel that nothing but the most undivided attention and entire devotion to them will ensure me even an ordinary standing in the profession. There is something false in such devotion — I already feel its chilling effects. I fear I shall fall into the wake of the profession which is in this section proverbially bestial. Law is a noble profession[,] it calls loudly for men of genius and integrity to fill its ranks. I do not aspire to be a great lawyer. I know I cannot be, but it is the sincere desire of my heart that I may be a true one.
>
> You are ready to ask — how I like the West. I must answer — not very well. I love New England so much that the West is comparatively odious to me. The part of Ohio that I visited was one dead Level — often did I strain my eyes to catch a glimpse of some distant mountain that should transport me in imagination to

the wild country of my birth, but the eternal level spread itself on & on & I almost felt myself launched forever
. . .

Since only exiled New Englanders are entertained by this sort of anguish, I cut short Isaiah's lamentation, noting merely that at this writing he could get no Transcendental joy even from the splendor of sunsets over Lake Erie. What concerns us is Thoreau's response; though dated, as I say, in our copy September 8, it is palpably answering Williams's letter bearing the date of September 24:

Concord Sept. 8th 1841

Dear Friend

I am pleased to hear from you out of the west, as if I heard the note of some singing bird from the midst of its forests, which travellers report so grim and solitary — It is like the breaking up of Winter and the coming in of Spring, when the twigs glitter and tinkle, and the first sparrow twitters in the horizon. I doubt if I can make a good echo — Yet it seems that if a man ever had the satisfaction to say once entirely and irrevocably what he believed to be true he would never leave off to cultivate that skill.

I suppose if you see any light in the east it must be in the eastern state of your own soul, and not by any means, in these New England States.

Our eyes perhaps do not rest so long on any as on the few who especially love their own lives — who dwell apart at more generous intervals, and cherish a single purpose behind the formalities of society with such steadiness that of all men only their two eyes seem to meet in one focus. They can be eloquent when they speak — they can be graceful and noble when they act. For my part if I have any creed it is so to live as to preserve and increase the susceptibleness of my nature to noble impulses — first to observe if any light shine on me, and then faithfully to follow it. The Hindoo Scripture says, "Single is each man born; single he dies; single he receives the reward of his good, and single the punishment of his evil deeds."

Let us trust that we have a good conscience[.] The steady light whose ray every man knows will be enough for all weathers. If any soul look abroad even today it will not find any word which does it more justice than the New Testament, yet if it be faithful enough it will have experience of a revelation fresher and directer than that, which will make that to be only the best tradition. The strains of a more heroic faith vibrate through the week days and the fields than through the Sabbath and the Church. To shut the ears to the immediate voice of God, and prefer to know him by report will be the only sin. Any respect we may yield to the paltry expedients of other men like ourselves — to the Church — the State — or the School — seems purely gratuitous, for in our most private experience we are never driven to expediency. Our religion is where our love is. How vain for men to go musing one way, and worshipping another. Let us not fear to worship the muse. Those stern old worthies — Job and David and the rest, had no Sabbath-day worship but sung and revelled in their faith, and I have no doubt that what true faith and love of God there is in this age will appear to posterity in the happy system of some creedless poet.

I think I can sympathize with your sense of greater freedom. — The return to truth is so simple that not even the muses can tell when we began to breathe healthily, but recovery took place long before the machinery of life began to play freely again when on our pillow at midnoon or midnight some natural sound fell naturally on the ear. As for creeds and doctrines we are suddenly grown rustic — and from walking in the streets and squares — walk broadly in the fields —

as if a man were wise enough not to sit in a draft, and get an ague, but moved buoyantly in the breeze.

It is curious that while you are sighing for New England, the scene of our fairest dreams should lie in the west — it confirms me in the opinion that places are well nigh indifferent. Perhaps you have experienced that in proportion as our love of nature is deep and pure we are independent upon her. I suspect that ere long when some hours of faithful and earnest life have imparted serenity into your Buffalo day, the sunset on lake Erie will make you forget New England. It was the Greeks made the Greek isle and sky, and men are beginning to find Archipelagos elsewhere as good. But let us not cease to regret the fair and good, for perhaps it is fairer and better than to [blank] them.

I am living with Mr. Emerson in very dangerous prosperity. He gave me three pamphlets for you to keep, which I sent last Saturday. The "Explanatory Preface" is by Elizabeth Peabody who was Mr. Alcott's assistant, and now keeps a bookstore and library in Boston. Pray let me know with what hopes and resolutions you enter upon the study of law — how you are to make it a solid part of your life. After a few words interchanged we shall learn to speak pertinently and not to the air. My brother and Mr Alcott express pleasure in the anticipation of hearing from you and I am sure that the communication of what most nearly concerns you will always be welcome to Yours Sincerely

H. D. THOREAU

Isaiah writes again on November 27. There has been a great change. He has little to say about Transcendentalism; what he would register upon his correspondent is his distress at becoming enslaved to "the Law." He composes one of those cries of heart which, over two centuries, have been uttered by American youths possessed of, or possessed by, "ideals," who have to make a living under "The Commercial Spirit." He was striving to merge himself in the profession. A little bit of his screaming will suffice:

> Time's devastating hand is beginning already to obliterate the traces of my youthful feelings — and I am becoming more & more contented with my present situation and feel less and less a desire inexorable to return and be a child once more.
>
> This I suppose to be the natural tendency of the circumstances in which I am placed. Man's ends are shaped for him and he must abide his destiny. This seems a little like fatality — yet, how can we avoid the conclusion that the Soul is Shaped by circumstances and many of those circumstances beyond man's control? I think that could I always be "true to the dream of Childhood" I should always be happy — I can imagine circumstances in which I think I might be so — but they are not my present circumstances — these are my fate — I would not complain of them did they not war against what I feel to be my highest interest and indeed I will not as it is — for I know not what is my highest good. — I know not the good whither I am bound, and as I do not know but all is well as far as the external is concerned I will trust to the author of my being — the author and creator of those beautiful fields and woods I so much enjoy in my morning and evening walks — the author of the glorious Lake Sunsets — that all is well.

Here was indeed a transformation, from September to November! Within two months, still an esteem for Emerson — though moderated — and kind regards to Alcott: and with this formality, a capitulation to the Being who governs us through circumstances, with at last an acceptance of Lake Erie's sunsets. Whereupon, Isaiah tells the full, the grim, details of his professional decision. Years later, Thoreau would assert that most men lead lives of quiet desperation; let us try to conceive how, having finished volume 3 and at work on volume 4, Henry would have received this from one who had been touched by the flame of Emersonian Concord:

> I love the profession. It presents a boundless field — a shoreless ocean where my bark may drift — and bound & leap from wave to wave in wild but splendid surge — without the fear of rock or strand. Yet I chose it not so much for the love I bore it — for I knew that in it my intercourse must be with the worst specimens of humanity — as knowing that by it, I might get more knowledge, discipline and intellectual culture than in any other which I could choose simply as a means of livelihood — have much more time to devote to literature and philosophy — and, as I have said, be better prepared intellectually for progress in these pursuits than in any other branch of business followed simply to provide for the bodily wants.

This confession — this pathos of Williams's surrender — is an old story. Was it Thoreau's first encounter with the prescribed pattern of American sensibility? Williams carried it off bravely, telling how he first sat down to Blackstone with a heavy heart, crying "Adieu, ye Classic halls — My Muse adieu," but how he achieved a modus vivendi: he would so conduct himself as a lawyer that he would still find a place within his profession for "Literature — philosophy theology or poetry."

If the manuscripts we now retain are, as they seem to be, the sum of this correspondence, then Thoreau did not find himself moved to counter Williams's effusion until March 14, 1842. During November and December of 1841 he was living — in "dangerous prosperity" — with Emerson, working around the house, reading proofs of *The Dial,* keeping his *Journal* — and, of course, making no progress in any visible "profession." On January 11, 1842, John Thoreau died. On January 27, Emerson's six-year-old son Waldo died of scarlet fever. There are no entries in Thoreau's volume 6 between January 9 and February 19. He had his ways of meeting social obligation. Williams professed to admire John, and Henry owed Williams a letter. He collected his energies, on March 14, to tell Isaiah about both John and Waldo.

This is not the place to worry about how Emerson the sage absorbed into his cosmic optimism the shock of bereavement. In the *Journals* he at first furiously declared that no law of compensation should ever solace him, could ever justify such wanton desolation. Eventually, he composed "Threnody," and later, in an essay entitled "Experience," told, with for him astonishing frankness, how he managed to reconcile himself to this horror.

But Emerson was obliged to make the wrong become a right. None among his expectant public was more concerned than Williams. He wrote Thoreau, out of his now engrossing profession, on June 25 — he had been tremendously busy — and was properly sympathetic about John, who, Isaiah commiserated, was not fitted for this cold, hardhearted world: "In such a nature I see a strong assurance of a better existence when this is over." But, that obeisance made, Mr. Williams came to what urgently concerned him and all who had been enticed by Emerson:

> And Mr. Emerson — how did he endure the loss of his child? It was a cruel stroke — did his philosophy come to his aid as does the Christian Faith to administer consolation to the bereaved? I wish to know what were his feelings, for the consolation that a Christian faith offers the bereaved & afflicted is one of its strongest holds upon my credulity. If there is consolation from his philosophy

in trials like those, it will do much toward settling my belief. I wish to know minutely in this point. I think much on Death & sometimes doubt if my early impressions upon that subject are ever effaced. The fear of it occasions a thousand folies — I feel it is unmanly — but yet "that undiscovered country" Who shall tell us whether to fear — or desire it?

Up to 1840 death had not come close to Henry Thoreau. His taciturn father, his voluble mother, his loquacious aunts, his two sisters, his gay brother had been there since first he came to consciousness. Even so, he was a child of New England: the "burying ground" was almost the center of that culture. One of the fascinations of volume 3 is that in it, for the first time, he tries to talk death down. The note on the front cover lining about death (below, p. 133) points toward the long entry of December 14 (p. 188), wherein we discover Thoreau's initial, as it was to remain his final, defiance of extinction.

We note here, as often in Thoreau, a rhetorical use of traditional phrases — our "spirits" must "ascend." But what the angry passage really demands is a purification out of which our "impurities" may join sun and wind, in which they wither and are consumed like a tree in the woods. It is a plea for death by "dry rot," by fire rather than by water. Why, we ask, this insistence? Emerson's method of accepting the fact of death, by weaving it into his lofty scheme of universal compensation, is at least comprehensible, raises no queries about hidden psychological motives. But Thoreau's attitude comes from some deep, twisted compulsion. Is the rejection of death that runs through the *Journal* truly a circumvention or the elaborate disguise of a wish? Thoreau takes no refuge in philosophy; he demands the pure process of decomposition, and he wants it over with quickly. In death as in friendship, pure hate must "underprop" cognition.

The Stratagems of Consciousness — Death

In February, six weeks after John died, Henry could resume the *Journal* with self-exhortation in Emersonian fashion: "The death of friends should inspire us as much as their lives." [2] In March, after rescuing from the front cover lining of volume 3 his thought about understanding animal death better by considering death in the vegetable,[3] he boldly (and unconvincingly) asserts that death is a transient affair, that the memory of departed friends is incrusted "with sublime and pleasing thoughts." He obviously was not succeeding in persuading himself.

Eventually death becomes as much a character in the *Journal* as in the poems of Emily Dickinson. When the *Journal* resumes continuity, with the confident manner of 1850, it remarks, for instance, "Friends are as often brought nearer together as separated by death." [4] What again reminds us of Emily, Henry had learned to treat the enemy with insolent familiarity:

> To the eyes of men there is something tragic in death. We hear of the death of any member of the human family with more than regret, — not without a slight shudder and feeling of commiseration. The churchyard is a *grave* place.[5]

This was working up to the point when, on his deathbed, to that Parker Pillsbury who harried him with talk of the future world, he could whisper, "One world at a time."

Between that final insouciance and his glib entry of August 14, 1840, Thoreau had come a long journey. The *Week*, we know, is a monument to John. Henry glorified the trip of August and September 1839 into a cosmic voyage; he put into it, as though moods and insights of these two short weeks (which he compressed into a fictional one), a hundred later entries of the *Journal*. Yet in the finished book, death is conspicuously evaded. The few references are therefore all the

67

more startling. Two weeks before John was stricken, on December 29, 1841, in the midst of a stilted salute to the homeliness of greatness (quite in the vein of volume 3), Henry praised innocence by declaring, "Death is that expressive pause in the music of the blast." [6] In the book, he concludes "Wednesday" by pretending that on that night he suffered the nightmare which actually is related in volume 4 as of January 26, 1841[7] — in which justice is symbolically rendered him for the miscarriage of the most disinterested act he ever performed. In the *Week*, this crime becomes "a difference with a Friend," and we surmise that the "Friend" is John. To introduce his contrivance, Thoreau reaches back to the entry of December 1841 and comes out with: "For our lifetime the strains of a harp are heard to swell and die alternately, and death is but 'the pause when the blast is recollecting itself.' " [8] Thus consciousness goes to extravagant lengths to insure itself against mortality!

The one point at which the *Week* must confront death is three heavily jocose pages in "Monday" about the old cemetery south of Nashua. These make fun of New England epitaphs (in a way that recalls Benjamin Franklin's satire), disclaim any competence for composing in the genre, and drop the subject by recommending that the farmer who has skimmed his farm ought to be plowed into it, "and in some measure restore its fertility." [9] Were this the complete story, we should say that Thoreau disposed of, or tried to dispose of, death by turning it into a joke. Since for most of us death is not a joke, we might say that Thoreau's gambit is simply shallow.

Fragments of the work-sheets for this portion of the *Week* exist: they indicate, even though they do not quite reveal, the agonized effort that lies behind the pages. He worked this passage over and over, and eventually discarded most of what he endeavored to say. The subject became too much for him, he could not master it. A study of the revisions, insertions, cancellations, which finally resulted in the three trivial pages of the *Week*, shows the intensity of the encounter. To recapitulate all these would be tedious, but one passage does, I feel, suggest what Thoreau had to conceal (all the more because this he suppressed):

Some nations even make it a matter of religion to bury their dead in the earth, and would think it sacrilege to treat them otherwise; but to my imagination the ancient practice of burning the dead is, on the whole, more taste-ful and beautiful, for so the body is most speedily and cleanly returned to dust again, and its elements dispersed throughout nature. Those saints who have been burnt at the stake, and their ashes cast into some stream, have made the cleanest departure. God says plainly, for even I hear him, lay not up this matter but disperse it. Go into a museum and look at a mummy and consider whether the man that did that work of embalming has not got something to answer for. Aye, the nation, with its fingers ever in its entrails, like the dog returning to his vomit. The most fearful thought of all is that there may, nay must, be a soul, a real living entity somewhere, ghastly and funest as that corpse. If we were to be our own undertaker, we should say, let the winds and the streams take our dust, or disperse it from the cannon's mouth so only it broad-cast, and so celebrate your inde-pendence. These condemned, these damned bodies, — what shall we do with them? Think of the living men that walk on this globe, and then think of the dead bodies that lie in graves beneath them, carefully packed away in chests, as if ready for a start! Whose idea was it to put them there? Is there any race of beetle bugs that disposes of its dead thus? In a sort of chrysalis state deep in the earth, as if any butterfly were about to issue thence! . . .[10]

I believe in a speedy resurrection of the body in some

other form, — in corn for fodder — in wood for fuel; in grain and flowers for use or beauty. Every wind blows the last trump which should call the lost atoms together. The last thing I should wish to preserve is an old man's body now for 30 years may have been wracked with the gout & rheumatism[.] Waste no time at funerals. Let the dead bury their dead. Festive viator memento vivere — make haste traveller, remember that you have got to live. P. S. But there comes some body.

Indeed, the shifts by which he tried to make this graveyard interlude come out right in the *Week* are fantastic. If I may cite one more: in that book, at the beginning of the sketch, occurs one of Thoreau's more unfortunate puns, "A monument should at least be stary-y-pointing";[11] in the manuscript draft, where this joke is first perpetrated, it is followed by:

This is my thought about grave yards. They are too highly manured. If I held, as I do not, to the practice which is prevalent, of manuring highly, I should remove all the stones — for though there is commonly a good crop of grass you cannot mow them conveniently ["on account of" is here crossed out] between the stones — and then plow deep, and plant corn for the first crop, and go on ploughing deeper & deeper every year. As it is I should recommend to a village to collect together and grind or burn up all its bones, and distribute the dust to its several families to be spread broadcast on the land as a top dressing. The first settlers of Concord owed their bodies to the

There he turned to the next page, which we do not have: what he was driving at is clear.

The young Thoreau took his position as regards the inevitable end of man on December 14 of 1840, and so was compelled to make of it what he could. Students of *Walden* marvel over the queries, in this rejected draft, about what race of "beetle bugs" would conceivably be so foolish as to bury its dead, in view of that "strong and beautiful bug" which at the end of the book comes out of the dry leaf of an old table of apple-tree wood, to the tune of: "Who does not feel his faith in a resurrection and immortality strengthened by hearing of this?" [12] Hence it becomes all the more important, if we hope to get below the surface of that hymn to resurrection, to go back to the year of John Thoreau's death, to apprehend how the fact of death did first and most grievously thrust itself upon Henry's unprotected consciousness. And as a witness to his reaction to that crisis, outside the silence of, or the later punning of, the *Journal*, we have this letter to Isaiah Williams, under the date of March 14, 1842. Again, we have only Blake's (?) copy, which we trust as much as we dare.

Concord   March 14th 1842

Dear Williams,

   I meant to write to you before but John's death and my own sickness, with other circumstances, prevented. John died of the lock-jaw, as you know, Jan. 11th[.] I have been confined to my chamber for a month with a prolonged shock of the same disorder — from close attention to, and sympathy with him, which I learn is not without precedent. Mr. Emerson too has lost his oldest child, Waldo, by scarlet fever, a boy of rare promise, who in the expectation of many was to be one of the lights of his generation.
   John was sick but three days from the slightest apparent cause — an insignificant cut on his finger, which gave him no pain, and was more than a week old — but nature does not ask for such causes as man expects — when she is ready there will be cause enough. I mean simply that perhaps we never assign the sufficient cause for anything — though it undoubtedly exists. He was perfectly calm, ever pleasant while reason lasted, and

71

gleams of the same serenity and playfulness shone
through his delirium to the last. But I will not disturb
his memory. If you knew him, I could not add to your
knowledge, and if you did not know him, as I think you
could not, it is now too late, and no eulogy of mine
could suffice — For my own part I feel that I could not
have done without this experience.

What you express with regard to the effect of time
on our youthful feelings — which indeed is the theme of
universal elegy — reminds me of some verses of Byron —
quite rare to find in him, and of his best I think. Probably you remember them.
"No more, no more,! Oh never more on me
    The freshness of the heart can fall like dew
Which out of all the lovely things we see,
    Extracts emotions beautiful and new,
Hived in our bosoms like the bag o' the bee,
    Think'st thou the honey with these objects grew
Alas! 'Twas not in them, but in thy power,
    To double even the sweetness of a flower.

No more, no more! Oh, never more, my heart!
    Cans't thou be my sole world, my universe
Once all in all, but now a thing apart,
    Thou canst not be my blessing, or my curse,
The illusion's gone forever —"

It would be well if we could add new years to our lives
as innocently as the fish adds new layers to its shell —
no less beautiful than the old. And I believe we may
if we will replace the vigor and elasticity of youth with
faithfulness in later years.

When I consider the universe I am still the youngest
born. We do not *grow* old we rust *old*. Let us not consent to be old, but to die (live?) rather. Is Truth old?
or Virtue — or Faith? If we possess them they will be
our *elixir vitae* and fount of youth[.] It is at least good

to remember our innocence; what we regret is not quite lost — Earth sends no sweeter strain to Heaven than this plaint. Could we not grieve perpetually; and by our grief discourage time's encroachments? All our sin too shall be welcome for such is the material of Wisdom, and through her is our redemption to come.

'Tis true, as you say, "Man's ends are shaped for him," but who ever dared confess the extent of his free agency? Though I am weak, I am strong too. If God shapes my ends — he shapes me also — and his means are always equal to his ends. His work does not lack this completeness, that the creature consents. *I* am my destiny. Was I ever in that straight that it was not sweet to do right? And then for this free agency I would not be free of God certainly — I would only have freedom to defer to him[.] He has not made us solitary agents. He has not made us to do without him[.] Though we must "abide our destiny," will not he abide it with us? So do the stars and the flowers. My destiny is now arrived — is now arriving. I believe that, what I call my circumstances will be a very true history of myself — for God's works are complete both within and without — and shall I not be content with his success? I welcome my fate for it is not trivial nor whimsical. Is there not a soul in circumstances? — and the disposition of the soul to circumstances — is not that the crowning circumstance of all?

But after all it is *intra*-stances, or how it stands within me that I am concerned about. Moreover circumstances are past, but I am to come, that is to say, they are results of me — but I have not yet arrived at my result.

All impulse, too, is primarily from within[.] The soul which does shape the world is within and central.

I must confess I am apt to consider the trades and professions so many traps which the Devil sets to catch men in — and good luck he has too, if one may judge. But did it ever occur that a man came to want, or the almshouse from consulting his higher instincts? All

73

great good is very present and urgent, and need not be postponed. What did Homer — and Socrates — and Christ and Shakespeare & Fox? Did they have to compound for their leisure, or steal their hours? What a curse would civilization be if it thus ate into the substance of the soul. — Who would choose rather the simple grandeur of savage life for the solid leisure it affords? But need we sell our birthright for a mess of pottage? Let us trust that we shall be fed as the sparrows are.

"Grass and earth to sit on, water to wash the feet, and fourthly, affectionate speech are at no time deficient in the mansions of the good."

You may be interested to learn that Mr. Alcott is going to England in April.

That you may find in Law the profession you love, and the means of spiritual culture, is the wish of your friend

HENRY D. THOREAU.[13]

Two facts in this letter are particularly arresting: Henry's sympathetic participation in John's disease and the studied quotation from Byron. For a moment we may suppose that he sank to the level of this Byronic posturing only out of consideration for his auditor. However, Thoreau was incapable of that sort of politeness; he lent Williams's first letter to Mrs. Lucy Brown in October, asking her advice, saying he had been glad to receive it, "though I hardly know whether my utmost sincerity and interest can inspire a sufficient answer to it." [14] If, then, the copying out of these verses must be taken as a gesture of sincerity, the clew is in the skunk-cabbage entry of 1838 (and in the many skunk-cabbage passages throughout the *Journal*). And if he cut down the lines of *Don Juan* (Canto I, ccxiv, ccxv) to give Williams only the sentimental import, he could hardly have been unaware that the last stanza ends with one of Byron's ironic twists, one of those devices of

consciousness by which *he* resisted the tug of time and of
decay:

> The illusion's gone forever, and thou art
>   Insensible, I trust, but none the worse,
> And in thy stead I've got a deal of judgement,
> Though heaven knows how it ever found a lodgement.

This, therefore, was no occasion for confessing a willingness
to submit to the will of God: on the contrary, let Him work
as He may, God Almighty must work through me, and so I
myself am my own destiny!

In his letter of June 25, 1842, after telling of his increased
(and delighted) absorption in the law, Isaiah Williams would
blandly recite his activities as a reformer and useful citizen:

> My race have an indisputable claim upon my best, all
> the services I am able to render while I live. I will not
> withhold from them the pittance due from me. With
> this thought before me I have endeavoured to join in
> the reforms of the day. I make Temperance speeches.
> . . . I go to Sabbath School.

This sad, uncomprehending creature thereupon asks Henry
Thoreau if he is taking the best course to "benefit" himself
and others! Here ends the correspondence. Williams drops
out of the Thoreau story; he prospered in the law at Buffalo,
specializing in admiralty, and in the Civil War he made
patriotic speeches. I am sure he never got the point of the last
paragraphs of Henry's letter, announcing his own resurrection.

The nature of *Walden* was thus predetermined. Consciousness in Concord had no Byronic fund of experience, sensation,
love affairs, riots to feast on. It had only a simple village life,
and in that restricted existence the supreme fact was death.

So the great book — the only book Thoreau could compile — would have to be, even though cunningly disguised, a song of death and a paean of resurrection: "Walden was dead and is alive again."

Before that could be written, it was clear that one condition had scrupulously to be observed. The delicate, the fragile, faculty for consciously savoring life — for living deliberately — could not for a moment be dulled by the slightest rasping upon it of any trade or profession.

We may doubt that earnest Isaiah really understood the letter of March 14; if he had, he would never have answered by describing his reformist doings. We should not be too hard on him — even Emerson never understood the seriousness of Thoreau's search for disengagement. All Thoreauvians hold Emerson culpable because he denigrated Thoreau for conducting huckleberry parties instead of becoming a powerful engineer, or at least attempting something "Napoleonic." But it is difficult for even the most ardent of his admirers — fortunately he had and still has few "followers" — to sound the depths of Thoreau's hatred of the very notion of a "profession." Or rather, only in this day of existential protest against the merging of existence with the role, of the man with the postman, can readers evaluate the severity of Thoreau's ordeal. It is easy to smile when we find him, on September 8, 1841, at the age of twenty-four, writing thus to Mrs. Lucy Brown (probably she smiled):

> I am as unfit for any practical purpose — I mean for the furtherance of the world's ends — as gossamer for ship-timber; and I, who am going to be a pencil-maker to-morrow, can sympathize with God Apollo, who served King Admetus for a while on earth. But I believe he found it for his advantage at last, — as I am sure I shall, though I shall hold the nobler part at least out of the service.[15]

Robert Louis Stevenson was exasperated over Thoreau's affectation of being Apollo. We may easily become equally annoyed, and wish that he might have varied it by leading a lobster on a red ribbon down the Mill Dam of Concord. But then, we recollect what in his America King Admetus had become.

"Who is King Admetus?" he asks on August 6, 1851. (This ten years after the letter to Mrs. Brown. *Walden* in substance is written. Does he not *yet* know?) "It is Business, with his four prime ministers Trade and Commerce and Manufactures and Agriculture." Whereupon Thoreau can add what, in view of his own sense of the *Journal* as a conscious fabrication, must be taken as another of his astonishing revelations: "And this is what makes mythology true and interesting to us." [16]

On September 16, 1851, he is once more "forcibly struck" with the truth of the worn-out fable; for the hundredth time he applies it to himself: "The poet must keep himself unstained and aloof." [17] To keep aloof in Concord, by showing no visible means of support and by concealing the trade-secret of the pencil manufactory, was a relatively simple game, and could fool even Emerson. But how then could deceptive Thoreau find the audacity to inform the Harvard Corporation, gullible as they were, that he had chosen a profession — "letters"? What sort of writer would he be — like his Raleigh ("a singularly perverted genius, with such an inclination to originality and freedom, and yet who never steered his own course") [18] — who should seek both a library and a publisher, and yet pretend to keep himself unstained and aloof?

The reader who gets deep into the *Journal*, through and beyond volume 3, looks back to the prophetic meaning of the undergraduate essay on William Howitt (among essays that have so little prophecy in them): the boy then declaimed about native American genius in what was soon to become Cornelius Mathews's regular oration. Actually, there is surprisingly little declamation on this theme in the *Journal* — one of Thoreau's instinctive responses to good taste. In the 1840's the New Yorkers so took over the cause, and so celebrated it in Cambyses' vein, that any New Englander, even Thoreau, would be embarrassed to sound it. But, though Professor Channing disliked such talk, and though Longfellow, Lowell and Holmes ridiculed it, the conception had become an integral part of Henry Thoreau's intelligence. We can appreciate what he wrote, and what little he published, only as we grasp the finality with which his enlistment in the "service" of national literature was the solution of both his artistic and his personal predicament.

His most explicit statement is entered on February 2, 1852, after he had read how Sir Francis Head attested that the moon looks larger in America than in Europe:

> At length, perchance, the immaterial heaven will appear as much higher to the American mind, and the intimations that star it will appear as much brighter. For I believe that climate does thus react on man, and that there is something in the mountain air that feeds the spirit and inspires. We shall be more imaginative; we shall be clearer, as our sky, bluer, fresher; broader and more comprehensive in our understanding, like our plains; our intellect on a grander scale, like our thunder and lightning, our rivers and our lakes, and mountains and forests. Are not these advantages? Will not man grow to greater perfection intellectually as well as physically under these influences? Or is it unimportant how many foggy days there are in his life? [19]

In the early 1850's, with the weight of an unpublished *Walden* heavy upon his awareness, Thoreau launches again and again into these celebrations of the "wild" which at the end of the decade were strung together to form the belated

"Walking." This was published in *The Atlantic Monthly* for June 1862, just after his death. Possibly because of its posthumous appearance — when the slogans of literary nationalism, in the forms that had excited Whitman and Melville, were submerged in the more mundane problem of preserving the Union — the pressure of this concern throughout Thoreau's formative years has not been recognized. Yet it is one of the keys to his strategy. He insists on November 15, 1850, that except for flashes of "uncivilized, free, and wild thinking" in Shakespeare the literature of England is tame.[20] In January of 1851, he exclaims, "There was need of America." [21] Hence literature in America would, if true to the landscape, not be a "profession." To become a writer would not be to concede with Isaiah Williams that man is governed by circumstances; it would be a device for escaping the gyves of Admetus:

> The fault of our books and other deeds is that they are too humane. I want something speaking in some measure to the condition of muskrats and skunk-cabbage as well as of men, — not merely to a pining and complaining coterie of philanthropists.[22]

Death, after all, was not the direst of threats: decomposition is supportable, a clean process. The temptations of success and philanthropy were more insidious. Henry Thoreau acquired, by contagion or by sympathy, his brother's disease; but he who could invoke Byron (the skunk-cabbage) against philanthropic Isaiah was well on his way toward becoming the one who, by a Yankee stratagem of intelligence, would on the last pages of *Walden* elude death's cosmic conspiracy.

7

The Stratagems of Consciousness—

Woman and Men

I had two friends. The one offered me friendship on such terms that I could not accept it, without a sense of degradation. He would not meet me on equal terms, but only be to some extent my patron. He would not come to see me, but was hurt if I did not visit him. He would not readily accept a favor, but would gladly confer one. He treated me with ceremony occasionally, though he could be simple and downright sometimes; and from time to time acted a part, treating me as if I were a distinguished stranger; was on stilts, using made words. Our relation was one long tragedy, yet I did not directly speak of it. I do not believe in complaint, nor in explanation. The whole is but too plain, alas, already. We grieve that we do not love each other, that we cannot confide in each other. I could not bring myself to speak, and so recognize an obstacle to our affection.

I had another friend, who, through a slight obtuseness, perchance, did not recognize a fact which the dignity of friendship would by no means allow me to descend so far as to speak of, and yet the inevitable effect of that ignorance was to hold us apart forever. (March 4, 1856; J, VIII, 199)

IF HISTORY SHOWS that the independence of self-conscious mind is perpetually assaulted by anxieties about death, it also declares that the bastion of freedom is attacked by another surging enemy: consciousness gives way to the importunities of love. Men yield to that enticement even more abjectly than the Isaiah Williamses of this world compromise their freedom by capitulating to a "profession."

One of the more amusing developments in the history of Thoreau's reputation has been the effort of his partisans to make him a little more acceptable to ordinary humanity by thrusting him into a sentimental posture. The more readers he gains, the more they try not to recognize his lineaments. Let a Lowell find him in 1865 conceited, selfish, unimaginative, crude, and his apologists rush to explain that all this was a pose, that he was an affectionate son, a loving brother, a faithful friend. But what for long especially outraged commentators was the supposition that Thoreau flouted the highest, the most sacred, duty of masculinity: he was not interested in women!

As his letters were printed — commencing with the volume Emerson edited in 1865 — champions of normality were further exacerbated by what seemed the only moment in his frigid history when he should have observed at least the common decencies of gallantry but when, by his own account, he behaved like a boor. At any rate, this is how he shows himself in a letter to Emerson, November 14, 1847:

> I have had a tragic correspondence, for the most part all on one side, with Miss ——. She did really wish to — I hesitate to write — marry me. That is the way they spell it. Of course I did not write a deliberate answer. How could I deliberate upon it? I sent back as distinct a *no* as I have learned to pronounce after considerable practice, and I trust that this *no* has succeeded. Indeed, I wished that it might burst, like hollow shot, after it had struck and buried itself there. *There was no other way.* I really had anticipated no such foe as this in my career.[1]

At best his paragraph calls up the picture of a comic New England anti-masque, a sex-starved spinster clutching at the village eccentric; at its worst, it betrays a neurotic panic which, in its impulsive imagery, shows itself the product of a complex of disease.[2] Add to this the rumor which darkly floated through Concord gossip about some woman whom Henry drove to suicide, and that the *Journal* (appearing in 1906) displays him answering someone who in 1852 was rash enough to report the accusation to him with what, even from a peasant, would be called callousness, "I said I did not know when I had planted the seed of that fact that I should hear of it."[3] The least suspecting reader feels uncomfortable when he finds that by the end of this August 1852, Thoreau is accusing himself of being a cuttlefish who darkens the atmosphere in which he moves, and astonishingly is writing, "To all parties, though they be youth and maiden, if they are transparent to each other, and their thoughts can be expressed, there can be no further nakedness."[4]

However, shortly after his death, and increasingly as the century waned, his friends circulated hints about Ellen Sewall — as though carefully putting out counter-propaganda. In 1880 Robert Louis Stevenson blasted him for being an egotist and skulker, "dry, priggish, and selfish." Six years later, Stevenson issued his "recantation" because he had been reliably informed that "Thoreau was once fairly and manfully in love, and, with perhaps too much aping of the angel, relinquished the woman to his brother."[5] By that "fairly and manfully," humanity was vindicated, the scandal was silenced! The mystery was happily resolved! Thoreau the congenital misanthrope had been insupportable (an American Jonathan Swift), but Thoreau the self-effacing lover (his Stella an Ellen), hiding in affected rudeness an excess of affection — this put him into a rubric of drama, removed the last sting from his aspersions upon the ordinary man's devotion both to profession and to family. It enabled, and still enables, mere human creatures to read Apollo without self-condemnation.

There is no longer any possibility of getting the facts of Ellen Sewall's story. If there really was any drama or melodrama, it took place during the months of this volume 3. In recent years, when the volume was known to exist but was not accessible, a legend circulated that it held the solution. Mr. Canby's *Thoreau* in 1939 reveled in the "romance." Announcing, "I have been fortunate enough to see the whole of this unpublished section," Mr. Canby "inferred" from some of our entries gory details. In this respect, as in others, Mr. Canby did his subject unforgivable disservice.

The nearest we can come to a firm source, outside the vague intimations of Sanborn and of Concord gossip-mongers, is a third-hand version of the narrative Ellen Sewall is alleged to have told, years later, to her two daughters. Mr. T. M. Raysor got it from them as late as 1926.[6] He was permitted to quote (whether from originals or copies is not clear) the two pieces of solid evidence. One is a letter Ellen wrote her father while visiting Concord in July 1839, describing walks and rowing excursions with the brothers Thoreau. The second is presented as a letter to her aunt, of November 1840, wherein she relates that her father wished her to write — in a short, explicit, and cold manner — to "H. T." This she has sorrowfully but dutifully done. All the rest is wild surmise.

Every reader of volume 3 must take several entries as he chooses, and may interpret them as elliptical references to this interlude — especially those for October 17, the end of October 18, October 19, November 1, and the verses for November 7. Since Miss Sewall lived in Scituate, repetitions of "eastern" seem significant. If in October 19 the "friend" is definitely masculine, this may be construed as a concealment of the disclosure which, on the preceding day, cannot be made. Mr. Raysor figured that Ellen's letter to her aunt would be written on November 5, and that this perfectly accounts for the lines of November 7 (which Raysor had seen). This would appear to explain the frustration of some "peculiar love."

83

These tantalizing bits, if only by the fact of mystification, tempt one to settle for the easy explanation. In that theory, we content ourselves with believing that Henry loved Ellen, held his tongue out of affection for John; when he learned in July that she had refused his brother, then, and not until then, did he offer himself. If this be so, two or three other mysteries are solved. In the *Week*, "Sunday" opens with a celebration of the Sabbath stillness, works into the assertion that our lives need suitable backgrounds, and for illustration says:

> On this same stream a maiden once sailed in my boat, thus unattended but by invisible guardians, and as she sat in the prow there was nothing but herself between the steersman and the sky.[7]

Because Thoreau follows this with a poem, supposedly addressed to her on the water, "Low in the eastern sky," he once more is supposed to mean Ellen of Scituate. And, of course, this hypothesis makes more plausible the strange insertion into the *Week* of the dream of January 25, 1841,[8] as though he had experienced it while sleeping beside his brother on the banks of the Merrimack in September 1839.[9] It then becomes transparently a trauma over having been a rival to his brother. Hence the undisclosed "secret" which haunts volume 3.

As I say, I forbid nobody to accept this fantasy. Mr. Canby accepted it and promulgated it, though he had to piece it out with inferences, guesses, and by granting that some parts of it — notably the idea that Ellen Sewall would even momentarily have accepted John — are "queer." Be that as it may, there are other considerations which a study of this and similar pieces of the early *Journal* call to our attention.

Take, to start with, that maiden in the boat. The two

paragraphs in the *Week* which culminate in her image are choice instances of Thoreauvian mosaic. On June 15, 1840, he had written:

> I stood by the river to-day considering the forms of the elms reflected in the water. For every oak and birch, too, growing on the hilltop, as well as for elms and willows, there is a graceful ethereal tree making down from the roots, as it were the original idea of the tree, and sometimes Nature in high tides brings her mirror to its foot and makes it visible.[10]

Now the so-called "Ellen passage" in the *Week*, incorporating a song by "one of our Concord poets," proceeds:

> For every oak and birch, too, growing on the hilltop, as well as for these elms and willows, we knew that there was a graceful ethereal and ideal tree making down from the roots, and sometimes Nature in high tides brings her mirror to its foot and makes it visible.[11]

The *Week* then, with simulated innocence, sets forth the stillness. In fact, the next sentences are also recastings, this time of an entry for June 16, 1840, recounting the effects upon a landscape as seen through "the bottom of a tumbler" [12] — which vehicle has entirely disappeared from the printed text. And in the *Week*, that paragraph ends with a sentence which is simply a condensation of a passage first entered into the *Journal* on February 27, 1841.[13]

Thus by indirection we come, in the next paragraph, to the maiden. In volume 2 of the *Journal*, for June 19, 1840 (and along with that drum), just before our volume 3 begins, we find:

> The other day I rowed in my boat a free, even lovely young lady, and, as I plied the oars, she sat in the stern,

and there was nothing but she between me and the sky. So might all our lives be picturesque if they were free enough, but mean relations and prejudices intervene to shut out the sky, and we never see a man as simple and distinct as the man-weathercock on a steeple.[14]

Whereupon we may truly begin to wonder if *this* be the language of a lover, open or concealed. Remembering what is the method of the early *Journal*, we may divine that here is one more instance of the process of collecting material out of limited experience, in which the predominant emotion is not a passion for anybody but a greed for tidbits.

Ellen, in short, could be moved at will from stern to prow, to meet a literary convenience. She is a "suitable background" for the polishing of sentences. At first she teaches her cavalier the difference between picturesqueness and mean relations, but on second thought she demonstrates how "character always secures for itself this advantage, and is thus distinct and un-related to near or trivial objects, whether things or persons" — including, we may be sure, herself! She is a literary prop, to be utilized — consciously, oh so consciously! — to furnish interest within a limited angle of vision.

However, passages about *her* could be facilely altered: it was not possible to do more with, once it had been written, "the clang of corselet and buckler from many a silent hamlet of the soul." It may at least be posed as a question whether Henry Thoreau in his Concord hamlet of 1840 had the slightest inclination to offer himself as husband to Ellen Sewall. If he did, then it was in the certainty of being refused, and so an inexpensive way to gain an increment in consciousness.[15]

The problem of trying to decipher, either as literary analyst or psychological surgeon, what "love" could have meant for Henry Thoreau leads abruptly into the still more complex problem of what he meant by "friendship." The theme appears in volume 1 with a poem of April 8, 1838; [16] the dissection commences in volume 2, somewhere in the fall of 1839, with, "Then first I conceive of a true friendship, when some rare specimen of manhood presents itself." [17] On February 18, 1840, he has come this far:

> All romance is grounded on friendship. What is this rural, this pastoral, this poetical life but its invention? Does not the moon shine for Endymion? Smooth pastures and mild airs are for some Corydon and Phyllis. Paradise belongs to Adam and Eve. Plato's republic is governed by Platonic love.[18]

The topic is a (rural) staple for more entries in volume 3 — not only those suspected of meaning Ellen Sewall, but also October 20, December 24 and 28, January 1, 11, 20. And it is often descanted upon in the remaining three volumes. To judge from the snippets we have of 1842 to 1844, it then became an obsession. The climax of these early meditations, not to say agonizings, is the long section inserted into "Wednesday" of the *Week*,[19] which in substance is another mosaic of the early *Journal*, and serves (as we have noted) as a prologue to the revised form of the passage about his dream of reconciliation with *the* friend above all his friends, brother John.

Let me insist, to begin with, that Henry Thoreau is not unique within the Transcendental community in addressing himself in so oratorical a tone, and so solemnly, to this topic. Emerson, we know, composed an essay on "Friendship" for the *First Series*. Curiously enough, he was working on it during the spring and summer of 1840; the next year he printed it as a sequel to "Love." His admirers read it with awe; the modern reader may well find it more enigmatic, or certainly more tepid, than all Henry's perverse pronouncements. Margaret Fuller, in the years of her "Conversations" and of editing *The Dial* (1839–1842), not to mention those when she was teaching girls in Timothy Fuller's school in Providence (1837–1839), voyaged so extravagantly into the uncharted oceans of "Friendship" that one wonders how she ever found a way back to dry land. When contributing in 1852 to the memorial volume to her, Emerson came up with the observation that she wore her friends as a necklace. Maybe he did not quite mean it this way — but a necklace, however brilliant, is something the wearer can remove, or, if bored with it, have redesigned.

These New Englanders, in their small communities, were children of the "Romantic Movement." They read avidly, but in America could put on no such show as *Hernani*. It is a truism that an elevation of friendship into something more "spiritual" than the eighteenth-century's admiration for a chap who would bail you out or serve as your second in an affair of honor — the ideal of friendship, let us say, in Restoration comedy — was everywhere a sign of the shift from that extroverted century to the introverted nineteenth. Jane Austen might wickedly satirize the new fashion in *Love and Freindship: Volume the First*, but the Napoleonic era gorged itself on such grandiose attachments as figure in Jean Paul's *Titan* — and so declaimed over the treason of Napoleon's marshals. Byron and Tom Moore gave the concept literary vitality; Wordsworth and Coleridge strove to play up to it. By the time we come to Transcendental New England, we enter a jungle almost tropical.

To catch our bearings, we must make two factual observations:

One, in this New England literature, love and friendship are interchangeable terms. For the Transcendental search of meaning on the plane of "Reason," the object of devotion may indifferently be of the same sex or of the other (this quite apart from the "Understanding's" giving in marriage).

Two, in this exotic circle — Francis Parkman termed it a combination of excited brains and cool emotions — the game of friendship became a method of setting up a standard so rarefied, so absolute (and so self-exonerating), that the inept vis-à-vis was bound to fall short.

We might call it a perfervid cult of friendship deliberately dedicated to causing the associate to come a cropper. What Madame de Staël and Benjamin Constant gained for the enrichment of literature by tormenting each other as sexual lovers, these Romantic Yankees squeezed out of thin, dry life by perfecting devices for being let down by their friends — so that the friends could then be accused of cowardice.

Isaiah Williams, apparently, proved to be no stuff amenable to the adventure. He clung to Christianity, resumed his hope of immortality, worked in his profession, tried to be a reformer. To be a friend in the Emersonian — much more in the Thoreauvian — sense, you had to be so appreciative of the ego in the beloved as never to require that anything explanatory be said between him and you. Yet at the same time you were expected to be so perverse and insensitive (you too having an ego) as to afford him (or her) provocations for denouncing you. Emerson, Margaret Fuller, the "lesser" Transcendentalists, but above all Thoreau, devoted a dismaying portion of their energies to attesting the paradox that the more they loved each other, the more they could do without each other.

"The higher the style we demand of friendship," Emerson would say in the *Essays*, "of course the less easy to establish it with flesh and blood. We walk alone in the world." [20] Harrison Blake devoted himself in the 1850's to becoming friend to Henry Thoreau (we suppose he might as well have taken a marriage vow), and had to pay the price: he had to receive, read and inwardly digest lectures upon his role. To take one of many pomposities, consider this in September 1852:

In love and friendship the imagination is as much exercised as the heart; and if either is outraged the other will be estranged. It is commonly the imagination which is wounded first, rather than the heart, — it is so much more sensitive.[21]

In this same sermon, on the supremacy of conscious concept over the instinct of the heart, in 1852, Thoreau launches another diatribe which devotees of the Ellen legend fondly quote as proof that his heart still suffered. It is at least of this interest: for once the object is avowedly feminine:

I require that thou knowest everything without being told anything. I parted from my beloved because there was one thing which I had to tell her. She *questioned* me. She should have known all by sympathy. That I had to tell it her was the difference between us, — the misunderstanding.[22]

Possibly Ellen in the boat may have asked which way the Concord River *does* flow. We can hardly imagine this minister's daughter pressing Henry Thoreau for anything embarrassingly intimate; but then — the self is compelled to invent defenses against the irrelevant, even where no attack is designed. At least, in a world where the frontal attacks of love are so finely modulated.

One who reads much (or little) in the *Journal* after 1850 must be impressed — indeed, appalled — not only by the obviously insatiable drive that brings Thoreau back, again and again, to "friendship," but by the monotony of his rhetorical devices for translating friendship into no friendship. These entries are variations, depressingly slight variations, on the motif that friendship is a threat to the integrity of Henry Thoreau. And yet, by their insistence, they seem to be pleading for the dreaded invasion. To take one out of several, here is one of February 15, 1851 (and remember, by this time the *Journal* is a soliloquy!):

> Alas! Alas! when my friend begins to deal in confessions, breaks silence, makes a theme of friendship (which then is always something past), and descends to merely human relations! As long as there is a spark of love remaining, cherish that alone. Only *that* can be kindled into a flame. I thought that friendship, that love was still possible between [us]. I thought that we had not withdrawn very far asunder. But now that my friend rashly, thoughtlessly, profanely speaks, *recognizing* the distance between us, that distance seems infinitely increased.[23]

The story is painfully clear, interpret it how one will: from the beginning Thoreau's frantic concern with the idea of friendship is a struggle to make it perverse, to make it a judgment on the faults of friends, to equate it with hatred. The verse in this volume 3 for January 1 is a good example of the early stage. We make out from the pages of diaries and work-sheets between 1842 and 1850 that he was then giving even more attention to the problem. For instance, a long passage, in what probably was a *Journal* of 1848–1849, goes, in part, thus:

> I had a friend, I wrote a book, I asked my friend's criticism, I never got but praise for what was good in it — my friend became estranged from me and then I got blame for all that was bad — & so I got at last the criticism which I wanted[.]
> While my friend was my friend he flattered me, but I never heard the truth from him but when he became my enemy he shot it to me on a poisoned arrow.

On the surface merely of empirical observation, one is obliged to declare that Henry clearly *wanted* the arrow of friendship to be poisoned, that he would brew the stuff and apply it himself. Thus he twisted the patronage of Emerson into a "rejection." Historians, innocent in these matters, accuse him of ingratitude, and quote, as the prime exhibit of his nastiness, the passage of May 23, 1853, recounting the failure of a talk with Emerson in which Thoreau says he lost his identity: "He, assuming a false opposition where there was no difference of opinion, talked to the wind — told me what I knew — and I lost my time trying to imagine myself somebody else to oppose him." [24]

It is not difficult to draw from the *Journal* ample proof of Thoreau's having put more rigorously into practice than any others the Transcendental doctrine of friendship as a ravishment which only gods could endure. However, when the student asks more closely the reasons for this peculiar stance, he lands in a morass of conjecture; he is tempted to turn and run. Of course, the literary conventions of a Romantic age have always to be borne in mind; even in the American gift-books there are sentimental lucubrations upon the friend which promote him or her to the lover. Furthermore, the Transcendental fellowship, as part of their protest against the materiality of commercial New England, found in their idealization of friendship an escape analogous to that which the younger romantics of France found in sexual promiscuity and in plucking the flowers of evil. Even so, granting that all this determines much of the vocabulary, we recognize that with Thoreau a luxuriating in friendship and in its inadequacies becomes simply monstrous.

Pascal observed that if friends knew what each says about the other behind his back, no friendship would endure. On February 1, 1852, Thoreau starts a long declamation by exclaiming: "When I hear that a friend on whom I relied has spoken of me, not with cold words perhaps, but even with a cold and indifferent tone, to another, ah! what treachery I feel it to be! — the sum of all crimes against humanity." Often the modern reader finds these tantrums of Transcendental friendship merely comic; reconsidering, he perceives that at the root of them there is something terribly black, something devouring. In the entry of 1852, Thoreau rejects any Christian notion that differences will be reconciled in a future world; he cries out for one moment of realization in this instant life, and berates his friends, with more (private) exclamation points: "They but express their want of faith in me or in mankind; their coldest, cruelest thought comes clothed in polite and easy-spoken words at last." [25] The reader can hardly help concluding, to put it crudely, that he is confronted with a hunger which dreads satisfaction more than it suffers from deprivation.

Psychologizing by laymen is dangerous; we have found in recent decades that even skilled analysts can make fools of themselves by trying to diagnose a work of art. We recognize that the *Journal*, limited in circulation, is about as much a contrivance as anything by Proust or Joyce. Wherefore, when we ask what lies beneath the surface, we have on the first level to realize, as fully as we can, that this is a literary performance; it is not a confession of lusts, but the unending search into a literary predicament. That the literary libido is related to some more biological or psychic neurosis goes without saying; but the precise nature of the not too artfully hidden connection is what concerns us. In fact, it so engrossed Henry Thoreau (who I suspect might honestly answer the question, could we put it to him, by saying he understood no more than we and was equally curious) that the whole *Journal* is a clinical study of it.

To look at still another crucial passage, here is this of January 30, 1852:

> Do nothing merely out of good resolutions. Discipline yourself only to yield to love; suffer yourself to be

attracted. It is in vain to write on chosen themes. We must wait till they have kindled a flame in our minds. There must be the copulating and generating force of love behind every effort destined to be successful. The cold resolve gives birth to, begets nothing. The theme that seeks me, not I it. The poet's relation to his theme is the relation of lovers. It is no more to be courted. Obey, report.[26]

There are an abundance of passages in Thoreau to warrant Stevenson's calling him a "prig." That lecture on sex he sent to Blake is ridiculously prudish, even when considered as an utterance of the Victorian period. For a man to orate thus in a letter to a "friend" is positively absurd.[27] Consequently, when Thoreau, in addressing himself about the purpose of his occupation, which by 1852 had become keeping the *Journal*, resorts to the language of sexual intercourse, and beholds in the objects which produce his entries those which make love to him, we get a glimmering of what the art of composition had become to him. The successive moments of realization which the *Journal* is — or which he tried to make it become — are efforts to sustain this passion. For this reason, among others, the inferior passions of human intercourse, love and friendship, are *required* to prove abortive!

It would be trite to say that the *Journal* is in any sense a "sublimation" of inhibited loves, or a "compensation" for a ghastly sense of inferiority, or a neurotic defense against a fear of humiliation. (All of which, in so far as literature can be, it is.) Supposing that elements in the drama can be so isolated, we have to insist that these are only factors in a complex of forces which focused the total being of Henry Thoreau upon realizing — to the point of exquisite torture — the delirium of self-consciousness. By 1858 he could say it straight-out: "Genius is inspired by its own works; it is hermaphroditic." [28] The one release from his compulsion, as well as the one control over it, was incessant writing. Out of such dank soil flowers the clarity and simplicity, the oratory, of his prose. Within the strict confines of a stringently limited knowledge of life, Thoreau did contrive to become an artist.

Students of Thoreau have been strangely reluctant to raise questions of this sort. They react as though even to suggest such considerations were to desecrate an idol. But he did work at explaining himself; he left the *Journal*, in its enduring box, as a work that should not be destroyed. What hope he cherished that someday others would read it, we know not; the point is, he had come in his own mind to where the writing of it was full and sufficient reason for doing it. Paradoxically, as long as we are interested in what makes a writer a great writer, we are not merely prurient in trying to probe below the topsoil of the *Journal*.

Biographers have belatedly admitted that the poem "Sympathy" — which Henry addressed to Ellen's brother on June 24, 1839, and which Emerson persuaded Margaret to print in the first *Dial* of July 1840 — was in truth written to a boy. Thoreau therefore knew his own mind, in the treatise on friendship devised for the *Week*, when he got under way by reprinting the poem:

> Lately, alas, I knew a gentle boy,
>   Whose features all were cast in Virtue's mould,
> As one she had designed for Beauty's toy,
>   But after manned him for her own stronghold.

For years, Emerson, Sanborn, Channing persisted in explaining these verses as directed to Ellen, as having used the "boy" for a disguise. We know not whether these worthies believed their contention — whether they were so bewildered that they could suppose no other hypothesis, whether they had some intimation about a truth which might be other, but which they were resolved to insist in public was heterosexual truth.

Introduction

Only within recent years have studies had the courage to call attention to the androgynous character of Thoreau's mono-maniac discussions of friendship.[29]

In all the pages through which participants in the loose federation we call Transcendentalism expatiate upon the joys — and agonies — of friendship, we are struck by their sublime assumption that nobody in the world had known this experience before them. Thoreau opens his digression in the *Week*[30] by asserting that, while all men use the term, "nevertheless, I can remember only two or three essays on this subject in all literature" (one being Emerson's, which he does not quote; his chief authority is Confucius). Yet there is considerable evidence in the literature of Transcendentalism that there was one "essay on the subject" which they all read — the Sonnets of William Shakespeare.

These had seemed to Emerson, as early as October 1831,[31] more wonderful than the plays, "and perhaps are even more valuable to the analysis of the genius of Shakespeare, and that is the assimilating power of passion that turns all things to its own nature." Again, on April 30, 1834, after his brother's remarking upon the common impression left by Jesus of Nazareth and by Shakespeare, Emerson got to thinking how remarkable were the Sonnets: "Those addressed to a beautiful young man seem to show some singular friendship amounting almost to a passion which probably excited his youthful imagination." Hence these poems are "invaluable for the hints they contain respecting his unknown self." [32]

There is comparatively little mention of Shakespeare in Thoreau's *Journal*; unlike Emerson, he did not use his record as a repository for casual thoughts on his reading. But he shared entirely the "Shakespeareolatry" which the Transcendentalists practiced as fervently as any in the era. And as everywhere in the Romantic cult, but especially in America (one thinks also of Herman Melville), Shakespeare's supposed deficiency in formal education was taken as proof positive of "Genius." In volume 2, on June 22, 1840, Thoreau is at work on the definition of that elusive quality, and so digresses:

> It is odd that people will wonder how Shakespeare could write as he did without knowing Latin, or Greek, or geography, as if these were of more consequence than to know how to whistle. They are not backward to recognize Genius, — how it dispenses with those furtherances which others require, leaps where they crawl, — and yet they never cease to marvel that so it was, — that it was Genius, and helped itself.[33]

Thoreau's transparent interest in himself which informs this apostrophe is another instance of what inspires all Romantic adulation: Goethe, Coleridge, Hazlitt, no less than Emerson, were primarily interested in Shakespeare the unknown self, less concerned with dramaturgy than with arriving at, by his help, a precise statement of the essence of "Genius." (Was it "the assimilating power of passion"? If so, let us all become passionate and assimilative!) Thoreau comes back to this theme again on October 27, 1857, when he commences (once more thinking only about himself), "The real facts of a poet's life would be of more value to us than any work of his art," which of course brings up the challenge of that omnipresent alter ego:

> Shakespeare has left us his fancies and imaginings, but the truth of his life, with its becoming circumstances, we know nothing about. The writer is reported, the liver not at all. Shakespeare's house, how hollow it is! No man can conceive of Shakespeare in that house. But we want the basis of fact, of an actual life, to complete our Shakespeare, as much as a statue wants its pedestal. A poet's life with this broad actual basis would be as superior to Shakespeare's as a lichen, with its base or thallus, is superior in the order of being to a fungus.[34]

Introduction

There is always the implication, in Transcendental circling round the enigma, of a great curiosity, and worry, about the Sonnets, much more than about the character of Hamlet (in fact, they all knew who Hamlet was: he was their own selves). More than any other masterpiece they perused, the poems spoke of friend and lover as synonymous:

> Had my friend's muse grown with this growing age,
> A dearer birth than this his love had brought . . . (xxxii)

But if the inquirer is not content to accept the Sonnets as virtuoso experiments within a series of conventional conceits, then he must wonder about the biography; in that case, what does he do with a Genius who advertises a passion so utterly self-abnegating that it is willing to turn in condemnation against itself should the friend tire of him?

> When love, converted from the thing it was,
> Shall reasons find of settled gravity;
> Against that time do I ensconce me here
> Within the knowledge of mine own desert,
> And this my hand against myself uprear,
> To guard the lawful reason on thy part:
> > To leave poor me thou has the strength of laws,
> > Since, why to love, I can allege no cause. (xlix)

Try to imagine how, in New England, friendship would render one liable to so utter a loss of self-esteem, if one were required to say (and to mean) to his friend,

> For thee, against myself I'll vow debate,
> For I must ne'er love him whom thou dost hate! (lxxxix)

Thoreau writes his essay in the *Week* (as to a lesser extent Emerson also wrote his) as a sort of handbook on how not to get so drastically entangled:

> The only danger in Friendship is that it will end. It is a
> delicate plant, though a native. The least unworthiness,
> even if it be unknown to one's self, vitiates it.[35]

Whereupon our puzzlement increases: Did these people who
so hungered for communion actually want friendship to prove
its transcendent quality by keeping its mouth tightly shut?
That seems to be what Thoreau demands: "It may be that
your silence was the finest thing of the two. There are some
things which a man never speaks of, which are much finer
kept silent about." [36] Did he and they mean, or did they
suppose that they meant, what one of the greatest of the
Sonnets (cii) concludes:

> Our love was new, and then but in the spring,
> When I was wont to greet it with my lays;
> As Philomel in summer's front doth sing,
> And stops his pipe in growth of riper days:
> Not that the summer is less pleasant now
> Than when her mournful hymns did hush the night,
> But that wild music burthens every bough,
> And sweets grown common lose their dear delight.
>   Therefore, like her, I sometime hold my tongue
>   Because I would not dull you with my song.

Would this be the inevitable penalty of confessing homage to
even a "gentle boy" — that the sweets would grow common?
And that the tongue must be held?

The point needs no belaboring: these New Englanders read
and loved the Sonnets, but being New Englanders, children of
Puritanism, they found themselves burdened with an instinctive resolution never to commit themselves irrevocably — even
though the hanging back was excruciating. One can study
the consequences for the drama of their passions in the
letters of Emerson and those of Margaret Fuller and Caroline

Sturgis from 1840 to 1844; but for us the crux of the imbroglio comes in July of 1841, when Emerson fled to Nantasket, to be alone, to get at least a respite not so much from family as from friends:

> In face of the grandeur of simple truth wh. changes not, but forever justifies itself & its adherent, I sometimes say, I am sick of love. Never let me be with lovers again, those capricious, unstable ridiculous fanatics, groping after they know not what — with their immense egotism measuring in every word & act of the other party how much refers to their sacred selves, avaricious of every personal regard beyond the fables of misers & counting all beside, dross, tho' it were God & his angels.[37]

Shakespeare reported, as though from bitter experience, "Lilies that fester smell far worse than weeds" (xciv). Emerson pled with Caroline, "Study how you can protect me." The Transcendental emotional scheme was resolutely determined that if these lilies were fated to fester, it would get the festering over with before the lilies had a chance to bloom. Emerson and Margaret Fuller were never successful in this stratagem: Henry Thoreau nipped every threatening stench in the bud. As he points out in the *Week* that the violence of love is as much to be dreaded as that of hate, that "its famous pains begin only with the ebb of love," [38] we gather that the lesson he learned early in life, and resolutely stuck to thereafter, was to contrive, at whatever cost, that nothing should ever rise so high about him as to permit any ebb at all.

The opportunity of presenting this strayed volume of the early *Journal* is not an occasion for further exploring these perplexities, though it be one for mentioning them. This volume 3 does contain what, if anything, we can expect to extract from Henry Thoreau about Ellen Sewall. But, I must add, this is not to say that the whole female species meant nothing more than is here conveyed. On the contrary, there is even in this booklet, entered as of January 4, 1841, a Thoreauvian love song in prose. At this writing, such an entry complicates the emotional mystery; but upon our central concern, which is the growth of the poet's consciousness, it sheds a flickering light.

Thoreau's household was dominated by women. Also, from all we can gather, he did seek the companionship of older women — Mrs. Brown, Mrs. Emerson, Elizabeth Hoar. Mr. Canby, noting the solicitude which Lidian Emerson felt for the perverse but affectionate youth, so sensationally exaggerated their relationship that he stifles any sane consideration of how the young writer was in fact operating. On that front, the explanation for Thoreau's strategy is not far to seek: he had it all under control when he gaily wrote to Emerson that he had not anticipated such a "foe" as a proposal of marriage. He could never have made a serious offer to Ellen Sewall. His concern was already defined: to avoid entanglement, either with professions or with women; to arrange experience so that both the labors of other men and the affections of women — mother, sister, friends — would minister to his egotism. Only by such exploitation could the Byron of Concord (the skunk-cabbage) become a major writer.

This is not to say that he had an easy time disposing of, circumventing, the demands of love. Had that been the case, he would not be the writer of such stature as, more and more, we comprehend him to be. There exists an almost incoherent fragment of a journal which, if Sanborn's notes can be believed, is his response to the death of his sister Helen in 1849. Some of it comes through clearly: "I still think of you as my sister." Other entries get out of control:

> . . . but you are part of me you are of me I of you
> I can not tell where I leave off and you begin — there

is such a harmony when your sphere meets mine. To you I can afford to be forever what I am, for your presence will not permit me to be what I should not be.

These strangulated pages can also sound like something out of the more lush of the contemporaneous giftbooks: "My sister, it is glorious to me that you live. Thou art transfigured to me, and I see a perfect being — O Do not disappoint me." He sees her dressed in white; she covers him like incense. "The feminine of me — who art magnanimous."

These notes are the crude material for another confrontation of death; the lesson is that this home-centered youth — whose great act of disseverance was to go two miles away, into "the woods" — was the same who as a junior in Harvard College wept when his mother told him he should leave home and become a peddler, who stopped crying only when Helen, putting her arms around him, assured him he need never leave. As he triumphed over John's death by absorbing it into his self-esteem, so within a year of Helen's he could surmount that excision:

> Woman is a nature older than I and commanding from me a sort of veneration — like Nature. She is my mother at the same time that she is my sister. I cannot imagine a woman no older than I. . . . Methinks that I am younger than aught I associate with. The youngest child is more than my coeval.[39]

The serious and sympathetic student, conning these *disjecta membra* of 1850, finds his thought echoing with a hundred earlier exclamations, but especially with a sentence of the second letter to Williams in 1842: "When I consider the universe I am still the youngest born." This mélange of woman, nature, friendship, death, and out of it the survival of a delicate child — this has become a syndrome of sensibility.

There is agony in it, but out of it proceed sentences. From so barren an experience, so insignificant as compared with Byron's, there could, by judicious management, be produced an egotism which would become, to the amazement of the universe, the "main difference."

8

The Stratagems of Consciousness — Anticipation

It is the spring note of the nuthatch. It paused in its progress about the trunk or branch and uttered this lively but peculiarly inarticulate song, an awkward attempt to warble almost in the face of the chickadee, as if it were one of its kind. It was thus giving vent to the spring within it. If I am not mistaken, it is what I have heard in former springs or winters long ago, fabulously early in the season, when we men had but just begun to anticipate the spring, — for it would seem that we, in our anticipations and sympathies, include in succession the moods and expressions of all creatures. (March 5, 1859; *J*, XII, 14)

IN ORDER to mount the drama of *Walden*, Thoreau denounces the drabness, the boredom, of village economy, and then plants what is to be the book's final revelation (consciously withheld through the intervening chapters): "To anticipate, not the sunrise and the dawn merely, but, if possible, Nature herself!" [1] The verb is "anticipate": all *Walden* is an adroitly suspended anticipation of the climax of thawing sand and clay in the railroad cut; all the *Journal* — earnestly before the completion of *Walden*, more stridently thereafter — is a stratagem to anticipate, and so to survive, the winter.

In New England of the 1840's, the governing concern in every walk of life was to collect in summer enough food, fuel, and fat to get through the winter. Henry Adams set the motifs for his *Education* as the arctic, congealing winter, dissolving into the tropical New England summer. Jonathan Edwards found the absolute "type" of the filthiness of man's sinful conception in the slush of New England's spring. Emerson, on the contrary, celebrated the frolic architecture of the snow, and so incorporated New England's severity into a Transcendental scheme of optimism.

Even so, New England's winters were a trial to Transcendentalists. In their heart of hearts, they all, like Margaret Fuller, thirsted for the Mediterranean, though only she (with about two others) mustered the courage to go there. In the first (and only) issue of *Æsthetic Papers* of 1849 — by which Elizabeth Peabody hoped to start a "journal" to carry on where *The Dial* had collapsed — some nameless "widow" moralized the region's seasons. After joyous summer and sad autumn, she got down to the serious issue:

> Winter, dread Undertaker, thou art come!
> And how unique are thy official deeds!
> The living and the dead, uncoffined, both
> Live in our meanest traversings concealed.

Of the aged it used to be said that if they could get through March they were good for another year. Thoreau himself was so stricken in November of 1861 that he could no longer journalize (he had written, "In November a man will eat his heart, if in any month"); he lasted through the winter, but winter killed him.

Openly to admit that life in New England was in danger of extinction every January would be to concede that circumstances shape man's purpose — a concession which, as Thoreau explained to Isaiah Williams, no self-appreciating consciousness would allow. But if this proposition were to be resisted, there was only one alternative. Death might seem inevitable, yet could be circumvented; woman might be a lure, and also friendship, yet these temptations could be withstood. But if the real enemy was the onset of winter, then the last citadel that could hold against that assault would be a consciousness barricaded within the *Journal*.

Introduction

In the first of the ex cathedra letters to which Harrison Blake exposed himself, he heard, as of March 27, 1848, that while Henry Thoreau did not congratulate himself on past performances, Thoreau relished faith and aspiration:

> I have sworn no oath. I have no designs on society, or nature, or God. I am simply what I am, or I begin to be that. I *live* in the *present*. I only remember the past, and anticipate the future. I love to live.[2]

This bit, I must say, wrenched from the context, may sound even more oracular than Henry intended; still, it shows what a load was imposed upon Harrison Blake, that of comprehending Thoreau's gigantic anticipation!

In this perspective, our volume 3 prepares for the siege. Later, its etchings of friendship are to be more deeply engraved, its notes on winter to become the intransigence of *Walden*. These preliminary fragments show that he already knew how he would need more than the blatant heroics of "The Service" in order to come through the winter. He would need some strategy of prefiguration; and this the book, his *Walden*, achieved. Yet even after it was published, Henry Thoreau had still to walk the wilderness of Concord.

We must then read the *Journal* as a retreat before the ever-pressing assault. Compare, for instance, the tone of this volume with the autumn of 1858: then, on October 29, nature is stripping herself for the contest with "her great antagonist Winter."[3] On November 8 he hears that snow has fallen in Manchester; he did not realize how near winter had approached: "It is as if a scout had brought word that an enemy were approaching in force only a day's march distant."[4] Implacably winter moves: on November 14 "the old she wolf is nibbling at your very extremities."[5] On Christmas Day, the ground is bare: "You come near eating your heart now."[6]

The Stratagems of Consciousness — Anticipation

Blake pieced together a volume of *Winter* in such a way as to give the impression that Thoreau loved the season. If you read the *Journal* consecutively you see that every winter is a retirement to prepared positions. At last there is only one stronghold: the mind can *anticipate* spring. This, in essence, is the design of *Walden*.

But that book, even when Thoreau could get it printed, did not end the contest. On November 4, 1858, for instance, he notes how only a sharpshooter can hit snipes and woodcocks, that he who fires at random gets nothing, and then deduces:

> And so it is with him that shoots at beauty. Not till the sky falls will he catch larks, unless he is a trained sportsman. He will not bag any if he does not already know its seasons and haunts and the color of its wing, — if he has not dreamed of it, so that he can *anticipate* it. . . .[7]

The italics are his. Further in the passage, he is succinct: the hunter "prays for, and so gets it." But the poignance of this assertion is that by 1858 the *Week* was long ago lost, *Walden* seemed to have hit not even a snipe, his lectures had met "with no marked success." ("Preaching? Lecturing?" he exclaims on November 16: "Who are ye that ask for these things? What do ye want to hear, ye puling infants?")[8] But even as the situation worsens, the *Journal* rings more valiantly with the word that is the clarion of *Walden* — "anticipate."

Anticipation, as conceived in these lonely years, became for Thoreau a consolation: someday he would be heard. As far as we can tell, his egotism never lost that assurance. In this respect he stands in American literature a contrast to Whitman — who ended his days amid a band of adorers assuring him that his fame would increase — and a stark contrast to Melville, who, we gather, abandoned all hope. Thoreau's sort of anticipation is in the grand Romantic convention: the genius is misunderstood in his own generation, but he shall, he *must*, become recognized by the next. Why else should he have labored? To consider 1858 again, Thoreau was able to tell himself on October 31, noting that an hour-glass apple shrub beside the Conantum house was full of fruit, that likewise would it be "with the rude, neglected genius from amid the country hills." Such a being suffers many a check at first; he grows broad and strong, "hopelessly stunted, you would say, and not like a sleek orchard tree all whose forces are husbanded and the precious early years not lost"; but eventually, "thanks to his rude strength," the rough genius attains full stature, his fame will spread for generations, "while that thrifty orchard tree which was his competitor will, perchance, have long since ceased to bear its engrafted fruit and decayed." [9]

Thoreau's competitors, such as Longfellow and Holmes, with their engrafted fruit, have decayed. In his day the conspicuous competitor was N. P. Willis, who was highly engrafted, and has emphatically decayed. We forget how intensely conscious of the competition Thoreau was. When composing volume 3, by placing in it preservable nuggets from the Ur-journal, he had to tell himself that his early years should not be lost. Every word is put down in confident anticipation that the rude genius from the country hills shall find a use for it, that every word someday shall bear the fruit of success.

From this vantagepoint we perceive how he worked, perfecting paragraphs with one purpose in mind: the future use, never to indulge in comment on the passing scene. This volume, along with the other early volumes (and, as far as we can calculate, the volumes before 1850), contains units of perception. In 1840 Thoreau was stacking his thoughts as he might pile logs during the summer in anticipation of the winter. Wherefore, what strikes us is the miserly, the niggardly way he scrapes his mind: every scrap is preserved — after, that is, an elimination of the junk. Nothing that looks as though it might be useful is thrown away (just as, in the course of time, almost everything is indeed used); nothing is given away, nothing squandered. Everything dug out of the ground, if it be solid and impermeable, is to serve against the she wolf.

What we have to deal with, to put it otherwise, is a method of composition which Margaret Fuller, to express her dislike of it, called a "mosaic." Thoreau builds his edifices out of bricks already baked. Contemporaries objected that the *Week* was a pastiche of bits previously printed, mostly in *The Dial*, stuck together by the artificial glue of the voyage. Some who noticed *Walden* sensed that it also was a conglomeration; such, in great part, it is. But in this one instance, and only this one, the devouring forces of ego and anxiety struck a balance; the pellets consolidated in expectation of a whole proved to be more than parts of a part. What could, in this unique instance, marshal them into coherent formation was the command that they vindicate the concept of anticipation.

Torrey and Allen made a conscientious effort to note particles of the *Journal* that Thoreau used in his books and essays. The third entry in volume 1, October 24, 1837, concludes thus:

> So this constant abrasion and decay makes the soil of my future growth. As I live now so shall I reap. If I grow pines and birches, my virgin mould will not sustain the oak; but pines and birches, or, perchance weeds and brambles, will constitute my second growth.[10]

Even though we know that this was siphoned off from the big notebook, we are tempted, when we find it in the preserved *Journal*, to interpret it as autobiography, as young Thoreau's self-dedication. But we learn wariness when, following Torrey's footnote, we turn to the close of "Friday" in the *Week*, and in the middle of a paragraph describing how the shadows chased one another over wood and meadow that day, we find:

> The constant abrasion and decay of our lives makes the soil of our future growth. The wood which we now mature, when it becomes virgin mould, determines the character of our second growth, whether that be oaks or pines.[11]

From its inception, the *Journal* was anticipating the books; what was squeezed out of experience referred not to the experience from which it came but to the project for which it was designed. As far as ingenuity could manage, every particle would be fitted in. It is hardly a caricature of the process to say that the fascination for us is that of watching a writer who was always at least one jump ahead of the game.

The similarity of Thoreau's method with Emerson's, and yet the radical differences from it, can be seen by comparing how the two were behaving in the time of this volume. At the end of 1839 and through this summer of 1840 Emerson was, we have noted, applying himself to the subject of friendship. By October he was to tell his brother that he had been idle, that he had been writing "romances of letters." Indeed he had: this is the summer of those letters, back and forth, with Caroline Sturgis and Margaret Fuller which in any other country, or by any other hands, would be called love letters. Emerson also had to get whatever he could from a fairly restricted field of sensation. He gave Margaret adequate warning in January: "I am intent some day to write out as I told you the whole chapter of friendship."[12] Possibly she was a willing victim, and probably believed that when it came to this sort of fencing she would prove the better swordsman. On August

14, while riding with him, she taxed him with "inhospitality of soul," said that she and Caroline would gladly be his friends, "yet our intercourse is not friendship, but literary gossip." [13] Gossip or earnestness, in August and September, while holding Margaret spellbound by saluting her as "O divine mermaid or fisher of men," Emerson completed his essay — which was what he really wanted. But as many a more experienced philanderer has discovered — as a more hospitable study of Byron would have warned him — Margaret, having been used, was not to be summarily dismissed. On September 29 she wails that his light shall never understand her fire: "I felt that you did not for me the highest office of friendship, by offering me the clue of the labyrinth of my own being." He had spiced their relation by asking for a "foe" in his friend; he was on the verge of getting one in all earnest: "But a beautiful foe, I am not yet, to you. Shall I ever be. I know not." In October he tried explaining to her that while he would always cherish his "dear romance," would worship it, he would not "use" it. Gentle hints worked as little here as elsewhere. On October 24 — a week or two before Henry would have proposed, if he ever did propose, to Ellen — his mentor was forced to become explicit: "I ought never to have suffered you to lead me into any conversation or writing on our relation, a topic from which with all persons my Genius ever sternly warns me away." [14] As we have seen, by the next summer Emerson was in full retreat, but even so, he gained his essay.

What really concerns us, as it did him, is how Emerson transmuted "romancing" into journalizing. A fair sample is Emerson's entry for June 21 (just before Thoreau's volume 3 begins, when the Thoreaus would be welcoming Ellen Sewall):

> Can we not be so great as to offer tenderness to our friend, — tenderness with self trust? Why should

we desecrate noble & beautiful souls by intruding on them. Can we not guard them from ourselves? Why insist on these rash personal relations? Why go to the houses or know the mothers & brothers of our friend? Leave this touching & clawing. Let him be a soul to me. A message a compliment a sincerity a glance from him, — that I want. I can get politics & news & convenience without these sunbright qualities. To my friend I write a letter, & from him I get a letter. It is a spiritual gift worthy of him to give & of me to receive. It profanes nobody. In these warm lines the heart will trust itself as it will not to the tongue and pour out the prophecy of a better & godlier existence than all the annals of heroism have yet made good. To us even the society of our friend is as yet far from poetic. We are not pure in passive universal as yonder bar of cloud that sleeps on the horizon or that clump of waving grass. Let us bring him & ourselves up to that standard of nature. Leave him alone. Defend him from yourself. That proud defying eye that scornful beauty of his mien & action do not pique yourself on reducing but rather fortify & enhance. Guard him as thy great counterpart: have a princed [*sic*] on a World to thy friend. Let him be to thee forever a sort of beautiful Enemy, untameable, infinitely revered, and not a trivial shift & convenience to be soon outgrown & cast aside. The hues of the opal the lights of the diamond are not to be seen if the eye is too near. And yet, as E.H. said, though I do not wish my friend to visit me, I wish to live with him.

Quite apart from the interest which, I am sure, attaches itself to the document as a memento of this (I am tempted to call it) fetid summer in Concord, it is also of interest as an illustration of Emerson's *Journals*: free, flowing, the thought moving steadily, the passage expanding so that, with a minimum of editing, it can become a paragraph or a section of the finished essay. He is not compelled to mine nuggets from underground and to hoard them until he has enough to make a mosaic. He knows what he wants, and that comes when he whistles. In the published essay this entry becomes:

> Let us buy our entrance to this guild by a long probation. Why should we desecrate noble and beautiful souls by intruding on them? Why insist on rash personal relations with your friend? Why go to his house, or know his mother and brother and sisters? Why be visited by him at your own? Are these things material to our covenant? Leave this touching and clawing. Let him be to me a spirit. A message, a thought, a sincerity, a glance from him, I want, but not news, nor pottage. I can get politics and chat and neighborly conveniences from cheaper companions. Should not the society of my friend be to me poetic, pure, universal and great as nature itself? Ought I to feel that our tie is profane in comparison with yonder bar of cloud that sleeps on the horizon, or that clump of waving grass that divides the brook? Let us not vilify, but raise it to that standard. That great defying eye, that scornful beauty of his mien and action, do not pique yourself on reducing, but rather fortify and enhance. Worship his superiorities; wish him not less by a thought, but hoard and tell them all. Guard him as thy counterpart. Let him be to thee for ever a sort of beautiful enemy, untamable, devoutly revered, and not a trivial conveniency to be soon outgrown and cast aside. The hues of the opal, the light of the diamond, are not to be seen if the eye is too near. To my friend I write a letter and from him I receive a letter. That seems to you a little. It suffices me. It is a spiritual gift, worthy of him to give and of me to receive. It profanes nobody. In these warm lines the heart will trust itself, as it will not to the tongue, and pour out

the prophecy of a godlier existence than all the annals of heroism have yet made good.[15]

Where Emerson is fluid, Thoreau is a carpenter. One example will suffice: throughout these six volumes a persistent theme is Thoreau's reaction to his first readings in Indian literature. Again and again, he transmits from the Ur-journal some brief perception, seldom more than two or three sentences. On August 30, 1841, he achieves this:

> The "Laws of Menu" are a manual of private devotion, so private and domestic and yet so public and universal a word as is not spoken in the parlor or pulpit in these days. It is so impersonal that it exercises our sincerity more than any other. It goes with us into the yard and into the chamber, and is yet later spoken than the advice of our mother and sisters.[16]

Noting, as we read, this "mother and sisters," let us then remark the entry on page 160 below (August 28, 1840, a year before the one just quoted) about the wild fowls of India. And then take another entry of August 1841, this time on the 30th:

> To our nearsightedness this mere outward life seems a constituent part of us, and we do not realize that as our soul expands it will cast off the shell of routine and convention, which afterward will only be an object for the cabinets of the curious. But of this people the temples are now crumbled away, and we are introduced to the very hearth of Hindoo life and to the primeval conventicle where how to eat and to drink and to sleep were the questions to be decided.[17]

Then, to finish the inventory, there is an entry for March 15, 1842, after John's death, which starts as a lament on the inadequacy of any book to be read in the woods:

None will sail as far forward into the bay of nature as my thought. They stay at home. I would go home. When I get to the wood their thin leaves rustle in my fingers. They are bare and obvious, and there is no halo or haze about them. Nature lies far and fair behind them all.[18]

Here then are four particles of the *Journal*, separated by a period of almost two years, from August 1840 to March 1842, composed in several moods and in different contexts. But in "Monday" of the *Week* — written at the earliest in 1845 and probably later — there appears, as a digression, a discourse on the Laws of Menu, and part of one paragraph is thus manufactured:

This of Menu addresses our privacy more than most. It is a more private and familiar, and at the same time a more public and universal word, than is spoken in parlor or pulpit nowadays. As our domestic fowls are said to have their original in the wild pheasant of India, so our domestic thoughts have their prototypes in the thoughts of her philosophers. We are dabbling in the very elements of our present conventional and actual life; as if it were the primeval conventicle, where how to eat, and to drink, and to sleep, and maintain life with adequate dignity and sincerity, were the questions to be decided. It is later and more intimate with us even than the advice of our nearest friends. And yet it is true for the widest horizon, and read out of doors has relation to the dim mountain line, and is native and aboriginal there. Most books belong to the house and street only, and in the fields their leaves feel very thin. They are bare and obvious, and have no halo nor haze about them. Nature lies far and fair behind them all.[19]

Examples of this sort of dovetailing and splicing of entries can be multiplied indefinitely (the page about the maiden in the boat is, we have seen, another); those who wish further to follow the process can do so by glancing from Torrey's footnotes (and I trust from mine, in the matter of volume 3) to the printed text. For our purpose, the first moral is that volume 3 played its part in the complicated operation, that it contributed, along with the other five, to the production. It was drawn upon for the *Week*, but by then was so gutted that it had little to offer for *Walden*.

The second lesson arising from this analysis of Thoreau's method is more important, and the contrast with Emerson's drives it home: this writer had to husband his energies, collect his pieces one by one, and steadily, consciously, anticipate the day when, by expert masonry, he could construct an edifice. His problem was not, as was Emerson's, to check a stream of expression, but to keep the crevices from showing after he laid one brick on top of another. His existence was an anticipation that the miracle would happen — that the inert bones would join together and become flesh, that the resurrection would come.

It is useless, though beguiling, to speculate about what Henry Thoreau might have become as a writer had he ever experienced in life any "success." He would not have needed a big success, such as that of N. P. Willis — merely such a moderate but substantial audience as Emerson won. It seems fair to say that had he worked for it, and wanted to pay the price, he could have had it. Margaret Fuller's *Summer on the Lakes* in 1844 was such an *omnium gatherum* as the *Week* (it may have been Thoreau's model), and it at least attracted attention (as the *Week* did not) — though this may have been because of the adventitious fact of Margaret's notoriety as a "feminist." Actually, as the texts of both the *Week* and *Walden* stand, they are concerned with topics then being widely discussed in the lyceums — genius versus talent, nature as revelation, the self and society, country as against city, intuition against tuition. An insoluble riddle about American society in the 1840's and 1850's is why the literary voices of the era were so terribly obliged to become, in Melville's word, "isolates." Poe, of course, was a madman — in the opinion of his contemporaries; Whitman offended in ways too numerous to relate. Hawthorne possibly sentimentalized the loneliness of the years spent in his Salem chamber, seeking to open an intercourse with the world; even so, he numbed his fingers, and though he won attention with *The Scarlet Letter* in 1850, he never could break out of his prison. Melville took the public by storm with *Typee* in 1846 (which both Thoreau and Channing read), but with *Pierre* in 1852 he alienated it (there is no evidence that Thoreau read this). Emerson toiled manfully at making himself understood; the horrendous rebel of "The Divinity School Address" became the darling of lyceum audiences, and in the end of all, in 1882, he would die revered by the literate of his country almost as much as Longfellow. Thoreau strove to convey the essence of the Emersonian message, and assuredly he made every effort to be a good lecturer. We can, as some do, accuse the American public for not appreciating him, but we have to recognize that while Thoreau's lectures may read well today, he delivered them atrociously. In his literary ambitions, as in his friendships, he sought failure (once one realizes this, he thinks also of Emily Dickinson). Otherwise, Thoreau could not so have anticipated a success greater than any worldly success among his contemporaries.

In the 1840's, young graduates from Harvard did not feel called upon, when they returned home, to demonstrate how at the college they had acquired aesthetic sensitivities so exquisite that they could no longer endure the philistinism of their parents or the banality of their parents' friends. In almost all cases where Emerson and "Transcendentalism"

117

wrought some such effect upon the undergraduate, and he became a rebel against parental precept, the issue was seriously intellectual. O. B. Frothingham's quarrel with his father, the Reverend Nathaniel Langdon Frothingham of the First Church in Boston, and his fleeing for sanctuary to the house of Theodore Parker, illustrate the usual pattern of disruption. As far as we can make out, Henry returned from Harvard to his beloved home in Concord without bringing into it ideas that disturbed the domestic harmony (though one of his aunts did sniff at his preference for Madame de Staël as against the Bible). Clearly he never had any sort of quarrel, least of all ideological, with his taciturn father. However, when he was in the house, unless he could retreat out of earshot to his attic (as apparently he often did), he was bombarded by the incessant chatter of his voluble mother, of his aunts and sisters. Fragments of drafts he worked up on the theme of "idle conversation" suggest that his nerves were constantly rasped. The writings are full of his contempt for the conversational limitations of his fellow townsmen (by implication, for those of his family?), but the work-sheets show that when he approached publication he exercised restraint. One of these suppressed tirades ends on what to many of his readers may be a startling note, if only because it confronts them with the apparition of Henry Thoreau in a parlor:

> Once at a tea-table, forgetting where I was, I whistled — whereupon the company would not be convinced that it was not meant for a hint that their conversation was frivolous. I thought that their suspicion was the best proof that it was so.

We are tempted to smile, as though assailed by the familiar rudeness of an adolescent intellectual. However, in Henry Thoreau we have to deal with a truculence more deeply rooted:

from the beginning he is dedicated to self-justification. I trust that I detract not an iota from his denunciatory prose by expounding it as a device for exoneration of the self. For a moment we may yield to the hypothesis that here is, if not simply the recalcitrant youth, a carryover of New England's Calvinistic heritage, in which the sinner was exonerated from his transgressions by the certainty of an election that had naught to do with his merit. But the young Thoreau was haunted by an anxiety which no Calvinism could lay to rest. "I never was so rapid in my virtue," he wrote to himself on February 8, 1841, "but my vice kept up with me." It seemed to him that every time he taught his virtue a new nobleness, his vice acquired a new cunning.[20] And eventually, in the specific context of the Concord community, he had to learn precisely wherein he could cleanse himself: in April 1844, five months after he fled back home from New York, Henry Thoreau — master of woodcraft — set fire to Concord woods and almost destroyed the town. His vice kept up with him.

Thoreau's biographers mention this accident, as they must, for the memory of it still remains in Concord, furnishing proof positive that he was not only shiftless but dangerously irresponsible. Whereupon his biographers minimize the seriousness of his conflagration. What they fail to note is that they base their accounts on a version of the disaster which Thoreau put into his *Journal* six years after the event, in the undated prologue to the volume commencing with June 1850.[21] Possibly he may have pondered on it in the now destroyed volumes before 1850; even if he did, we must stand amazed that after all these years, after the sojourn by the Pond, and after his bitter humiliation with the failure of the *Week*, he was thus internally compelled to vomit forth the cancer of his guilt.

Thoreau tells his story apropos of nothing that seems to call for the telling, after remarking how Concord herdsmen drive their cattle to New Hampshire in the summer. He breaks in upon himself: "I once set fire to the woods." He had gone, in this April of 1844, upstream with "a single companion." He does not say that this companion was Edward Hoar, then a student at Harvard; Sanborn later disclosed that had not the son of Samuel Hoar been implicated, Thoreau would have been prosecuted for criminal negligence. They caught some fish, tried to cook them over a fire which spread to the dry grass (there had been no rain) and which raced to the woods. Edward, according to Thoreau's soliloquy, cried out, "Well, where will this end?" Thoreau says he answered, "It will go to town," but whether with terror or glee he reveals not. Thoreau ran two miles to arouse the populace — who perfectly understood, as would those in any New Hampshire village of today, the gravity of the threat — and then retired to Fair Haven Cliff to contemplate the spectacle.

What he may actually have experienced at the moment is a matter for speculation. What he says he felt amounts to a stupendous gesture of exculpation:

> Hitherto I had felt like a guilty person, — nothing but shame and regret. But now I settled the matter with myself shortly. I said to myself: "Who are these men who are said to be the owners of these woods, and how am I related to them? I have set fire to the forest, but I have done no wrong therein, and now it is as if the lightning had done it. These flames are but consuming their natural food." (It has never troubled me from that day to this more than if the lightning had done it. The trivial fishing was all that disturbed me and disturbs me still).

The *Journal* by 1850 had become, as he was to declare in November of the next year, a "says I to myself." Were he really secure in that proposition, would he have needed in 1850 to tell himself how virtuous he had been in 1844?

When he assures himself in 1850, he contends that the mob who fought the fire (and saved the town) were less concerned about loss of property than with the excitement of conflagration. This may, in our age, become a profoundly sociological insight, but we are struck with Thoreau's remembering that some citizen, ascertaining the facts, called him "a damned rascal." We notice the logic by which this rascal staved off the judgment of the community:

> I at once ceased to regard the owners and my own fault — if fault there was any in the matter, — and attended to the phenomenon before me, determined to make the most of it. To be sure, I felt a little ashamed when I reflected on what a trivial occasion this had happened, that at the time I was no better employed than my townsmen.

Had Thoreau announced this position in 1844, we might admire it as impulsive. But he relived the violence, in cold blood, in 1850. Later in that June he came back to it, as though finally to rid himself of the specter, and told himself, "When the lightning burns the forest its Director makes no apology to man, and I was but His agent." Still, the *Journal* thereafter is resonant with unuttered references to this escapade. He lied in 1850 when he said that he was never troubled, as though the lightning and not he had done it. He knew that he figured in the shrewd estimation of the town as the damned rascal who, pretending to be at home in the forest, had set fire to the dry woods.

Relations with fellow-citizens came under the generic heading of "friendship." Early in Wednesday's digression on this topic in the *Week* Thoreau took care to address "my most serene and irresponsible neighbors," in order to show that mere neighborhood had nothing to do with true friendship. We may now perceive, from isolated bits of an early draft, that he wrote this essay with a vehemence which he strove, in the final version, to restrain. Again, he drew upon the *Journal*. In the *Week* the passage goes thus:

> Nothing can shock a brave man but dullness. Think how many rebuffs every man has experienced in his day; perhaps fallen into a horse-pond, eaten fresh-water clams, or worn one shirt for a week without washing. Indeed, you cannot receive a shock unless you have an electric affinity for that which shocks you.[22]

The first sentence comes almost intact from an entry of June 22, 1840, but the *Journal* continues, "what mean these sly suspicious looks, as if you were an odd fish, a piece of crockery-ware to be tenderly handled." [23] The rest of the entry is cut down to make the three sentences of the *Week*, but in the *Journal*, another sentence follows the last: "Have no affinity for what is shocking."

We happen to possess the work-sheet for this page. It reveals how he compressed the passage, but it also shows that after cleaning up the verbiage, leaving out the reference to himself as an odd fish, he tried a different conclusion. Seeking to improve on what the *Journal* gave him, Thoreau wrote, "When we are shocked at vice, we express a lingering sympathy with it." Then he crossed this sentence out, but the evidence remains that he ventured on the idea.

Sensitive as Thoreau was to cadence, and hating prolixity, he may have erased both the final sentence from the *Journal* — "Have no affinity for what is shocking" — and the tentative substitute — our lingering sympathy for vices at which we are shocked — because he felt that in "electric affinity" he had said all he needed. Still, the thwarted revision tells more than he may have realized, or rather more than he would wish to betray. Even in his experiments, Thoreau did nothing by inadvertence. This foray, though he suppressed it, points up the problem of Thoreau the justifier of conflagration. He had two choices, only two: he could declare himself perfect and so never apologize; or he could so inure himself against his own vices as never to let himself be shocked by them. In the second case, if the stratagem might work (or could be made to work), Henry Thoreau would be as discharged from sympathy with his vices as though they never existed.

This was a complex dialectic, and we may well ask whether Thoreau knew precisely what he was doing. Still, he had his inklings. On March 2, 1842, some two years before his inadvertence, he told himself that a man was fortunate who could get through life with no reputation. But, he then followed the logic, such freedom is not a matter of "character." It is entirely a prerogative of genius, and "Genius, strictly speaking, is not responsible, for it is not moral." [24]

Readers of the published *Journal* become accustomed to, even bored by, the rhetorical patterns of this self-justification — repetitive insistence that mild meadows of Concord are more impressive than the Roman compagna, why should we go to Paris? etc., etc. In the last years these exclamations on the bigness of the little become a nervous tic, cease to carry any conviction. But the young Thoreau had to make his decisions, little realizing how he would be imprisoned by them. The volume before us, emerging out of 1840, speaks for the time when the consequences of self-immolation, daring to become the "damned rascal," were accepted with bravado, with no realization of the penalties. Wherefore, though its value to literature may be slight, its meaning is in poignance.

There is a page of the dissevered journalizing sometime after 1842 — I would guess before 1845 — which has never been published, but which more than anything in print displays the state of mind he was fast (faster than he realized) approaching, even as he put down these refined thoughts in 1840. We may see it as an adumbration of the self-portraiture which eventually became the staple of the *Journal*; because it is early, and because it does "anticipate" the career of failure, it is worth recalling along with our volume 3:

> Is there such virtue in raking cranberries that those men's employment whom I now see in the meadow can rightly reprove my idleness? Can I not go over these same meadows after them & rake still more valuable fruits — rake with my mind? Can I not rake a thought perchance which shall be worth a bushel of cranberries? . . .
>
> It is pathetic for one far in the fields in mid [word obscure] to hear the village clock striking. The bees in the flowers [seem to (pencil insertion)] reprove my idleness yet I ask myself to what end do they labor? Is there so much need of honey & wax? Is the industry of mankind truly respectable? [(crossed out:) Can it rightly reprove my idleness?] I will not mind the village clock. It makes time for the dead & dying. It sounds like a knell; as if one struck the most sonorous slates in the churchyard with a mallet, & they rang out the words which are engraved on them — tempus fugit irrevocabile. I harken for the clock that strikes the eternal hours. What though my walk is [word obscure] and I do not find employment which satisfies my hunger & thirst, and the bee probing the thistle & loading himself with honey & wax seems better employed than I, my idleness is better than his industry. I would rather that my spirit hunger & thirst than that it forget its own wants in satisfying the hunger & thirst of the body.
>
> I would fain hunger & thirst after life forever & rise from the present enjoyment unsatisfied. I feel the necessity of treating myself with more respect than I have done — of washing myself more religiously in the ponds & streams if only for a symbol of our inward cleansing & refreshment — of eating and drinking more

abstemiously and with more discrimination of savors
— recruiting myself for new and worthier labor. There
are certain things which only senses refined and purified
may take cognizance of — May such senses be mine!
O that I might truly worship my own body as the
worthiest temple of God — bow down with reverence
to his image graven in it — & so love and reverence the
very persons of my friends. May I love and revere myself above all the gods that men have ever invented, and
never let the vestal fire go out in my senses.

Comment is mute in the presence of such declamation.
Still, our curiosity persists. Do we here have a piece of what
I call the Ur-journal — a spontaneous first utterance which
Thoreau, in his circumspect years, would refine into more
usable, more impersonal, building blocks? That this burst
was a yielding to an emotion of the moment, more than he
considered seemly, more than he could overcome by stratagem,
may be seen in a penciled annotation at the end: "What shall
it profit etc." What indeed was his profit?

My excuse for excavating this quotation out of the chaos
of Thoreau's manuscripts is that it exemplifies the devices
of his early writing, what I call his "stratagems." He labored
faithfully, and in high hopes, upon the books; he endeavored to
give acceptable lectures. Hardly in the history of literature,
wherever we enter the workshop, is there such devotion to
duty. But nowhere, I venture, can we find a creature dedicated
to the art of composition — which after all is designed to
communicate with one's fellows — so resolved, at the very
beginning of his career, to inquire, "Is there so much need of
honey & wax?" And assuredly, there are few, if any, who mix
anticipations of failure with reflections on the knell that
sounds from striking with a mallet slates in a New England
graveyard.

Above all, this effusion is an apology for what the town took to be idleness. In Thoreau's most governed statement, at the end of *Walden*, an idle bug, even though "strong and beautiful," comes out of the old table. However, what at the conclusion of that book is even more remarkable is the scene chosen for the demonstration of revivification. The Pond, the water, we have heard, was dead, but now is alive. Poets and artists for centuries have hailed resurrection in the flowering of plants, the melting of ice, the risen Christ, the glory of love consummated, the rebirth of nature. Thoreau lived in "the woods": but for him, the recrudescence of animal vigor is beheld not in some billowy meadow but in the rude gash of the railroad cut, a wound to the earth — not in any blossoming pasture but in "thawing sand and clay." [25] He who may or may not have offered marriage to Ellen Sewall fixes his image of renascence upon this sterility, upon "the silicious matter," [26] and concludes his hymn to death with a resuscitation neither of love nor of maidens, not even of vineyards, but of "thawing clay." [27] This, and only this phenomenon — "multiplied since railroads were invented" — imparts the assurance (for blood vessels were formed out of mud) that even in winter we may loiter, in the anticipation that "in a pleasant spring morning all men's sins are forgiven." [28] As an afterthought, but a serious and calculated one, this self-constituted enemy of the people and of his friends, might then find a roundabout way to pleading, "Through our own recovered innocence we discern the innocence of our neighbors." Even so, the precondition of the "traveller's" charity is the anticipation of his own salvation. God, Thoreau will assert, offers his pardon freely to all, but not to man born of woman: "What is man but a mass of thawing clay?"

The pages by which Henry Thoreau — deliberately, we may be sure! — brings his book about Walden Pond to its climax in a slime of sand demand more analysis than they have received. Once more, every reader is on his own. But none can blink the fact that in this return of fertility the scene is predestined to sterility. Anticipation is the cause for living, and for beating the game, but also the assurance of failure. Still, the frost is coming out of the ground: "this is Spring." This afterbirth of mud and clay is filthy, because it precedes (and must precede) the flowery spring of youth and music: "I know of nothing more purgative of winter fumes and indigestions."

Toward this ultimate — this derisive, tortured — irony, at the end of *Walden*, Henry Thoreau was conducting himself through his early *Journal:* circumventing death, evading woman, discounting friendship, he anticipated the impossible, so as never to be seduced by the moments he loved so passionately. Our fragile volume 3 is a chapter in this perverse pilgrimage.

9

A Note on the Editing

BRADFORD TORREY had to contend with a vast manuscript, and further was burdened by the knowledge that Harrison Blake had taken unforgivable liberties with it. Being an ornithologist of established reputation, Torrey was frequently shocked by what he read in Thoreau's reporting. He did the best he could, and nobody can blame him. He calculated that the proper method would be to print the original form, and to assume that changes made between that and what ultimately appeared in the *writings* would automatically show how Thoreau had refashioned his pristine material.

What Torrey therefore left out are the portions of the *Journal* in which Thoreau fiddled with paragraphs for which he never found any publishable use. What worries us even more, Torrey was not consistent: he sometimes gives us, without previous notice, the amended rather than the original entry.

The student who has no ambition beyond reading the fourteen volumes of the *Journal* — most find this chore enough — will not cavil over Torrey's editorial decisions. Some who have worked on the manuscripts complain about his inconsistency. Is what we read Thoreau's first, second, or later thought? The problem would not seem to be too difficult: Thoreau generally wrote the distillations which we call his *Journal* in ink; when he revised, he used a pencil. To the extent to which this rule prevails, as it does in 1840, we can read the *Journal* intelligibly.

A Note on the Editing

For example: there is an amusing response on August 27, 1838, to his loss of a tooth. It appears, ignominiously, that Thoreau swallowed it! In Torrey's transcript, the last sentence runs: "But let him who has lost a tooth open his mouth wide and gabble, lisp, and sputter never so resolutely." In this case, the sentence happens to be a penciled alteration: what the young Thoreau, in his humiliation, first put down, in ink, was: "If you are toothless and speak a lingo — open your mouth wide and gabble never so resolutely." [1] Surely there is something, albeit slight, to learn about Thoreau's apprenticeship to language by a comparison of these early efforts.

Or again — considering his relation to the children he led (Emerson disapproving) on huckleberry parties — it is rather a shame to confine us to Torrey's rendition of the ink original of November 7, 1839, which says "Children appear to me as raw as the fresh fungi on a fence rail," [2] and so to miss the penciled insertion, "To remember of children that they exist as poets."

In several cases (so far as I have followed him, not too many), Torrey's use either of the ink or of the pencil is a bit capricious. No harm is done to Thoreau, and Torrey did have to consider space. Since our volume 3 is short, and I have room in which to turn around, I have thought it worth while to indicate most of the revisions, to show what happened to our passages.

The most expeditious way seems to be to give in my printed text Thoreau's revised version, wherever his changes make a coherence, and to indicate in the "Notes on Textual Variants," at the back of the book, what was earlier or what was suppressed. Several of the situations are, however, so complex that I can do little more than elucidate them *ad hoc*.

Torrey and Allen found it incumbent upon them, "if the *Journal* was to be of comfortable use by ordinary readers," to impose upon it a rational system of punctuation. They were wise, especially in the later volumes, which otherwise would be difficult for ordinary readers to follow. In these first volumes, where Thoreau is painfully extracting his more rounded ideas from the Ur-journal, he worked slowly, and is fairly orthodox in punctuating. But since, again, our volume 3 is a brief segment, and the peculiar circumstances of its belated appearance make it a curiosity, I have reproduced Thoreau's own (however eccentric) punctuation. One can readily see, by comparing any portion which he later made use of, that he subjected his notes to rigorous discipline, his commas no less than his adjectives.

I have done as little "silent" editing as possible, but I have assumed that pedantry should be avoided. Where, for instance, Thoreau writes "the the," obviously intending only one "the," I see no point in documenting his slip. I have eliminated most of these minor inadvertencies, but have used the conventional (which I hate) brackets to indicate corrections or omissions that may be of interest to infatuated Thoreauvians. He did not bother, when dating his entries, to punctuate them consistently; rather than distract the reader unnecessarily, I have supplied the periods. After all, our concern is, as far as possible, to read what Henry Thoreau wrote.

PART II

The Journal

July 30, 1840, to January 22, 1841
(volume 3)

Nov, 1st 1840

The days' won by the blushes of the dawn

I thought that the sun you love should have risen as noiseless as the sun out of the sea, and we sailors have found ourselves steering between the tropics as if the broad day had lasted forever. If you knew how the sun comes up from the sea when you stand on the cliff, and does'nt startle you, but everything, and you too are helping it.

Monday, Nov 2d 1840.

It is well said that the "attitude of inspection is prone." The soul does not inspect but behold. Like the lily or the crystal in the rock, it looks in the face of the sky.

Page 64 of the "Lost" Journal

The entry for November 1 contains the enigmatic passage which may or may not be a disguised reference to Ellen Sewall. The precision of the penmanship and phrasing illustrates the strong probability that these entries were made after the first draft had been composed and perfected on some other paper.

N_{EXT} to having lived a day well is a clear & calm over-looking of all our days.

I have seen a sage hold up one finger to express individuality, and two for dualism without injuring the effect of his action by speech — so that his audience got a clearer notion of the difference than they ever had before, or you would believe possible.*

What is "leisure["] but opportunity for more complete and entire action: our energies pine for exercise, and demand leisure.

We can understand the phenomenon of death in the animal better, if we first consider it in the order next below us — the vegetable.

All men are really most attracted by the beauty of plain speech, & they even write in a florid style in imitation of this. They prefer to be misunderstood rather than come short of its exuberance. Hussein Effendi praised the epistolary style of Ibrahim Pasha to the French traveller Botta because of "the difficulty of understanding it: there was he said but one person

---

* This seems clearly an indication of the awesome effect Emerson in 1840 was making on Thoreau, setting him a model for lecture technique which he strove in vain to achieve. However, the sage may have been Alcott.

at Jidda who was capable of understanding and explaining the Pasha's correspondence." *

The man of genius as such, is not an artist. Art deals in that which the man knows. The man of Genius referred to mankind is an originator or Creator who produces a perfect work in obedience to laws as yet unexplored. The artist is he who detects & applies for himself the law from observation of the works of Genius. The artisan is he who merely applies the rules which others have detected.[2]

The woods make an admirable fence to the landscape.[3]

You see some trees in the fields which are but overgrown bushes.[4]

The true laborer is recompensed by his labor not by his employer.†

---

* Since these early *Journals* were transcribed out of the rough notebooks, Thoreau tried to make them as neat and definitive as possible; irresistibly he would be carried away by some momentary impulse which he would jot down, as here, with a pencil, and then commence to rework it. He rewrote this passage — inserting a first sentence, "Plain speech is always a desideratum" — in volume 6 on March 23, 1842, and out of it developed further paradoxes on the exuberance of simplicity. This revision he used in "Sir Walter Raleigh"; when Margaret Fuller would have none of that, he put the paragraph in storage. For the *Week* he reworked it, recasting the language of both the *Journal* of 1842 and the "Raleigh," but interestingly enough he went back to the front cover lining of volume 3 for these sentences and used them verbatim.[1]

. . .

† Thoreau has already cast himself as Apollo, is obsessed with figuring out schemes for escape. This sentiment is worried over

The Journal

A peculiar style of Beauty
the Persian lilack grafted on the ash.

A rich man's house is a *sedes*, that is a place to sit in, a *seat* or *residence*. The poor man's a *lectum*, a *roof* or *shelter*. These humble dwellings yet homely & sincere in which a hearth was still the essential part were more pleasing to our eyes than palaces would have been.[6]

Lydgate's "Story of Thebes", intended for a Canterbury Tale, is a specimen of most unprogressive and unmusical verse — Each line rings the knell of its brother as if it were introduced but to dispose of him. No mortal man could have breathed to that cadence without long intervals of relaxation — the repetition would have been fatal to his lungs. No doubt there was much healthy exercise taken in the meanwhile.*

and over in the *Journal*, eventually (in the essay "Life Without Principle," put together out of *Journal* passages to make a lecture — unsuccessful — in 1854, published in *The Atlantic Monthly* for October 1863) to become this:

If the laborer gets no more than the wages which his employer pays him, he is cheated, he cheats himself.[5]

· · ·

* Thoreau copied this exercise off the flyleaf of volume 3 almost exactly into volume 6 for March 31, 1842.[7] To it he added, "He should forget his rhyme and tell his story, or forget his story and breathe himself." The whole miniature essay is one of many he was attempting as a result of his comprehensive reading of Chambers's *Edinburgh Journal*. He made copious notes on the then neglected fourteenth century, but the material proved (as he ought to have foreseen) intractable. In the back of his mind seems to have been the thought of an essay on the poetry of Gower, Lydgate and Skelton. In the 1840's either in England or America, there was hardly any audience for these forgotten geniuses — which underscores Thoreau's perverse independence.

I've heard my neighbor's pump at night,
Long after Lyra sunk her light,
As if it were a natural sound,
And proper utterance of the ground —
Perchance some bittern in a fen —
Or else the squeak of a meadow hen.

Who sleeps by day and walks by night,
Will meet no spirit but some sprite.*

July 30th 1840.

No fresher tints than this morning's witnessed the valor
of Hector and Idomeneus, and some such evening as this the
Greek fleet came to anchor in the bay of Aulis; but alas; it is
not to us the eve of a ten years' war, but of a sixty years'
idleness and defeat.†

---

* Of these lines Thoreau salvages the last two to make a gnomic
utterance for the end of "Saturday" in the *Week*.[8] We may
or may not make something of the fact that within the next
few pages, in "Sunday," he copes with the maiden who once
"sailed" in his boat.[9] The American bittern, or "stake-driver,"
would become a considerable figure in the later *Journal*; see, for
instance, June 16, 1852: "Most would suppose the stake-driver
the sound of a farmer at a distance at his pump, watering his
cattle." [10] If one is avid for music, he has to make the most of
what he can hear.

. . .

† This is the first dated entry in volume 3; the last in volume 2
is July 27. In this month and the next Thoreau is assiduously
carving gems of ideas to ornament the essay he is intending for
The Dial, "The Service." He probably conceived the idea in the
spring of 1840 when he would know that *The Dial* had become
assured. As was always to be his practice, he began by searching
through everything he had so far deposited in his manuscript; he
reached all the way back into volume 1, to September 3, 1838.[11]

Our peace is proclaimed by the rust on our swords, and our inability to draw them from their scabbards — She does not so much work as to keep these swords bright and sharp. Let

Out of his production of the two years he could find enough stridency to serve his intention, but, as that intention became precise in 1840, he was reeling off defiance, reaching a crescendo in this July.

We make out from this volume that sometime in August he completed his draft, and expectantly sent it, via Emerson, to Margaret Fuller. In the press of business, she got around to pronouncing her Sibylline judgment only on December 1 (we can imagine Thoreau's nervous expectation and his chagrin):

> Last night's second reading only confirms my impression from the first. The essay is rich in thoughts, and I should be pained not to meet it again. But then, the thoughts seem to me so out of their natural order, that I cannot read it through without pain. I never once felt myself in a stream of thought, but seem to hear the grating tools on the mosaic. It is true, as Mr. Emerson says, that essays not to be compared with this have found their way into *The Dial*. But then, these are more unassuming in their tone, and have an air of quiet good-breeding, which induces us to permit their presence. Yours is so rugged that it ought to be commanding.[12]

Here indeed was a lesson in Transcendental "friendship"! Remembering this officiously friendly chiding, we comprehend how cool was the objective mood in which Thoreau obeyed Emerson's command in July 1850 to go to Fire Island — he who hated to travel in the direction of New York — to see what could be found of the wrecked *Elizabeth*, aboard which Margaret, her Italian husband and her baby perished, and with what complacency he beheld a button ripped from a coat of the "Marquis of Ossoli." "I do not think much of the actual," he would then muse, or eventually posture as musing in the *Journal*'s representation of the moment: "It is something which we have long since not ours be such nonresistance as the chaff that rides before the gale.*

The time lapses without epoch or era, and only a half score of mornings and evening are remembered — Almost the night grieves, and leaves her tears on the forelock of the day.

Sometimes I think I could find a foe to combat in the morning mist, and fall on its rear as it withdraws sluggishly to its daylight haunts —.

July 31st 1840.

The very dogs that sullenly bay the moon from farm yards

---

done with. It is a sort of vomit in which the unclean love to wallow." [13] The vocabulary is, to say the least, interesting. The barb had struck home: "the grating tools on the mosaic." A writer of Thoreau's temper can forgive anything except being found out!

In the manuscript of "The Service," this entry had become:

> Idomeneus would not have demurred at the freshness of the last morning that rose to us, as unfit occasion to display his valor in; and of some such evening as this, methinks, that Greecian fleet came to anchor in the bay of Aulis. Would that it were to us the eve of a more than ten years' war, — a tithe of whose exploits, and Achillian withdrawals, and godly interferences, would stock a library of Iliads. [14]

What is most striking about the revision is his substitution of such pseudo-Homeric rhetoric for the *Journal*'s contemptuous characterization of the sixty years since the American Revolution as nothing but "idleness and defeat"!

. . .

* In the completed essay this passage becomes an exhortation: "Let not our Peace be proclaimed . . ." The overtones of *Othello* are obvious.

o' these nights, evince more heroism than is tamely barked forth in all the civil exhortations and war sermons of the age.*

Our actions should make the stars forget their sphere music, and chant an elegiac strain — that heroism should have departed out of their ranks, and gone over to humanity.

If want of patriotism be objected to us, because we hold ourselves aloof from the din of politics, I know of no better answer than that of Anaxagoras to those who in like case reproached him with indifference to his country because he had withdrawn from it, and devoted himself to the search after truth — "On the contrary," he replied pointing to the heavens, "I esteem it infinitely." My country is free — my country 'tis of thee sweet land of liberty to thee I sing.

The very laughter and jokes of a sober man are sober in their effects — They shake the firmament.

Any melodious sound apprises me of the infinite wealth of God.

Aug. 1st 1840.
The divinity in man is the vestal fire of the temple, which is never permitted to go out, but burns as steadily, and with as pure a flame, on the obscure provincial altar, as in Numa's temple at Rome.[16]

Aug. 4th 1840.
Why let our lives be a cheap and broken hour, which should be an affluent eternity?

---

* In "The Service" this sentence is annexed to the exhortation against rust on the swords.[15]

July & August, 1840.

Spes sibi quisque. Virgil.*

The brave man is the elder son of creation, who steps boyantly into his inheritance, while the coward, who is the younger, waits patiently till he decease.†

He is that sixth champion against Thebes, whom, when the proud devices of the rest have been recorded, the poet describes as "bearing a full-orbed shield of solid brass."

> "But there was no device upon its circle,
>   For not to seem just but to be is his wish." ‡

"Discretion is the wise man's soul" saith the poet. His prudence may safely go many steps beyond the utmost rashness of the fool.§

There is as much music in the world as virtue — At length music will be the universal language, and men greet each other in the fields in such accents as a Beethoven now utters but rarely and indistinctly.❨

---

* In Sanborn's edition, this serves as the motto, with (presumably) Thoreau's own translation: "Each one his own hope."

. . .

† In the final text, this is the opening sentence.[17] Thoreau consistently writes "boyantly."

. . .

‡ This becomes the end of the first paragraph.[18]

. . .

§ Verbatim in the essay, except that "fool" becomes "coward." [19]

. . .

❨ As Sanborn printed the essay, it is divided into three chapters, the second entitled "What Music Shall We Have?" This entry

It entails a surpassing affluence on the meanest thing.*

Let not the faithful sorrow that he has no ear for the more fickle and rabble harmonies of creation — if he be awake to the slower measure of virtue and truth. If his pulse does not beat in unison with the musician's quips and turns — it may yet accord with *their* larger periods.†

We too are dwellers within the purlieus of the camp. The soul is a sterner master than any King Frederick, for a true bravery would subject our bodies to rougher usage than even a grenadier can bear — When the sun breaks through the morning mist I seem to hear the din of war louder than when his chariot thundered on the plains of Troy.[21]

It behoves us to make our life a steady progression and not be defeated by its opportunities[.] The stream which first fell a drop from heaven, should be filtered by events, till

---

is incorporated into page 12. We wonder what, if anything, of Beethoven Thoreau had heard.

. . .

* This also is on page 12, followed by: "riding over the heads of sages, and soothing the din of philosophy."

. . .

† This appears on page 15 of *The Service*, with the last clause changed to: "it accords with the pulse-beat of the ages." Within a few years this developed into one of the great passages of *Walden*:[20]

> If a man does not keep pace with his companions, perhaps it is because he hears a different drummer. Let him step to the music which he hears, however measured or far away.

Sanborn printed "fickle and subtle" instead of "fickle and rabble" — which makes nonsense of Thoreau's Shakespearean invocation.

it burst out into springs of greater purity, and extract a diviner flavor from the accidents through which it passes.[22]

Our task is not such a piece of day labor that a [man] must be thinking what he shall do next for a livelihood, but such that as it began in endeavor, so will it end only when nothing in heaven or on earth, remains to be endeavored.*

Of such sort then be our crusade, that, while it inclines chiefly to the heartiness and activity of war, rather than the insincerity and sloth of peace, it may set an example to both of calmness and energy; we will be as unconcerned for victory as careless of defeat, not seeking to lengthen our term of service, nor to cut it short by a reprieve, but earnestly applying ourselves to the campaign before us. Nor let our warfare be a boorish and uncourteous one, but a higher courtesy attend its higher chivalry, though not to the slackening of its sterner duties and severer discipline — that so our camp may be a palaestra for the exercise of the dormant energies of men.†

---

* As used in the essay,[23] this is introduced with "Nor need we fear that the time will hang heavy when our toil is done. . . ." The involuntary omission in the manuscript of "man" again suggests that Thoreau was copying from a text already in existence, not inventing *de novo*.

. . .

† Substantially this is reproduced in the essay,[24] except that a new twist is given the ending:

> That so our camp may be a palaestra, wherein the dormant energies and affections of men may tug and wrestle, not to their discomfiture, but their mutual exercise and development.

We appreciate something of the "tug and wrestle" between Henry and Margaret when we note that she, after reading his

Methink[s] I hear the clarion sound, and the clang of corselet and buckler from many a silent hamlet of the soul. The morning gun has long since sounded, and we are not yet at our posts.*

Oftener from lone caves and over bogs and fens gleams the ray which cheers and directs us, than from lighted saloons.

---

profession of a high courtesy, of eschewing boorishness, refused his piece because it lacked the "quiet good-breeding" of admittedly lesser ones!

.   .   .

* Here we have the essence of the young Thoreau. He used this entry for what he supposed would be the resounding end of "The Service," adding to it: "Let us make such haste as the morning, and such delay as the evening." [25] Thus he first entered upon "anticipation"! But even if Margaret thought it boorish, he would thrust it at her again in the second effort, "Sir Walter Raleigh." Therein it became:

> In our lonely chambers at night we are thrilled by some far-off serenade within the mind, and seem to hear the clarion sound and clang of corselet and buckler from many a silent hamlet of the soul, though actually it may be but the rattling of some farmer's waggon rolling to market against the morrow.[26]

But even with the wagon to make it more "unassuming," she would not have it. So, at the end of "Monday," when in the *Week* a distant drum is supposedly sounding — a drum which assuredly was not rolled on any Monday of 1839 — Margaret Fuller was paid off:[27]

> The clarion sound and clang of corselet and buckler were heard from many a hamlet of the soul, and many a knight was arming for the fight behind the encamped stars.

"The grating of tools on the mosaic" — forsooth!

The age is resigned. Everywhere it sounds a retreat, and the word has gone forth to fall back on innocence. Christianity only *hopes*. It has hung its harp on the willow and cannot sing a song in a strange land. It has dreamed a sad dream and does not yet welcome the morning with joy.*

Surely joy is the condition of life. Think of the young fry that leap in ponds — the myriads of insects ushered into being of a summer's evening — the incessant note of the hyla with which the woods ring in the spring, the *nonchalance* of the butterfly carrying accident and change painted in a thousand hues upon his wings — or the brook-minnow stemming stoutly the current, the lustre of whose scales worn bright by the attrition is reflected upon the bank.†

---

* At this point Thoreau is finished with "The Service." Since he is still writing under the general head of "July & August," he may have planed this entry in the expectation of its fitting that essay; in any event, he found no hole there in which to insert it, so he kept it for "Sunday" of the *Week*,[28] and there slightly adjusted it to fit with, ahead of it, a passage from 1838 and, after it, one of 1841. Here indeed is the mosaic method!

• • •

† In April 1842, Emerson was concentrating his reading upon the natural sciences, and subscribed to a series of reports issued by the Commonwealth of Massachusetts on the flora and fauna of the state. These were dryly factual, simply scientific catalogues. By this time he had agreed with Margaret Fuller that editing *The Dial* was too great a burden for her shattered nerves; as he prepared to assume the task, a thought struck him: he "set Henry Thoreau on the good track" (as he considered it) of doing an essay review of these inventories. We are bound to wonder about two strange facts: one, why Emerson did not now, since Margaret could not oppose him, print either "The Service" or "Sir Walter Raleigh" (both manuscripts were in his desk); and two, what Henry secretly felt about being thus arbitrarily assigned a mission not of his own devising.

The Journal

Let us hear no more of peace at present — There is more of it in fiercest war than any Amiens or Utrecht ever compounded.

We have need to be as sturdy pioneers still as Miles Standish or Church. We are to follow on another trail, perhaps, but one as convenient for ambushes, and with not so much as a moccasin print to guide us. What if the Indians are exterminated? Do not savages as grim defile down into the clearing to-day?

The danger is that we be exterminated.*

Emerson was serenely assured that he was doing Thoreau a favor, devising a task suited to his genius, by which his "work & fame may go out into all lands." Thoreau went dutifully to work: he related the contents of the dull volumes, but wherever some fact gave him a chance, he asserted his independence by taking flight. As we should now suspect, most of these flights had already been taken in the *Journal*. He was careful to use nothing he had already used in the two rejected essays (was he expecting that Emerson would remember them?). Indeed, he was generally meticulous about employing an entry in only one publication. To do this essay, Thoreau went over all his little volumes, and into his mosaic description of winter in New England put passages from as early as November 1837. The result was his first piece of original prose, "Natural History of Massachusetts," [29] which remains some of his freshest writing.

This entry becomes the conclusion of a paragraph, combined with snippets from the *Journal* of December 1841 and January 1842.[30] So his initial prose publication is prophetic of what would always be his method.

. . .

* Here is a pretty instance of Thoreau's resolution to let nothing go to waste. On "Monday" of the *Week* the brothers reach Dunstable, from which Captain Lovewell marched to his fatal battle in 1725. Thoreau indulges his hobby of dredging up New

The Journal

What if our music be the sough of the wind. — In the deepest silence, I hear the distant din of conflict, and the sound of clarion and trumpet comes wafted to me upon the breeze.

Aug. 7th 1840.

When my senses are awake, I hear a "Battle of Prague" played in these tame fields.

When sitting in my chair I hear "Hero's Quick-step" played on the piano — I am convinced that music was invented for a stirring bravery — and not for an armchair stateliness.*

England folklore, quotes verses from the old ballad, and then has to finish his digression. Inserting Lovewell's name after that of Church, he makes this fragment from the mood of 1840 serve.[31]

.   .   .

* This is one of those passages in Thoreau that break your heart. As is well known, Thoreau had an insatiable hunger for music (the entries of this summer of 1840 are enough to testify to it); his untutored flute-playing has become a legend. He could invoke Beethoven, but he knew little about music, had virtually no chance to learn. In later years his solace was the twanging of the telegraph wire along the railroad — the "telegraph harp" he called it — to which he listened enraptured by putting his ear to a pole, most poignantly in the bitterest of winter. The second chapter of "The Service," that on heroic music, is pathetic in its revelation of musical illiteracy. What he could learn of music, aside from his little "music box" and Emerson's Aeolian harp, was only what he might hear through the windows of some burgher's house wherein a daughter of respectability was practicing her piano lessons.

"The Battle of Prague" was composed in London, about 1788, by a Bohemian refugee, Franz Kotzwara, who later hanged himself. It is an onomatopoetic rendition of a Prussian-Austrian battle — flying bullets are staccato notes, sobbing treble wails are cries of the wounded, and so on, complete with trumpets, drums, cavalry charges. By 1840 it had become a standard gambit in the student's torment. In 1842, *Punch* ran a cartoon showing the daughter of the house banging away at it, over the caption "Social Misery." Thackeray satirized it in *Vanity Fair* (Chapter 21). It is only just to say that Thoreau may have had some inkling that this was not the highest form of musical utterance, for in a very early entry, November 18, 1837, labeled "Harmony," he noted the essential silence of nature and concluded: "When I would muse I complain not of a rattling tune on the piano — a Battle of Prague even — if it be harmony, but an irregular, discordant drumming is intolerable." [32] Still, the contrast between his attitude to the composition and that of our other great enemy of the genteel tradition is instructive. In order that Huck Finn may innocently convey to us the cultural atmosphere of the Grangerfords, Mark Twain has him, after admiring the mortuary poetry of Emmeline, give the whole game away by marveling at the piano with tin pans in it, "and nothing was ever so lovely as to hear the young ladies sing 'The Last Link is Broken' and play 'The Battle of Prague' on it" (Chapter 17). In *Life on the Mississippi*, in the chapter which heaps up *all* the horrors of "The House Beautiful," he lists, along with the gift-books and the bouquets of still flowers under glass French domes, the music on the stand, including "She Wore a Wreath of Roses the Night When Last We Met" and — inevitably — "The Battle of Prague" (Chapter 38). But in *A Tramp Abroad*, forty years after Henry heard it sound in the tame fields of Concord, Mark Twain at the Jungfrau Hotel in Interlaken paid his final respects to the masterpiece (II, Chapter 3). A bride sits before the drawing-room piano and

> turned on all the horrors of the "Battle of Prague," that venerable shivaree, and waded chin deep in the blood of the slain. She made a fair and honorable average of two false notes in every five, but her soul was in arms and she never stopped to correct. The audience stood it with pretty fair grit for a while, but when the cannon-

A wave of happiness flows over us like sunshine over a field.*

Society is fragrant.†

Aug. 8th 1840.

Music is a flitting maiden, who now lives just through the trees yonder, and now at an oriental distance.‡

---

ade waxed hotter and fiercer, and the discord average rose to four in five, the procession began to move. A few stragglers held their ground ten minutes longer, but when the girl began to wring the true inwardness out of the "cries of the wounded," they struck their colors and retired in a kind of panic.

One is bound to suspect that what Henry heard in his chair was performed with equal skill. "Hero's Quick-Step," as the title indicates, was another of these representations.[33]

．　．　．

* Mr. Canby, fixing August as the time of Ellen's breaking off her engagement to John Thoreau, quotes this line as proof of Henry's secret joy, by having the wave flow over "me." [34] The manuscript clearly reads "us."

．　．　．

† Thoreau's first lecture, before the Concord Lyceum in the Masons' Hall, on April 11, 1838, was on "Society."

．　．　．

‡ What relation the mélange in this August of music, heroism and the flitting maiden may have to the presence of Ellen Sewall in Concord is open to speculation. As I have indicated, to my reading the *Journal* is so thoroughly a literary exercise that I am wary of biographical interpretations. At any rate, we can make out that in what once was the volume for the end of 1843 Thoreau was descanting upon this theme; a passage that seems to emerge out of another of his discourses on "Genius" comes to this:

I believe that the office of music is to remind us continually of the reality and necessity of these fine ele-

Floating in still water, I too am a planet, and have my orbit, in space, and am no longer a satellite of the earth.

As summer wanes the chirp of the crickets seems to come from further under the sod, and the frogs croak from beneath the pads, but more complacently, as if they had struck a league with time, and were unanxious for the future.

Just before sunset the light in the west is purer — deeper — and more memorable than the noon.

Far in the eastern horizon I seem to glimpse the domes and minarets of an oriental city — and men lead a stately, civil life there, as poetical as the pastoral.*

---

ments of love and friendship. One mood always forgets another. And till we have loved we have not imagined the heights of love. Love is an incessant inspiration. By the dews of love the arid desert of life is made as fragrant and blooming as a paradise.[35]

I find it difficult to conceive a more "literary," less experiential, utilization of passion than this, unless it be among the Elizabethan sonneteers!

• • •

* For a poet to behold in the flaming sunset some vision of an "oriental" pageant had long since become a cliché of romantic poesy. However, to show both how far Thoreau could develop and yet how miserably he was confined to his parochial round, compare this entry with a sunset-piece of September 18, 1858:

. . . Some long amber clouds in the horizon, all on fire with gold, were more glittering than any jewelry. An Orient city to adorn the plates of an annual could not be contrived or imagined more gorgeous. And when you looked with head inverted the effect was increased tenfold, till it seemed a world of enchantment. We only regretted that it had not a due moral effect on us scapegraces.

We hear it muttered of some village far up amid the hills, and look to our chart and guide book to learn of its mountains, and caves, and rivers. For the livelong day there skirts the horizon the dark blue outline of Crotched Mountain, in Goffstown, as we are told. Every sweep of the oar brings us nearer to "the far blue mountain." *

> Nevertheless, when, turning my head, I looked at the willowy edge of Cyanean Meadow and onward to the sober-colored but fine-grained Clamshell Hills, about which there was no glitter, I was inclined to think that the truest beauty was that which surrounded us but which we failed to discern, that the forms and colors which adorn our daily life, not seen afar in the horizon, are our fairest jewelry. The beauty of Clamshell Hill, near at hand, with its sandy ravines, in which the cricket chirps. This is an Occidental city, not less glorious than that we dream of in the sunset sky.[36]

The several kinds of pathos of this passage — the still unavailing effort to feed his imagination on merely Concord stimulants, the incessant effort to compensate for lack of the immense by heightening the values of the small — are capped by the fact that "Cyanean Meadow" and "Clamshell Hills" are Thoreau's private names for two ordinary spots on the Sudbury River, about half a mile above the railroad bridge, where he took his moonlight walks, places which he thus invested with romantic dignity.

.   .   .

* Again, we remember that the voyage of the brothers took place in September 1839. Thoreau here is still trying to capture a present-tense feeling for it. Eventually the sight of Uncanoonuc Mountain would thus be presented:[37]

> It is the northernmost in the horizon which we see from our native town, but seen from there is too ethereally blue to be the same which the like of us have ever climbed.

The man of genius as such is not an artist. Art deals in that which two may know — that degree of truth only whose law has been ascertained from observation of the works of genius. It is not lonely as Genius is. He is the artist who applies the laws already learned from observation of the works of genius.

The rich man's house is a *sedes* — that is a place to sit in — a *seat* or *residence* [—] the poor man's a *lectum* — a roof or shelter. So in English we say a gentleman's *seat* or *residence*, but a poor man's *house* or *roof*.*

He is the artist who detects & applies for himself the true laws from observation of the works of Genius. — He is the artisan who merely applies the rules which others have detected. The man of Genius is he who performs a perfect work in obedience to laws as yet unexplored — an originator or creator.†

---

* While volume 3 contributed much to the *Week*, it was about exhausted in the effort; yet such was Thoreau's tenacity that, since he found no place for this gem of an idea in his first book, he reached back for it in describing his *Walden* hut:[38]

> Wherever I sat, there I might live, and the landscape radiated from me accordingly. What is a house but a *sedes*, a seat? — better if a country seat.

The progress in "egotism" from *Journal* to book is monumental.

. . .

† Noting all the tinkering he did both on the flyleaf and on the page which contains this entry and the second above it, we should find the ultimate result interesting:[39]

> The Man of Genius may at the same time be, indeed is commonly, an Artist, but the two are not to be confounded. The man of Genius, referred to mankind, is an originator, an inspired or demonic man, who pro-

Aug. 10th 1840.

Between the hills, as in a crucible, a gleaming flood of light undulates.

Aug. 12th 1840.

A brave soul will make these peaceful times dangerous — and dangerous times peaceful.

We strive to prolong our moments of comfort and leisure — as if that were life and not a stagnation of life — Life is current and not stagnant, and cannot afford to repeat a certain past cheapness, to the sacrifice of a possible future affluence.*

When the accents of wisdom and eloquence have died away — I discover that the chirp of the crickets is still clear in advance.

A good book will not be dropped by its author — but thrown up. It will be so long a promise that he will not overtake it soon. He will have slipped the leash of a fleet hound.

When I hear a strain of music from across the street, I put away Homer and Shakspeare, and read them in the original.

---

duces a perfect work in obedience to laws yet unexplored. The artist is he who detects and applies the law from observation of the works of Genius, whether of man or nature. The Artisan is he who merely applies the rules which others have detected. There has been no man of pure Genius, as there has been none wholly destitute of Genius.

By such devious labor did the disguised Apollo ascertain the "spontaneous" essence of his Genius!

. . .

* I cannot help feeling that this casts light on the psychological origins of what I have called his striving for "anticipation."

When with pale cheek and sunken eye I sang
Unto the slumbering world at midnights hour,
How it no more resounded with war's clang,
And virtue was decayed in Peace's bower;

How in these days no hero was abroad,
But puny men, afraid of war's alarms,
Stood forth to fight the battles of their Lord,
Who scarce could stand beneath a hero's arms;

A faint, reproachful, reassuring strain,
From some harp's strings touched by unskilful hands
Brought back the days of chivalry again,
And the surrounding fields made holy lands.

A bustling camp and an embattled host
Extending far on either hand I saw,
For I alone had slumbered at my post,
Dreaming of peace when all around was war.

Aug. 13th 1840.
When I listen to the faint creaking of the crickets, it seems
as if my course for the future lay that way.

These continents and hemispheres are soon run over — but
always an unexplored and infinite region makes off on every
side from the mind — further than Cathay. We can make
no high way or beaten track into it, but immediately the grass
springs up in the path.

To travel and "descry new lands" is to think new thoughts,
and have new imaginings. In the spaces of thought are the
reaches of land and water over which men go and come. The
landscape lies fair within. The deepest and most original
thinker is the farthest travelled.*

---

* This in 1840: both the glory and the sorrow appears when it is
linked to the famous sentence of *Walden* in 1854: "I have
travelled a good deal in Concord." [40]

A man should be collected and earnest in his bearing — moving like one and not several, like an arrow with a feather for its rudder — and not like a handful of feathers bound to a rod — or a disorderly equipage which does not move unanimously. Addison says somewhat to the purpose, when lamenting the "Preference of Wit and Sense to Honesty and Virtue." — "I lay it down therefore for a rule, that the whole man is to move together;" — otherwise, he says, a man "is hopping instead of walking, he is not in his entire and proper motion."

A worm is as good a traveller as a grasshopper or cricket; with all their activity they do not hop away from drought nor forward to summer. No hopping animal migrates.

We do not avoid evil by hurry-skurry and fleetness *in extenso*, but by rising above [or] diving below its plane. As the worm escapes drought and frost, by boring a few inches deeper, but the grasshopper is overtaken and destroyed — By our suppleness and speed we only fly before an evil, by the height or depth of our characters we avoid it.*

The geniuses have been a hard-favored race of immigrants, who have had no landed interests.†

Aug. 14th 1840.

How many miles of hill and valley and expanded plain between George Minot and Mr. Alcott — Within the hour I am in Scythia and in the στοα at Athens.

For my Tyre and Sidon, I have only to go a shopping. The Penobscots by the river are my Britains come to Rome.

---

* This and the previous entry are combined to make a passage with an amusingly different emphasis in the *Week*.[41]

. . .

† At the end of this, apparently an afterthought, Thoreau writes "squatters." We think ahead to "Economy," with its meager list of essential materials: "excepting the timber, stones, and sand, which I claimed by squatter's right." [42]

I cannot attach much importance to historical epochs — or geographical boundaries — when I have my Orient and Occident in one revolution of my body.

While one hour lapses I am conversing in George Minot's barn while the sun is disappearing from the prospect of its wide door, upon pigeons and raccoons, and corn and potatoes, and snuffing the odor of new hay, and the wholsome breath of the cow, and again, in a parlor, hear discussed the philosophies of Greece and Rome.

The day came in so forwardly that the morning was without dawn. The sun vaulted into the heavens at a bound. — So clear and liquid was the air that you could almost discover a pulse in the sky. The whole heavens palpitated like a vast blue artery, wherein the blue blood circulated in floods. A deeper silence brooded over the earth as at the approach of evening — and the morning was as the eve of a celestial day. The sun seemed to shine reflectedly like the moon — Day slumbered yet, but had left his candle lit —. We flowed as one drop in the veins of the slumbering earth — and our thoughts were dreams.

Aug. 16th 1840.

A strain of music reminds me of a passage of the Vedas.[43]

Aug. 17th 1840.

When Robert, afterwards Lord, Clive, with one hundred and twenty Europeans, and two hundred Sepoys, was invested in the fort of Arcot by ten thousand native and French soldiers, and, after a siege of fifty days, began to feel the pressure of hunger, "The Sepoys came to Clive — not to complain of their scanty fare, but to propose that all the grain should be given to the Europeans, who required more nourishment than the natives of Asia. The thin gruel, they said, which was strained away from the rice, would suffice for themselves."

When I revolve it again in my mind, looking into the west at sunset, whether these ordinances of the Hindoos are to be passed by as the whims of an Asiatic brain, I seem to see the divine Brahma himself sitting in an angle of a cloud, and revealing himself to his scribe Menu, and imagine that this fair modern creation is only a reprint of the Laws of Menu with the Gloss of Culluca. Tried by a New England eye, or the more practical wisdom of modern times they are simply the oracles of a race already in its dotage, but held up to the sky, which is the only impartial and incorruptible ordeal, they are of a piece with its depth and serenity, and I am assured that they will have a place and significance, as long as there is a sky to test them by. They are not merely a voice floating in space for my own experience is the speaker.*

Aug. 19th 1840.

Some events in history are more remarkable than important — like eclipses of the sun by which all are attracted, but whose effects no one calculates.

Homer was a greater hero than Ajax or Achilles.

Sir Thomas Overbury, who says that Raleigh followed the sherriff out of court "with admirable erection, but yet in such a sort as became a man condemned," has a share in that

---

* This entry, with most of the first sentence and all of the last omitted, forms the conclusion of the long paragraph in "Monday," [44] which is a spectacular mosaic of passages constructed at various times from 1840 to 1842 (and probably in the dismembered volumes of 1843 and 1844). One can see how the mosaic was constructed, piece-by-piece, by comparing these pages of the finished *Week* with what probably was the first draft of the book, into which this unit of volume 3 was already incorporated, though not as yet the other pieces from the later volume, which eventually found their place.[45]

exploit by his discernment. We admire equally him who could do the deed, and him who could see it done.*

When nobleness of soul is accompanied by grace and dignity of action — then especially has it a current stamp and value.

Aug. 20th 1840.

The historian of Greece and Rome is usually disabled and unmanned by his subject — as a peasant cringes and crouches before Lords. — From specimens I should judge that Raleigh had done better than this. — When the best man takes up the pen then will the best history be written. He will shake all men by the hand from Adam down, looking them familiarly in the face. He will stalk down through the aisles of the past as through the avenues of a camp, with poets and historians for his guides and heralds, and from whatever side the faintest trump reaches his ear, that way will he turn though it lead to the purlieus of the camp, to the neglect of many a gaudy pavilion.[47]

It was a maxim of Raleigh — "that good success admits of no examination.["]

Aug. 21[st] 1840.

In fact, good success can only spring from good conduct.

The age in which Sir Wa[l]ter Raleigh lived was indeed a

---

* This was used with little change in the Raleigh essay.[46] There is surprisingly little "Raleigh" material in the *Journal*; possibly this is because Thoreau did his writing and rewriting on another set of papers, since at least two complete manuscript versions survive, suggesting that still another one preceded them. Presumably the last of these drafts was done in 1844. The mystery remains as to why under Emerson's editorship it never appeared in *The Dial*.

stirring one. The discovery of America and the successful progress of the reformation afforded a field both for the intellectual and physical energies of his generation. Its fathers were Calvin — and Knox — and Cranmer, and Pizarro and Garcilasso; and its immediate forefathers Luther and Raphael, and Bayard; and Angelo and Ariosto — and Copernicus — and Machiavel, and Erasmus — and Cabot, and Ximenes — and Columbus. Its device should have been an anchor — a sword — and a quill. The Pizarro laid by his sword and took to his letters. The Columbus set sail for newer worlds still, by voyages which did not need the patronage of princes. The Bayard alighted from his steed to seek adventures no less arduous in the western world. The Luther who had reformed religion began now to reform politics and Science.

In his youth, however it might have concerned him, Camoens was writing a heroic poem in Portugal, and the arts still had their representative in Paul Veronese of Italy. He may have been one to welcome the works of Tasso and Montaigne to England, and when he looked about him found such men as Cervantes and Sidney, men of like pursuit and not altogether dissimilar genius from himself — a Drake to rival him on the sea, and a Hudson in western adventure — a Halley — a Gallileo, and a Kepler — for his astronomers — a Bacon — a Behmen — and a Burton, for his book of philosophy — and a Spenser and Shakspeare for his refreshment and inspiration.*

He wields his pen as one who sits at ease in his chair, and has a healthy and able body to back his wits, and not a torpid and diseased one to fetter them. In whichever hand is the pen, we are sure there is a sword in the other.

---

* This passage was used substantially, with punctuation cleaned up, in the essay.[48]

He sits with his armor on, and with an ear open to hear if the trumpet sound, as one who has stolen a little leisure from the duties of a camp. We are confident that the whole man sat down to the writing of his books — as real and palpable as an Englishman can be, and not some curious brain only. Such a man's mere daily exercise in literature might well astonish us — and Sir Robert Cecil has said, "He can toil terribly." [49]

The humane society will not make the hunter despicable so soon as the butcher nor the grouse shooter so soon as he who kills sparrows — I feel great respect for the English deer stalker on reading that " 'His muscles must be of marble, and his sinews of steel.' He must not only 'run like the antelope, and breathe like the trade wind;' but he must be able 'to run in a stooping position with a grey-hound pace, having his back parallel to the ground, and his face within an inch of it for miles together.' He must have a taste for running, like an eel through sand, *ventre à terre*, and he should be accomplished in 'skilfully squeezing his clothes after this operation, to make all comfortable.' "

Aug. 24th 1840.

Man looks back eastward upon his steps till they are lost in obscurity, and westward still takes his way till the completion of his destiny. Whence he came or whither he is going nor history nor prophecy can tell — He sprang where the day springs and his course is parallel with the sun. History gives no more satisfactory answer to the one inquiry than the sun which is the latest messenger from those parts, nor prophecy a clearer revelation than the sunset. In the east we expect to see the earth scarred with his first footsteps. It is that point in the horizon on which our eye finally rests. No doubt there are as fit fields there as anywhere to be inhabited by a primitive race and men who lived like gods.

Aug. 25th 1840.

In imagination I seem to see there the grey temples and hoary brow of the earth. The great plain of India lies like a cup between the Himmaleh and the ocean, on the north and south — and the Indies and Brahmapoutra, on the east and west, wherein the primeval race was received. — as if it were the cradle of the human race.*

Aug. 28th 1840.

I like to read of the "pine, larch, spruce, and silver fir," which cover the southern face of the Himmaleh range — of the "gooseberry, raspberry, strawberry," which from an imminent temperate zone overlook the torrid plains. So did this active modern life have even then a foothold and linking place in the midst of the primeval stateliness, and contemplativeness of the plain. In another era the "lilly of the valley, cowslip, dandelion," were to work their way down onto the plain, and bloom in a level zone of their own, reaching round the world. Already has the era of the temperate zone arrived, the era of the pine, and the oak, for the palm and the Banyan do not supply the wants of the foremost races. The lichens too on the summits of the rocks are to find their level ere long.

The fowls which are elsewhere domesticated run wild in India, and so I think of these domestic thoughts and fashions when I read the Laws of Menu.[51]

Sep. 21st 1840.

In the old Chinese book which the French call "L'Invariable Milieu" occurs this sentence — "L'ordre ètablie par

---

* In his disquisition on Hindu scriptures, Thoreau joined this with the following entry to make a paragraph.[50]

le ciel s'appelle *nature*; ce qui est conforme à la nature s'appelle *loi*; l'etablissement de la loi s'appelle *instruction*." *

God's order is nature — man's order is law — and the establishment of law is the subject of instruction.

Some of these old distinctions imply a certain grandeur and completeness in the view, far better than any modern acuteness and accuracy — They are a thought which darted through the universe and solved all its problems.

The French call writing a dead speech — une parole morte — and articulated language a living speech — une parole vive.

To Thales is attributed the saying — "It is hard, but good, to know oneself; virtue consists in leading a life conformable to nature."

Sep. 25th 1840.

Social yearnings unsatisfied are the temporalness of time.

Birds were very naturally made the subject of augury — for they are but borderers upon the earth — creatures of a subtler and more etherial element than our existence can be supported in — which seem to flit between us and the unexplored.

As I sat on the cliff today the crows, as with one consent, began to assemble from all parts of the horizon — from river and pond and field, and wood, in such numbers as to darken

---

* The accents are Thoreau's. Note that there is a break in volume 3 from August 28 to September 21; those attached to the Ellen legend may suppose it was she who distracted him; it is equally likely that the comments he was then making on Hindu scriptures in the Ur-journal seemed not worth his copying.

the sky — as if a netting of black beads were stretched across it — after some tacking and wheeling the centre of the immense cohort was poised just over my head. Their cawing was deafening, and when that ceased the winnowing of their wings was like the rising of a tempest in the forest. But their silence was more ominous than their din. — At length they departed sullenly as they came.

Prosperity is no field for heroism unless it endeavor to establish an independent and supernatural prosperity for itself.

In the midst of din and tumult and disorder we hear the trumpet sound.

Defeat is heaven's success. He cannot be said to succeed to whom the world shows any favor. In fact it is the hero's point d'appui, which by offering resistance to his action enables him to act at all. At each step he spurns the world. He vaults the higher in proportion as he employs the greater resistance of the earth.

It is fatal when an elevation has been gained by too wide a concession — retaining no point of resistance, for then the hero like the aeronaut, must float at the mercy of the winds — or cannot sail for calm weather, nor steer himself for want of waves to his rudder.

When we rise to the step above, we tread hardest on the step below.

My friend must be my tent companion.

Saturday   Sep. 26th 1840.

The day, for the most part, is heroic only when it breaks.

Every author writes in the faith that his book is to be the final resting place of the sojourning soul, and sets up his fixtures therein as for a more than oriental permanence — but

it is only a caravansery which we soon leave without ceremony
— We read on his sign only — refreshment for man and
beast — and a drawn hand directs us to Isphahan or Bagdad.

"Plato gives science sublime counsels, directs her toward the
region of the ideal; Aristotle gives her positive and severe laws,
and directs her toward a practical end." Degerando.[52]

Sept. 27th 1840.
Ideas which confound all things must necessarily embrace
all.

Virtue will be known ere long by her elastic tread. — When
man is in harmony with nature.

Monday   Sep. 28th 1840.
The world thinks it knows only what it comes in contact
with, and whose repelling points give it a configuration to the
senses — a hard crust aids its distinct knowledge. But what we
truly know has no points of repulsion, and consequently no
objective form — being surveyed from within. We are acquainted with the soul and its phenomena, as a bird with the
air in which it floats. Distinctness is superficial and formal
merely.

We touch objects — as the earth we stand on — but the
soul — as the air we breathe. We know the world superficially
— the soul centrally. In the one case our surfaces meet, in
the other our centres coincide.

Tuesday   Sep. 29th 1840.
Wisdom is a sort of mongrel between Instinct and Prudence, which however inclining to the side of the father, will
finally assert its pure blood again — as the white ram at length
prevails over the black. It is minister plenipotentiary from

earth to heaven — but occasionally Instinct, like a native born celestial, comes to earth and adjusts the controversy.

All fair action in man is the product of enthusiasm — There is enthusiasm in the sunset. The shell[s] on the shore take new layers and new tints from year to year with such rapture as the bard writes his poems. There is a thrill in the spring, when it buds and blossoms — there is a happiness in the summer — a contentedness in the autumn — a patient repose in the winter.

Nature does nothing in the prose mood, though sometimes grimly with poetic fury, as in earthquakes &c and at other times humorously. All the birds & blossoms & fruits are the products of enthusiasm.*

---

* Thoreau adds the last sentence, employing his efficient, sharp pencil, as an afterthought, an example of the way he read and reread his units. Then he hunts for a place to put the entry. In the essay on Raleigh he injects a blast against sour-faced reformism as compared with his hero's cheerful bravery, and continues thus:

We fear that much of the heroism which we praise nowadays is dyspeptic. When we consider the vast Xerxean army of reformers in these days, we cannot doubt that many a grim soul goes silent, the hero of some small intestine war; and it is somewhat to begin to live on cornbread solely, for one who has before lived on bolted wheat; — but of this sort surely are not the deeds to be sung. These are not the Arthurs that inflame the imaginations of men. All fair action is the product of enthusiasm, and nature herself does nothing in the prose mood, though sometimes grimly with poetic fury, and at others humorously. There is enthusiasm in the sunrise and summer, and we imagine that the shells on the shore take new layers from year to year with such rapture as the bard writes his poems.[53]

Saturday   Oct. 3^d 1840.

No man has imagined what private discourse his members have with surrounding nature, or how much the tenor of that intercourse affects his own health and sickness. While the head goes star gazing the legs are not necessarily astronomers too, but are acquiring an independent experience in lower strata of nature. How much do they feel which they do not impart — How much rumor dies between the knees and the ears! Surely Instinct uses this experience of the dumb members.

I am no more a freeman of my own members than of universal nature. After all the body takes care of itself — it saves itself from a fall — It eats — drinks — sleeps — perspires — digests — grows — dies — and the best economy is to let it alone in all these.

Why need I travel to seek a site and consult the points of compass[?] My eyes are south windows, and out of them I command a southern prospect.

But pray what has seeing to do with the soul that she must sit always at a window? — for I find myself always in the rear of my eye.

The eye does the least drudgery of any of the senses. It oftenest escapes to a higher employment — The rest serve, and escort, and defend it — I attach some superiority even priority to this sense. It is the oldest servant in the soul's household — it images what it imagines — it ideates what it idealizes. Through it idolatry crept in — which is a kind of *religion*. If any joy or grief is to be expressed the eye is the swift runner that carries the news. In circumspection double — in fidelity single — it serves truth always, and carries no false news. Of five cast[e]s it is the Brahmin — it converses with the heavens. How man serves this sense more than any

— when he builds a house he does not forget to put a window in the wall.

We *see* truth — We are children of *light* [—] our destiny is *dark*. No other sense has so much to do with the future. The body of science will not be complete till every sense has thus ruled our thought and language, and action, in its turn.

Oct. 4ᵗʰ 1840.

Every countryman and dairymaid knows that the coats of the fourth stomach of the calf will curdle milk — and what particular mushroom is a safe and nutritious diet. You cannot go into any field or wood but it will seem as if every stone had been turned, and the bark on every tree ripped up. Surely men are busy and knowing enough after their fashion. One would suppose that he who had counted the eyes of a fly and the nerves of a caterpillar, must have learned the whole duty of man in his youth. But alas, it is easier to make a white rose black, or pears grow on an apple tree, than to do one's duty for five minutes. It is vastly easier to discover than to see when the cover is off.*

A true poem is not known by a felicitous expression, or by any thought it suggests, as much as by the fragrant atmosphere

---

* This is the first of five particles of volume 3 which Thoreau joined together (using only the first two sentences and the last one of this entry) to make his conclusion for "Natural History of Massachusetts," [54] another remarkable example of the grating of his mosaic tools. He contrives to introduce them with a topic sentence he had put in the earliest volume:[55] "Let us not underrate the value of a fact; it will one day flower in a truth." In the context, it and the rest of the paragraph constitute an apology for reviewing mere catalogues of fact, but it is a portent of his whole endeavor, even unto the disastrous end, the *Journal* of 1859, when he was left abysmally with facts, when he had more and more to force them into stunted flowerings.

which surrounds it — Most have beauty of outline merely, and stand distinct on the page. They are striking as the form and bearing of a stranger but true verses come toward us indistinctly as the very kernel of all friendliness. They have an air of Comeliness which makes us long to be with them — but they do not want our company.

Oct. 5th 1840.

There is one thing which a man cannot wheedle nor overawe, and that is his genius. It requires to be conciliated by purer and loftier conduct than the world asks or can appreciate. — The moon is on the path of her unconscious duty, when the sun lets the light of his genius fall on her.

The visitations of genius are unbribed as the dawn. It is by patient and unanxious labor at the anvil that fairer mornings are to be compelled.*

A part of me which has reposed in silence all day, goes abroad at night, like the owl, and has its day.

At night we recline, and nestle, and infold ourselves in our being. Each night I go home to rest. Each night I am gathered to my fathers. The soul departs out of the body, and sleeps in God, a divine slumber. As she withdraws herself, the limbs droop and the eyelids fall, and nature reclaims her clay again. Men have always regarded the night as ambrosial or divine. The air is then peopled — fairies come out.

---

* Note what wonders accrue to this entry when it becomes a paragraph toward the close of the *Week*:[56]

A man cannot wheedle nor overawe his Genius. It requires to be conciliated by nobler conduct than the world demands or can appreciate. These winged thoughts are like birds, and will not be handled; even hens will not let you touch them like quadrupeds. Nothing was ever so unfamiliar and startling to a man as his own thoughts.

The Journal

Tuesday   Oct. 6ᵗʰ 1840.

If we were to see a man die naturally and greatly, we should learn that the sunset is but a reflection of his withdrawing aspect.

The revolution of the seasons — is a great and steady flow — it reminds me of the undulation of the back in animals of the cat kind — a graceful — peaceful — motion like the swell on lakes and seas. No-where does any rigidity grow upon nature — no muscles harden, no bones protrude — but she is supple-jointed now and always. No rubbish accumulates from day to day, but still does freshness predominate in her cheek, and cleanliness in her attire. The dust settles on the fences and the rocks — and pastures by the roadside — from year to year — but still the sward is just as green, nay greener, for all that. The world is well kept no rubbish accumulates [—] the morning air is clear even at this day — & no dust has settled upon the grass[.] It is not begrimmed with all the dust that has been raised. The dew makes all clean again. Nature keeps her besom always wagging — she has no lumber room no dust hole in her house. No man was ever yet too nice to walk in her woods and fields. His religion allows the Arab to cleanse his body with sand, when water is not at hand.*

I have not read any great literary criticism yet — nothing is considered simply as it lies in the lap of eternal beauty. Love the truth and write earnestly needs to be said. The flowing drapery of genius is too often tucked up and starched lest it offend against the fashions of the time. What is sacrificed

---

* Of this long and repetitious effort Thoreau used only the three lines beginning with "The world is well kept" (a good example of how severely he could discard as well as preserve), which he fits into another of his mosaics,⁵⁷ wherein he lifts the thesis of the original meditation to a loftier plane.⁵⁸ "Begrimmed" is his spelling.

to time is lost to eternity. This architectural civility and refinement will disappear with the plaster and white-wash —
but depth and solidity will abide with the granite. I want no
politeness nor ceremony in books — there is no laughing nor
sneezing in their company. Our thoughts as well as our bodies
are dressed after the latest fashion.*

To the rarest genius or talent it is the most expensive to
succumb and conform to the ways of the world. Talent is the
worst of lumber if the poet would float upon the breeze of
popularity. The bird of paradise in consequence of his gay
trappings is obliged constantly to fly against the wind, else his
long feathers pressing close to his body impede his free
movements. He can strike with gracefuller and steadier wing
in proportion as the atmosphere is more palpable and offers
greater resistance. The great man fronts the storm and steers
in the eye of the wind — so that his greatness is expanded,
and floats around him, like the plumage of the bird of paradise.†

---

* Out of this discourse Thoreau would rescue for the conclusion
of the *Week* only the beginning and end:[59]

> There is no just and serene criticism as yet. Nothing
> is considered simply as it lies in the lap of eternal beauty,
> but our thoughts, as well as our bodies, must be dressed
> after the latest fashions.

But even the peelings are not thrown away. In "Life Without
Principle," the sentence, "What is sacrificed to time is lost to
eternity," became the injunction: "Read not the Times. Read
the Eternities." [60] By then, of course, his deepening concern
with the function of newspapers in American life — manifested
by his denunciations of wasting attention upon them — had
taught him how to pun upon the *New York Times*.

• • •

† The *Week*[61] uses the first three sentences (they are marked off
with penciled parentheses in the manuscript) for a tight con-

He is the best sailor who can steer within the fewest points of the wind, and extract a motive power out of the greatest obstacles. Most begin to veer and tack as soon as the wind changes from aft — and as within the tropics it does not blow from all points of the compass — there are some harbors they can never reach.*

If I were to write some account of history before it had a muse assigned it, I should remember this sentence in Alwákidi's Arabian chronicle. "I was informed by *Ahmed Almatîn Aljorhami*, who had it from *Rephâa Ebn Kais Alámiri*, who had it from *Saiph Ebn Fabalah Alchátquarmi*, who had it from *Thabet Ebn Alkamah*, who said he was present at the action." Where was Clio?†

Wednesday   Oct. 7th 1840.

When one hears a strain of music he feels his blood flow in his veins.

Saturday   Oct. 10th 1840.

All life must be seen upon a proper back ground — else, however refined, it will be cheap enough — Only the life of some anchorite or nun or moody dweller among his fellows will bear to be considered — Our actions lack grandeur in the prospect — they are not so impressive as objects in the desert, a broken shaft or crumbling mound against a limitless horizon.

---

struct out of volume 3; the rest of the passage he saw, on critical review, was expendable.

. . .

* In the *Week*[62] this follows hard upon the previous entry, both of them after the entry of October 5 (above, p. 168), the whole constituting another example of Thoreau's parquetry.

. . .

† Thoreau contrived to fit this exotic bit into the surface of the *Week*,[63] but then gave up what in our version is the real point, the final interrogation. The accents are as in the manuscript; for the book he took pains to get them correct.

The fuel on the hearth sings a requiem — its fine strain tells of untrodden fields of virtue.

Oct. 11th 1840.

It is always easy to infringe the law — but the Bedouin of the desert find it impossible to resist public opinion.

The traveller Stevens had the following conversation with a Bedouin of Mount Sinai. "I asked him who governed them; he stretched himself up and answered in one word, 'God.' I asked him if they paid tribute to the pasha; and his answer was, 'No, we take tribute from him.' I asked him how. 'We plunder his caravans.' Desirous to understand my exact position with the sheik of Akaba, under his promise of protection, I asked him if they were governed by their sheik; to which he answered, 'No, we govern him.' ["]

The true man of science will have a rare Indian wisdom — and will know nature better by his finer organization. He will smell, taste, see, hear, feel, better than other men. His will be a deeper and finer experience. We do not learn by inference and deduction, and the application of mathematics to philosophy but by direct intercourse. It is with science as with ethics — we cannot know truth by method and contrivance — the Baconian is as false as any other method. The most scientific should be the healthiest man.*

---

* As an entry in the context of 1840 this may be fairly ordinary; but when, seeking an ending for his first venture into published prose, he turned back to it, Thoreau showed at once what he could do with resounding revision:[64]

> . . . the Baconian is as false as any other, and with all the helps of machinery and the arts, the most scientific will still be the healthiest and friendliest man, and possess a more perfect Indian wisdom.

The important shift is the placing of "Indian."

Deep are the foundations of all sincerity — even stone halls have their foundation below the frost.

Aristotle says in his "Meteorics"[:] "As time never fails, and the universe is eternal, neither the Tanais, nor the Nile, can have flowed forever." [65]

Strabo, upon the same subject, says, "It is proper to derive our explanations from things which are obvious, and in some measure of daily occurrence, such as deluges, earthquakes, and volcanic eruptions, and sudden swellings of the land beneath the sea." — Geology.

Marvellous are the beginnings of philosophy — We can imagine a period when "Water runs down hill" may have been taught in the schools. That man has something demoniacal about him who can discern a law, or couple two facts.*

Every idea was long ago done into nature as the translators say — There is walking in the feet — mechanics in the hand [—] climbing in the loose flesh of the palms — boxing in the knuckles &c, &c.

In a lifetime you can hardly expect to convince a man of an error — but must content yourself with the reflection that the progress of science is slow. If he is not convinced his grandchildren may be. It took 100 years to prove that fossils are organic, and 150 more, to prove that they are not to be referred to the Noachian deluge.†

---

* This was reworked to make a paragraph in "Natural History of Massachusetts." [66]

. . .

† In the *Week*[67] this becomes the prologue for a curious pastiche of *Journal* extracts, drawn from 1838 to 1845, which adds up to a quite different effect from the originals. For example, on March 4, 1838, Thoreau simply notes how in Homer Pallas Athene

Oct. 12th 1840.

The springs of life flow in ceaseless tide down below, and hence this greenness everywhere on the surface. But they are as yet untapped — only here and there men have sunk a well.

One of the wisest men I know, but who has no poetic genius — has led me round step by step in his discourse this afternoon, up to the height of land in these parts; but now that I am left alone, I see the blue peaks in the horizon, and am homesick.*

Tuesday   Oct. 13th 1840.

The only prayer for a brave man is to be a doing — this is the prayer that is heard. Why ask God for a respite when he has not given it. Has he not done his work and made man equal to his occasions, but he must needs have recourse to him again? God cannot give us any other than self help.

The workers in stone polish only their chimney ornaments, but their pyramids are roughly done — There is a soberness in a rough aspect, in unhewn granite — which addresses a depth in us, but the polished surface only hits the ball of the eye.

---

glides down from heaven to calm the irate Achilles,[68] but in the *Week*, launched by this passage upon his paragraph, he turns the thought into an angry rejection of so masculine a divinity as "my country's God," Jehovah — who has "no sister Juno, no Apollo, no Venus, nor Minerva, to intercede for me." [69] That there should be no provision for "me" in American Protestantism encourages him to the blasphemy of preferring, against "the Hebrew fable," the Grecian one: it "is infinitely more sublime and divine." This is a Byronism less strident than Byron's but more unrepentant.

.   .   .

* There can be little doubt the man was Alcott.

In all old books the stucco has long since crumbled away, and we read what was sculptured in the granite.*

Our etiquette is for little men —
To study style in the utterance of our thoughts, is as if we were to introduce Homer or Zoroaster to a literary club thus, — Gentlemen of the societies — let me make you acquainted with Sir Homer. — Think you if Zoroaster or Homer or Socrates were to come on earth, they would bring letters of introduction to the prominent characters? But a better than Socrates speaks through us every hour and it would be a poor story if we did not defer as much to him by ending impertinent ceremony.

True politeness does not result from a hasty and artificial polishing, but grows naturally from the roots upwards by a long fronting of circumstances and rubbing on good and bad fortune.

The elements are yet polishing the pyramids.†

---

* This was interestingly reworked and combined with the following entry for the ending of the *Week*.[70]

· · ·

† The first sentence, about etiquette, is a penciled addition; Thoreau may have wanted to insert it somewhere, or to make it serve as title for the entry (by this volume he is no longer formally entitling his thoughts, as he did in 1837 and 1838). In the index of topics which he scribbled inside the back cover, he wrote "etiquette for little men," with the page reference. He similarly indexed all his volumes; of these early ones, when he did so, we generally find the topic lodged either in the *Week*, or in *Walden*, or in an essay. Here, however, he apparently found the topic unusable; so he took his second paragraph and his final sentence, joined these onto the previous entry, and achieved the marvel of ingenuity on page 402 of the *Week*. It is indeed ironic that the discarded portion is an oration against studying "style"!

The draft of my stove sounds like the dashing of waves on the shore, and the lid sings like the wind in the shrouds.

The steady roar of the surf on the beach is as incessant in my ear as in the shell on the mantelpiece — I see vessels stranded — and gulls flying — and fishermen running to and fro on the beach.

Wednesday   Oct. 14th 1840.

I arose before light
To work with all my might,
With my arms braced for toil
Which no obstacle could foil,
For it robbed me of my rest
Like an anvil on my breast.

But as a brittle cup
I've held the hammer up,
And no sound from my forge
Has been heard in the gorge.
I look forward into night,
And seem to get some light;
E're long the forge will ring
With its ding-dong-ding,
For the iron will be hot
And my wages will be got.

Oct. 15th 1840.

There is not a chestnut in the wood but some worm has found it out. He will seem to be at home there, and not far from the highway. Every maggot lives down town.

Men see God in the ripple but not in miles of still water. Of all the two-thousand miles that the St. Lawrence flows — pilgrims go only to Niagara[.]

The Journal

Saturday   Oct. 17th 1840.

In the presence of my friend I am ashamed of my fingers and toes. I have no feature so fair as my love for him. There is a more than maiden modesty between us. I find myself more simple and sincere than in my most private moment to myself. I am literally true *with a witness*.

We would sooner blot out the sun than disturb friendship.

Sunday   Oct. 18th 1840.

The era of greatest change is to the subject of it the condition of greatest invariableness. The longer the lever the less perceptible its motion. It is the slowest pulsation which is the most *vital*. I am independent of the change I detect. My most essential progress must be to me a state of absolute rest. So in geology we are nearest to discovering the true causes of the revolutions of the Globe, when we allow them to consist with a quiescent state of the elements. We discover the causes of all past change in the present invariable order of the universe.

The pulsations are so long that in the interval there is almost a stagnation of life. The first cause of the universe makes the least noise. Its pulse has beat but once — is now beating. The greatest appreciable revolutions are the work of the light-footed air — the stealthy-paced water — and the subterranean fire. The wind makes the desert without a rustle.

To every being consequently its own first cause is an insensible and inconceivable agent.

Some questions which are put to me, are as if I should ask a bird what she will do when her nest is built, and her brood reared.

I cannot make a disclosure — you should see my secret. — Let me open my doors never so wide, still within and behind them, where it is unopened, does the sun rise and set — and day and night alternate. — No fruit will ripen on the common.

Monday   Oct. 19th 1840.

My friend dwells in the distant horizon as rich as an eastern city there. There he sails all lonely under the edge of the sky, but thoughts go out silently from me and belay him, till at length he rides in my roadsted. But never does he fairly come to anchor in my harbor. Perhaps I afford no good anchorage. He seems to move in a burnished atmosphere, while I peer in upon him from surrounding spaces of Cimmerian darkness. His house is incandescent to my eye, while I have no house, but only a neighborhood to his.

Tuesday   Oct. 20th 1840.

My friend is the apology for my life. In him are the spaces which my orbit traverses.

There is no quarrel between the good and the bad — but only between the bad and the bad. In the former case there is inconsistency merely, in the latter a vitious consistency.

Men chord sometimes, as the flute and the pumpkin vine — a perfect chord — a harmony — but no melody. They are not of equal fineness of tone.

For the most part I find that in another man and myself the key note is not the same — so that there are no perfect chords in our gamuts. But if we do not chord by whole tones, never-the-less his sharps are sometimes my flats, and so we play some very difficult pieces together, though the sameness at last fatigues the ear. We never rest on a full natural note — but I sacrifice my naturalness and he his. We play no tune through — only chromatic strains — or trill upon the same note till our ears ache.[71]

The Journal

Sunday   Oct. 25th 1840.

To yield bravely is infinitely harder than to resist bravely. In the one course our sin assists us to be brave, in the other our virtue is alone. True bravery has no ally yet all things are with it.

We do not see in a man all he promises but yet all he is. The aspirations do not completely appear in the features, (but they are always in a transition state —) The past is in the rind, but the future is in the core. The promise of a man must have become experience and character before it can be expressed in his face.

So this outward expression is after all a fair index of his present state, for virtue is not all van, but needs to be viewed both before and behind. The virtue is but a superficies, and we know not if it be thick or thin — the features whatever they are are made up of successive layers of performance — and show the thickness of the character. The past and future met together make the present. — Virtue is not virtue's face[.]

Nov. 1st 1840.

The day is won by the blushes of the dawn.

I thought that the sun of our love should have risen as noiselessly as the sun out of the sea, and we sailors have found ourselves steering between the tropics as if the broad day had lasted forever. You know how the sun comes up from the sea when you stand on the cliff, and doesn't startle you, but every thing, and you too are helping it.

Monday   Nov. 2^{d} 1840.

It is well said that the "attitude of inspection is prone." The soul does not inspect but behold. Like the lily or the crystal in the rock, it looks in the face of the sky.*

---

* This, along with other passages from volume 3, becomes part of the tesselation which is the final, resounding paragraph of

Francis Howell says that in garrulous persons "The supply of thought seems never to rise much above the level of its exit." Consequently their thoughts issue in no jets, but incessantly dribble. In those who speak rarely, but to the purpose, the reservoir of thought is many feet higher than its issue. It takes the pressure of a hundred atmospheres to make one jet of eloquence. For the most part the thoughts subside like a sediment, while the words break like a surf on the shore. They are being silently deposited in level strata, or held in suspension for ages, in that deep ocean within — Therein is the ocean's floor whither all things sink, and it is strewed with wrecks.

Tuesday   Nov. 3ᵈ 1840.

The truth is only contained, never withheld — As a feudal castle may be the headquarters of hospitality, though the portal is but a span in the circuit of the wall. So of the three circles on the cocoa nut one is always so soft that it may be pierced with a thorn, and the traveller is grateful for the thick shell which held the liquor so faithfully.

Wednesday   Nov. 4ᵗʰ 1840.

By your few words show how insufficient would be many words. If after conversation I would reinstate my thought in its primary dignity and authority, I have recourse again to my first simple and concise statement.

In breadth we may be patterns of conciseness, but in depth we may well be prolix[.]

We may have secrets though we do not keep them.

Dr. Ware Jr. said today in his speech at the meeting house — "There are these three — Sympathy — Faith — Patience"

"Natural History of Massachusetts" — a flight that would on the surface appear to be, if anything in Thoreau is, a creation of the passionate moment; passionate it may be, but an improvisation it is not.[72]

— then proceeding in ministerial style, "and the greatest of these is," but for a moment he was at a loss, and became a listener along with his audience, and concluded with "Which is it? I don't know. Pray take them all brethren, and God help you." *

Nov. 5th 1840.

Truth is as vivacious and will spread itself as fast as the fungi, which you can by no means annihilate with your heel, for their sporules are so infinitely numerous and subtle as to resemble "thin smoke; so light that they may be raised into the atmosphere, and dispersed in so many ways by the attraction of the sun, by insects, wind, elasticity, adhesion, &c., that it is difficult to conceive a place from which they may be excluded."

---

* Only something so special as a visit of Henry Ware, Jr., to the Concord pulpit could induce Thoreau to come to church — and this, presumably, was a weekday lecture, not a Sabbath service. Ware (son of the distinguished theologian whose appointment to the Hollis Professorship in 1805 declared the Unitarianism of Harvard College) was Emerson's colleague at the Second Church of Boston; in 1840, though in failing health, he was professor of pulpit eloquence and pastoral care in the Harvard Divinity School. Though a solid Unitarian, Ware disdained to join the hue and cry raised by Norton and Bowen against Emerson's "Divinity School Address," but was even more dismayed by it; he wrote Emerson an urgent letter begging him to desist, in answer to which Emerson memorably defined himself "a chartered libertine free to worship & free to raile." [73] Though the younger Ware was thus an adversary of Transcendentalism, all New England knew him for a saint; on his tour of Europe he had visited Wordsworth.

About the only other time that Thoreau is on record as attending a church service, this time on a Sunday, was June 13, 1841, when he came to hear Samuel Ripley deliver a farewell sermon to the old church edifice. Emerson found the spectacle of Henry at divine worship "droll." [74]

Saturday   Nov. 7th 1840.

I'm guided in the darkest night
By flashes of auroral light,
Which over-dart thy eastern home
And teach me not in rain to roam.
Thy steady light on t'other side
Pales the sunset, makes day abide,
And after sunrise stays the dawn,
Forerunner of a brighter morn.

There is no being here to me
But staying here to be.
When others laugh I am not glad,
When others cry I am not sad,
But be they grieved or be they merry
I'm supernumerary.
I am a miser without blame,
Am conscience striken without shame
An idler am I without leisure,
A busy body without pleasure.
I did not think so bright a day
Would issue in so dark a night,
I did not think such sober play
Would leave me in so sad a plight,
And I should be most sorely spent
When first I was most innocent.

I thought by loving all beside
To prove to you my love was wide,
And by the rites I soared above
To show you my peculiar love.

Monday   Nov. 9th 1840.

Events have no abstract and absolute importance, but only
concern me as they are related to some man. The biography
of a man who has spent his days in a library, may be as interest-

ing as the Peninsular campaigns. Gibbon's memoirs prove this to me. To my mind he travels as far when he takes a book from the shelf, as if he went to the barrows of Asia. If the cripple but tell me how like a man he turned in his seat, how he now looked out at a south window then a north, and finally looked into the fire, it will be as good as a tour on the continent or the prairies. For I measure distance inward and not outward. Within the compass of a man's ribs there is space and scene enough for any biography.

My life passes warmly and cheerily here within while my ears drink in the pattering rain on the sill. It is as adventurous as Crusoe's — as full of novelty as Marco Polo's, as dignified as the Sultan's, as momentous as that of the reigning prince.*

Thursday   Nov. 12th 1840.

Mathematical truths stand aloof from the warm life of man — the mere cold and unfleshed skeletons of truth.

Perhaps the whole body of what is now called moral or ethical truth may have once existed as abstract science, and have been only gradually won over to humanity. — Have gradually subsided from the intellect into the heart.

The eye that can appreciate the naked and absolute beauty of a scientific truth, is far rarer than that which discerns moral beauty. Most demand that the truth be clothed in flesh and blood & have the warm colors of life. They naturally prefer the partial statement, because it fits and measures them and their commodities best — but they forget that Science still exists as the sealer of weights and measures.†

---

* Here we have in full cry that thematic device of making a big world out of little Concord which is to become persistent (often tediously insistent) throughout the *Journal*.

•　　•　　•

† The future of this entry, as well as its past, is a revelatory example of Thoreau's method. In this manuscript the last para-

graph is already extensively revised.[75] By the time he excavates
it from the *Journal*, to roll into place within the *Week*,[76] he has
been reading Aristotle, and so must take his construct apart and
build it over again around a new center:

> The eye which can appreciate the naked and absolute
> beauty of a scientiffic truth is far more rare than that
> which is attracted by a moral one. Few detect the
> morality in the former, or the science in the latter.
> Aristotle defined art to be Λόγος τοῦ ἔργου ἄνευ ὕλης, *The
> principle of the work without the wood;* but most men
> prefer to have some of the wood along with the princi-
> ple; they demand that the truth be clothed in flesh
> and blood and the warm colors of life. They prefer
> the partial statement because it fits and measures them
> and their commodities best. But science still exists
> everywhere as the sealer of weights and measures at
> least.

This passage, along with the problem he confronted when ex-
ecuting Emerson's commission in "Natural History of Massachusetts," is prophetic of what was to become the incessant, the
destructive, concern. A consecutive reading of the last portions
of the *Journal* conveys the intolerable anguish of his sense "That
there hath passed away a glory from the earth." His luxuriating in
the lines of Byron he quoted to Isaiah Williams was only a
premonition. By 1850 (when we find the *Journal* most spacious)
he was already frightened: "I fear that the character of my
knowledge is from year to year becoming more distinct and
scientific; that, in exchange for views as wide as heaven's cope,
I am being narrowed down to the field of the miscroscope." [77]
By 1852 the agony is becoming intense: "Once I was part and
parcel of Nature; now I am observant of her." [78] Hence the
fury with which he responded (to himself) when in 1853 a
secretary of the Association for the Advancement of Science
included him in the mailing-list of a circular questionnaire as
to what branch of science he was specially interested in:

> The fact is I am a mystic, a transcendentalist, and a
> natural philosopher to boot. Now I think of it, I should

Sunday   Nov. 15th 1840.

Over and above a man's business there must be a level of undisturbed serenity, only the more serene as he is the more industrious — as within the reef encircling a coral isle, there is always an expanse of still water, where the depositions are going on which will finally raise it above the surface.

He must preside over all he does — If his employment rob him of a serene outlook over his life, it is but idle though it be measuring the fixed stars. He must know no distracting cares.

The bad sense is a secondary one.[80]

Nov. 11th I obtained a levelling instrument and circumferentor combined, and have since ascertained the height of the cliff-hill — and surveyed other objects.

Height of Cliff Hill above the River

Progress		Position	Elevation.
1st rise	12.10		12.10
2d	12.91		25.01
3d	12.63		37.64
	11.49		49.13
	12.80		61.93
	12.50		74.43
	13.26	Bars in wall	87.69
	12.41		100.10
	12.40		112.50

---

have told them at once that I was a transcendentalist. That would have been the shortest way of telling them that they would not understand my explanations.[79]

This was whistling to keep courage up, but toward the end he could barely whistle.

11.80	Pointed Rock.	124.30
12.18	Turned "	136.48
13.20	Near split Rock	149.68
12.47	stone in path	162.15
12.31		174.46
11.44	Stone by bars	185.90
13.26	Stone in path near rock on right.	199.16
12.64	Two birches by wall	211.80
12.		223.80
7.29	Top of Rock in Woods	231.09

The river was about three feet above low-water mark.

Wednesday   Dec. 2nd 1840.

The lake is a mirror in the breast of nature, as if there were there nothing to be concealed. All the sins of the wood are washed out in it. See how the woods form an amphitheatre about it — and it becomes an arena for all the genialness of nature. It is the earth's liquid eye — it is blue or grey, or black as I choose my time. In the night it is my more than forty feet reflector. It is the cynosure of the wood, all trees direct the traveller to its brink — all paths seek it out — birds fly to it — and quadrupeds flee to it — and the very ground inclines toward it. It is nature's saloon, or where she has sat down to her toilet. The sun dusts its surface each morning by evaporation. Always a fresh surface wells up. I love to consider the silent economy and tidiness of nature, how after all the filfth of the wood, and the accumulated impuritie[s] of the winter have been rinsed herein, this liquid transparency appears in the spring.

I should wither and dry up if it were not for lakes and rivers. I am conscious that my body derives its genesis from their waters, as much as the muskrat or the herbage on their brink. The thought of Walden in the woods yonder makes me supple jointed and limber for the duties of the day. Sometimes I thirst for it.

There it lies all the year reflecting the sky — and from its surface there seems to go up a pillar of ether, which bridges over the space between earth and heaven.

Water seems a middle element between earth and air. The most fluid in which man can float.

Across the surface of every lake there sweeps a hushed music.*

My body is invigorated by the cones and needles of the pine seen against this frosty air — This is no thin diet.

Dec. 3ᵈ 1840.

Music in proportion as it is pure is distant. The strains I now hear seem at an inconceivable distance, yet remotely within me. Remote[nes]s throws all sound into my inmost being, and it becomes music, as the slumbrous sounds of the village, or the tinkling of the forge from across the water or

---

* Much compressed, then somewhat revised, this entry becomes the center of a mosaic made up of units from volume 3 in "A Winter Walk," the second product of the *Journal* which Thoreau got Emerson to print in *The Dial*[81] for October 1843. Thoreau still had to submit to tuition: Emerson had hesitated about the piece, objecting to the *"mannerism"* — Thoreau's calling a cold place sultry, a solitude public, a wilderness *"domestic."* (Emerson noted that the last was "a favorite word.") But, Emerson says, "by pretty free omissions, however, I have removed my principal objections." Possibly he made the omissions from this entry that we now find in the printed text.[82] It is worth noting that the next July 13, when Emerson fled to Nantasket to get away from the importunities of Margaret and other friends, he explained his frigidity once more to Caroline Sturgis by indirection: "You know I was baptised in Walden Pond." [83] "Filfth" is not a slip of the pen: that is the way Thoreau wrote it and the way he thought of it.

the fields. To the senses that is farthest from me which addresses the greatest depth within me.*

Friday   Dec. 4th 1840.

Methinks I have experienced a joy sometimes like that with which yonder tree for so long, has budded and blossomed — and reflected the green rays. The opposite shore of the pond seen through the haze of a September afternoon, as it lies stretched out in grey content, answers to some streak in me.

I love to look aslant up the tree tops from some dell, and finally rest myself in the blueish mistiness of the white pines.

Many's the pine I know — that's a greybeard and wears a cocked hat.

Thursday   Dec. 10th 1840.

I discover a strange track in the snow, and learn that some migrating otter has made across from the river to the wood, by my yard and the smith's shop, in the silence of the night. — I cannot but smile at my own wealth, when I am thus reminded that every chink and cranny of nature is full to overflowing. — That each instant is crowded full of great events. Such an incident as this startles me with the assurance that the primeval nature is still working and makes tracks in the snow.

It is my own fault that he must thus skulk across my premises by night. — Now I yearn toward him — and heaven to me consists in a complete communion with the otter nature.

Mere innocence will tame any ferocity.

---

* The last sentence is fascinatingly compounded with one from August 16, about the association of the Vedas and music (see above, p. 155), to make a thoroughly Thoreauvian sentence in the *Week*.[84]

He travels a more wooded path, by water-courses and hedgerows — I by the highway — but though his tracks are now crosswise to mine, our courses are not divergent, but we shall meet at last.

Dec. 11th 1840.

A man who had failed to fulfil an engagement to me, and grossly disappointed me, came to me tonight with a countenance radiant with repentance, and so behaved that it seemed as if I was the defaulter, and could not be satisfied till he would let me stand in that light. — How long a course of strict integrity might have come short of such confidence and goodwill! — Such a "Roman recovery" was worth a thousand tons of coal. The crack of his whip was before attractive enough, but such conciliatory words from that shaggy coat and coarse comforter I had not expected. I saw the meaning which lurked far behind his eye all the better for the dark, as we see some faint stars better when we do not look directly at them with the full light of the eye. A true contrition when witnessed will humble integrity itself.

Dec. 12th 1840.

Society seems very natural and easy — can I not walk among men as simply as in the woods? I am greeted everywhere with mild looks and words, and it seems as if the eaves were running and I heard the sough of melting snow all around me.

The young pines springing up in the corn fields from year to year are to me a much more refreshing fact than the most abundant harvests.

My last stronghold is the forest.

Dec. 14th 1840.

How may a man most cleanly and gracefully depart out of nature? At present his birth and death are offensive and unclean things. Disease kills him, and his carcass smells to heaven. It offends the bodily sense, only so much as his life offended the moral sense. It is the odor of sin.

His carcass invites sun and moisture, and makes haste to burst forth into new and disgusting forms of life with which it already teemed. It was no better than carrion before but just animated enough to keep off the crows. The birds of prey which hover in the rear of an army are an intolerable satire on mankind, and may well make the soldier shudder. The mosquito sings our dirge — he is Charon come to ferry us over the styx — He preaches a biting homily to us. He says put away beef and pork — small beer and ale, and my trump shall die away and be no more heard. The intemperate cannot go nigh to any wood or marsh but he hears his requiem sung — all nature is up in arms against him. He who will dance must pay the fiddler. Gnats and mosquitos are the original imps and demons.

Man lays down his body in the field and thinks from it as a stepping stone to vault at once into heaven, as if he could establish a better claim there when he had left such a witness behind him on the plain. — Our true epitaphs are those which the sun and wind write upon the atmosphere around our graves so conclusively that the traveller does not draw near to read the lie on our tombstones. Shall we not be judged rather by what we leave behind us, than what we bring into the world? The guest is known by his leavings. When we have become intolerable to ourselves shall we be tolerable to heaven? — Will our spirits ascend pure and fragrant from our tainted carcasses?

May we not suffer our impurities gradually to evaporate in sun and wind, with the superfluous juices of the body, and so wither and dry up at last like a tree in the woods, which possesses a sort of embalmed life after death, and is as clean as the sapling or fresh buds of spring. Let us die by *dry* rot at least. The dead tree still stands erect without shame or offence amidst its green brethren, the most picturesque object in the wood. The painter puts it into the foreground of his picture, for in death it is still remembered.

When nature finds man returned on her hands, he is not simply those pure elements she has contributed to his growth, but with her floods she must wash away and with her fires burn up the filfth that has accumulated, before she can receive her own again. He poisons her gales, and is a curse to the land that gave him birth — she is obliged to employ her scavengers in self-defence to abate the nuisance.

May not man cast his shell with as little offence as the muscle, and it perchance be a precious relic to be kept in the cabinets of the curious? May we not amuse ourselves with it, as when we count the layers of a shell, and apply it to our ear, to hear the history of its inhabitant in the swell of the sea — the pulsation of the life which once passed therein still faintly echoed?

We confess that it was well done in nature thus to let out her particles of lime to the muscle and coral, to receive them back again with such interest.

The ancients were more tidy than we who subjected the body to the purification of fire before they returned it upon nature — for fire is the true washer, water only displaces the impurity. Fire is thorough — water is superficial.

Tuesday   Dec. 15th 1840.

In the woods one bough relieves another, and we look into them, not with strained, but relaxed, eyes. Seeing has a holiday in their maze. — But as soon as man comes into nature, by running counter to her, and cutting her off where she was continuous, he makes her angular and formal, and when we would bathe our eyes in the prospect it only makes them ache.

I saw today where some pines had been felled at various angles with the rest of the wood, and on that side nature offended me, as a diagram. It seemed as if man could not lay his tree gracefully along the earth as the wind does, but my eye as well as the squirrel's would detect it. I saw squares and triangles only.

When most at one with nature I feel supported and propped on all sides by a myriad influences, as trees in the plain and on the hillside are equally perpendicular — The most upright man is he that most entirely reclines — (the prone recline but partially). By his entire reliance he is made erect. Men of little faith stand only by their feet — or recline on the ground, having lost their reliance on the soul.

Nature is right, but man is straight. She erects no beams, she slants no rafters, and yet she builds stronger and truer than he. Everywhere she preaches not abstract but practical truth — She is no beauty at her toilet, but her cheek is flushed with exercise. The moss grows over her triangles. Unlike the man of science she teaches that skeletons are only good to wear the flesh, and make fast the sinews to — that better is the man than his bones.

There seem to be some qualities of the mind, which, like the size and strength of the bones — cannot be altered by the will of the possessor — while the most are less stubborn and in more rapid flux like the flesh.

In health all the senses receive enjoyment and each seeks its own gratification. — it is a pleasure to see, and to walk, and to hear — &c.

In the fields lights and shadows are my diet. How all trees tell of the sun. — It is almost the only game the trees play at — this tit for tat — now this side in the sun, then that.

The Journal

It is pleasant to work out of doors — My penknife glitters in the sun — my voice is echoed from the woods, if an oar drops I am fain to drop it again, if my cane strikes a stone, I strike it again — Such are the acoustics of my workshop.

Wednesday   Dec. 16th 1840.
Nothing is so beautiful as the tree tops at this season. A pine or two, with a dash of vapor in the sky — The forest is full of attitudes, & every character in history is here represented. Yonder pine stands like Caesar. I see Cromwell, and Jesus, and George Fox in the wood, with many savages beside. A fallen pine, with its green branches still freshly drooping, lies like Tecumseh with his blanket about him. So the forest is full of attitudes, which give it character. In its infinite postures I see my own erectness, or humbleness — or sneaking — I am posture master to the wood. I duck with the willow and hold up my head with the pine. The fair proportions of a great man like those of a tree are but the balancing of his accidents[,] the vicissitudes of fortune are his sun[,] wind, and rain.

Speech is fractional, silence is integral.

Beauty is where it is perceived. When I see the sun shining on the woods across the pond, I think this side the richer which sees it.

The motion of quadrupeds is the most constrained and unnatural; it is angular and abrupt, except in those of the cat tribe, where undulation begins. That of birds and fishes is more graceful and independent — they move on a more inward pivot. The former move by their weight or opposition to nature, the latter by their boyancy, or yielding to nature. Awkwardness is a resisting motion, gracefulness is a yielding motion. The line which would express the motion of the former would be a tangent to the sphere, of the latter a radius. But the subtlest and most ideal and spiritual motion is undulation. It is produced by the most subtle element falling on the next subtlest — and the latter impelling itself. Rippling is a more graceful flight. If you consider it from the hill top you will detect in it the wings of birds endlessly repeated. The two waving lines which express flight seem copied from the ripple. — There is something analogous to this in our most inward experiences. In enthusiasm we undulate to the divine spiritus — as the lake to the wind.*

Thursday   Dec. 17 1840.

The practice of giving the feminine gender — to all ideal excellence personified, is a mark of refinement, observable in the mythologies even of the most barbarous nations. Glory and victory even are of the feminine gender, but it takes manly qualities to gain them. Man is masculine, but his manliness (virtus) feminine. It is the inclination of brute force to moral power.

Dec. 18th 1840.

I find Gibbon to have been less a man and more of a student than I had anticipated — I had supposed him a person of more genius with as much learning, more an enthusiast than a pedant, better fitted to influence an active and practical people like the English, than to lead in a German School.

He had very little greatness. His Roman History, by his own confession, was undertaken from no higher motive than the love of fame. In his religious views he did not differ nobly from mankind, but rather apologized and conformed. He was ambitious and vain. It was a quite paltry ambition that inspired his first Essay — his observations on the Ænead, and

---

* Thoreau assays this ore, can find only four sentences of value for the Week.[85]

the Decline and Fall — and vanity inspired his memoirs of his own life. In his letters he was more literary than social, they are moments grudgingly given to his friends, whom he kept in pay to inform him how that world went on from which he had retired.

I hear him smack his lips at the prospect of a pipe of wine to be sent from England to Lausanne. There is not recorded of him, that I know, a single reckless and heroic action, which would have been worth a. thousand histories. That would have been to Rise and Stand. He withdrew into retirement in Switzerland, not to perfect his culture, but be more at leisure to build up a reputation undisturbed. He respected and courted the doctors and learned, not the learning. I think of him only as the laborious ambitious student who wrote the Decline & Fall, during those 56 years — which after all it does not concern me to read.

Dec. 19th 1840.

This plain sheet of snow which covers the ice of the pond, is not such a blancness as is unwritten, but such as is unread. All colors are in white. It is such simple diet to my senses as the grass and the sky. There is nothing fantastic in them. Their simple beauty has sufficed men from the earliest times — they have never criticised the blue sky and the green grass.

Dec. 20th 1840.

When I see lines set to catch pickerel through the ice, and men moving about over the white ground like pieces of forest furniture, I am pleased to think how they are domesticated in nature. The pond is their deal table or sanded floor, and the woods rising abruptly from its edge their walls.

My home is as much of nature as my heart embraces, if I only warm my house, then is that only my home. But if I sympathise with the heats and colds — the sounds and silence of nature and share the repose and equanimity that reigns around me in the fields then are they my house, as much as if the kettle sang — and the faggots crackled, and the clock ticked on the wall.*

---

* One cannot resist speculating whether this passage, in its present form or something like it, went into "A Winter Walk," and so became a target for Emerson's annoyance over the *"mannerism."* [86] Whether Emerson remodeled it, or whether Thoreau himself did (under Emerson's tutelage), we do not know; whatever the secret history, this is what the entry became in *The Dial*: [87]

> We fancy ourselves in the interior of a larger house. The surface of the pond is our deal table or sanded floor, and the woods rise abruptly from its edge, like the walls of a cottage. The lines set to catch pickerel through the ice look like a larger culinary preparation, and the men stand about on the white ground like pieces of forest furniture. The actions of these men, at the distance of half a mile over the ice and snow, impress us as when we read the exploits of Alexander in history. They seem not unworthy of the scenery, and as momentous as the conquest of kingdoms.

We also notice that, in the revision, the "domestic" word "home" has disappeared: the self-centered fantasy of domesticity in the winter wild has all but evaporated. We are bound also to speculate as to whether Emerson's irritation over Thoreau's favoring the word *"domestic"* was simply his sensitiveness to repetition or whether he, in some measure, divined the (to us) embarrassing revelation of Thoreau's primal urge to find a "mother-substitute" in impersonal nature. However, even though speculations of this sort come to nothing, the contrast between the entry and the finished passage, taken along with our certain knowledge of Emerson's editorial instruction, is a neat illustration of how Henry Thoreau learned to write.

I am as much moved and elevated when I consider men fishing on Walden Pond in the winter, as when I read the exploits of Alexander. Their actions are very nearly related. The occasions and scenery are so similar that the difference is unimportant.[88]

I rarely read a sentence which speaks to my muse as nature does. — Through the sweetness of his verse, without regard to the sense, I have communion with Burns. His plaint escapes through the flexure of his verses. It was all the record it admitted.

Dec. 21st 1840.

Wherever I walk I seem to have come upon ground where giants have been at play. Nature looks too big to fit me, and I would fall contentedly into some crevice along with leaves and acorns.

Thursday Dec. 24th 1840.

The same sun has not yet shined on me and my friend. — He would hardly have to look at me to recognize me — but glimmer with half-shut eye, like some friendly distant taper when we are benighted. — I do not talk to any intellect in nature, but am presuming an infinite heart somewhere — unto which I play — Nature has many rhymes, but friendship is the most heroic of all.

Dec. 25th 1840.

The character of Washington has after all been undervalued, simply because not valued correctly. He was a proper Puritan hero. It is his erectness and persistency which attract me. A few simple deeds with a dignified silence for background and that is all. He never fluctuated, nor lingered, nor stooped, nor swerved, but was nobly silent and assured. He was not the darling of the people, as no man of integrity can ever be, but

was as much respected as loved. His instructions to his stew-
ard — his refusal of a crown — his interviews with his officers
at the termination of the war, — his thoughts after his retirement, as expressed in a letter to La Fayette — his remarks
to another correspondent on his being chosen president —
his last words to Congress — and the unparalled respect which
his most distinguished contemporaries — as Fox and Erskine,
expressed for him — are refreshing to read in these unheroic
days.

His behavior in the field and in council, and his dignified
and contented withdrawal to private life — were great. He
could advance and he could withdraw.

But we are not sorry he is dead.*

The thought there is in a sentence is its solid part, which
will wear to the latest times.

Sat. Dec. 26 1840.

There is as good as a mine under my feet wherever I go. —
When the pond is frozen and covered with snow, I do not
suspect the wealth under my feet. How many pickerel are
poised on easy fin fathoms below the loaded wain. — The
revolution of the seasons must be a curious phenomenon to
them. Now the sun and wind brush aside their curtain and
they see the heavens again.†

Sunday Dec. 27ᵗʰ 1840.

The wood gaily wears its burden of snow. It is glad and

---

* At this point the reader realizes how far by December Thoreau
has journeyed past the operatic heroism of "The Service" with
which he started in July.

. . .

† This was reworked for "Natural History of Massachusetts." [89]
Compare a variant on the theme, "A Winter Walk." [90]

warm always, sometimes even more genial in winter than in summer. The snow melts round every tree.*

In a little hollow between the hills, some twenty feet higher than the village, lies Walden pond, the expressed genie of the hills and trees whose leaves are annually steeped in it. Its history is in the lapse of its waves, in the rounded pebbles on its shore, and the pines which have grown on its brink. It has its precessions and recessions, its cycles and epicycles — it has not been idle, though sedentary as Abu Musa — who says that "Sitting still at home is the heavenly way. The going out is the way of the world." Yet by its evaporations and by a thousand unimagined ways it has travelled as far as any.†

Dec. 28th 1840.

(The moss hangs on the trees as the fruit of the season. In those twigs which the wind has preserved naked, there is a warmer green for the contrast.) The whole tree exhibits a kind of interior and household comfort — a sheltered and covert aspect — It has the snug inviting look of a cottage on the moors, buried in snow.

How like your house are the woods, your voices ring hollowly through them as through a chamber & The twigs crackle under feet with private and household echoes.

---

* Broken up, to be used in another piecing-together in "A Winter Walk." 91

. . .

† Thoreau slightly reworked this for "A Winter Walk," 92 with the name of the Pond concealed, as a poet might conceal the name of his mistress. It is entirely evident that Thoreau's yearning for Walden Pond — and for the Pond in winter — has psychological origins long anterior to any "economical" decision to go live with it.

They are glad & on a clear winter morning the woods have their southern window as well as the house, through which the first beams of the sun stream along their aisles and corridors. The sun goes up swiftly behind the limbs of the white pines, as the sashes of a window. (The sun reflected from the red leaves of the shrub oak on the hill side is as warm as a fire.) The oaks have more heat than the pines, green is a cold color. It has the ancient principle of heat in it — a gentle simmering to eternity. There is a slumbering fire, an infinite eternal warmth in nature which never goes out, and no cold can chill. It melts the *great snow.**

Only the fates intercede between friends.

Tuesday   Dec. 29th 1840.

An echo makes me enunciate distinctly — So the sympathy of a friend gives plainness and point to my speech. This is the advantage of letter writing.†

Dec. 30th 1840.

In the sunrise I see an eastern city with its spires, in the sunset a western forest. —

The woods are an admirable fence to the landscape — every where skirting the horizon.‡

---

* Of this passage, with which, as the revisions show, Thoreau struggled, he seems to have been able to utilize only a few phrases for "A Winter Walk" [93] — unless it may be that this is another of those "wilderness *domestic*" bits of which Emerson made a "pretty free" omission.[94] For the "Great Snow" see *Walden*.[95]

· · ·

† Here we foresee what later became the great usefulness of Harrison Blake!

· · ·

‡ Here he takes the "fence" idea from the flyleaf recto (above, p. 134); it finds ultimate lodgment in the *Week*.[96]

You see some trees in the fields which are but overgrown bushes; no matter how large they are, for character is of no dimensions.*

The western landscape early of a winter's morning reminds me of the shadowy realms of Pluto — it is clothed in such a sombre Tartarran light. The trees stand very much as Dante and Virgil have described them. They are only infernal sounds that you hear — the crowing of cocks — the barking of dogs — the chopping of wood — the lowing of kine — all come from Pluto's barn-yard.

The elegance of Virgil's digressions, though too often to flatter his age or patron, is admirable.

Our Golden Age must after all be a pastoral one, we would be simple men in ignorance, and not accomplished in wisdom. We want great peasants more than great heroes. The sun would shine along the highway to some purpose, if we would unlearn our wisdom, and practice illiterate truth henceforth. The great dwell in cottages on the moor, whose windows the sun visits from day to day with his ray, and of their greatness none knoweth but that there they dwell. They write no Iliads nor Hamlets more than the Columbine at their doors.

Let us grow to the full stature of our humbleness — ere we aspire to be greater.†

It is great praise in the poet to have made husbandry famous. —

---

* Again he is rescuing an impromptu from the flyleaf recto (above, p. 134), giving it a little development; though the idea seems promising, he evidently never found a use for it.

· · ·

† I cannot resist interposing to suggest that for any understanding of Thoreau's literary career, this is a basic passage.

"In the new spring, when cool moisture from the hoary
    mountains flows,
"And the mouldering clod is dissolved by the zephyr,
"Then straightway let the bull with deep pressed plough
    begin
"To groan, and the share, worn by the furrow, to shine.

Georg. 1st 43^d.

And again when the husbandman conducts water down the
slope to restore his thirsty crops.

"That falling makes a hoarse murmur among the smooth
rocks, and tempers the parching fields with its bubbling
streams." ibid. 109th.

Describing the end of the Golden Age and the commencement of the reign of Jupiter, he says —

"He shook honey from the leaves, and removed fire,
"And stayed the wine everywhere flowing in rivers;
"That experience by meditating might invent various arts
"By degrees, and seek the blade of corn in furrows,
"And strike out hidden fire from the veins of the flint.

131st

Thursday   Dec. 31st 1840.

To discover a gleam in the trenches, and hear a music in
the rattling of the tools we work with — is to *have* an *eye* and
an *ear* — We should not be sad on account of the sins of men,
but glad in our own innocence. Another man's sin never made
me sad, it was my own. A burnishing of spades and plough-
shares the country over would be symbolic of the true reform.

There must be respiration as well as aspiration — We
should not walk on tiptoe, but healthily expand to our full
circumference on the soles of our feet.*

---

* Compare the entry of December 26, 1841: "The whole duty
of life is contained in the question of how to respire and aspire
both at once." 97

This sickly preaching of love, and a sympathy that will be tender of our faults, is the dyspepsia of the soul.

If aspiration be repeated long without intervals of respiration — it will be no better than expiration or simply losing one's breath — In the healthy for every aspiration there will be a respiration, which is to make his idea take shape, and give its tone to the character. Every time he steps boyantly up — he steps solidly down again, and stands the firmer on the ground for his independence upon it. We should fetch the whole — heel — sole — and toe — horizontally down to earth.

Let not ours be a wiped virtue, as men go about with an array of clean linnen, but unwashed as a fresh flower. Not a clean Sunday garment, but better as a soiled work-day one.

January —— 1841
Friendship ———— in The Dial Dec. 28th 1840.*

Friends —
They cannot help,
They cannot hurt,
Nor in indifference rest,
But when for a host's service girt,
They are a mutual guest.

They are a single power
Plenipotentiary,
No minister of state,
Anxious and wary
Decides their fate.

Where interest's self is
There is no go-between,

---

* This is a somewhat enigmatic heading, since Thoreau's "Friendship" was not published by *The Dial* until October 1841.[98]

But where another reaps,
They do but glean
In scanty heaps.

They have learned well to hate,
And never grant reprieve,
Nor e'er succumb to love,
But sternly grieve,
And look above.

If faults arise, my friend will send for me
As some great god,
Who will the matter try,
Holding the scales, even or odd,
Under the sky —

Who will award strict justice
All the while,
Confounding mine and thine,
And share his smile,
When they 'gainst me incline.

When in some cove I lie,
A placid lake at rest,
Scanning the distant hills,
A murmur from the west,
And gleam of thousand rills
Which gently swell my breast,
Announce the friendly thought,
And in one wave sun-lit
I'm softly brought
Seaward with it.

Jan. 1st 1841.

All men and women woo me. There is a fragrance in their breath —

"*Nosque — equis oriens afflavit anhelis.*"

And if now they hate, I muse as in sombre cloudy weather, not despairing of the absent ray.

"*Illic sera rubens accendit lumina Vesper.*"

Jan. 2nd 1841.

My virtue loves to take an airing of a winter's morning — it scents itself, and snuffs its own fragrance in the bracing atmosphere of the fields more than in the sluggishness of the parlor.

The searching wind drives away all contagion, and nothing can stand before it in the fields, but what has a virtue in it, and so if I meet anything in very cold and bleak places, as the tops of mountains, I respect it for a sort of sturdy innocence, and Puritan toughness — At such times it seems as if all God's creatures were called in for shelter, and what stayed out must be part of the original frame of the universe, and of such valor as God himself — There is a very warm fire under the traveller's fear-naught.*

The shrub oaks rustling in the thin cold breeze are a simmering crackling fire. They have more heat than the pines. Green is a cold color.†

---

* This was interestingly reworked for "A Winter Walk." [99] Readers of Thoreau will think ahead to the terrifying revelation of brute nature, in 1846, on the top of Ktaadn. [100]

. . .

† Thoreau here tries to make better use of the sentence he wrote on the margin for insertion December 28 (above, p. 198). His worrying it is another instance of what I have called his doggedness. In his college exercise on Howitt's *Seasons* he had written, speaking of October:

The richness of the outline of the wood against the sky is in proportion to the number of distinct interstices through which the light straggles to us.

> Nothing can be more pleasing to the eye than the appearance of the woods at this season. Green is allowed by most occulists to be the color which the eye may dwell upon with the least injury, as it is certainly that to which it is most accustomed. The trees have now thrown off their green costume and assumed a variegated dress.[101]

By February 10, 1855, his progression is completed: "The drooping oak leaves show more red amid the pines this wet day, — agreeably so, — and I feel as if I stood a little nearer to the heart of nature." [102]

He who reads the *Journal* must be struck by the way in which this or that phenomenon, which may figure casually from time to time, suddenly becomes the object of a consuming passion; then, day after day, Thoreau will address prose sonnets to it, until the frenzy dies down. Were these the diaries of any other writer, we would say that he was having a series of "affairs." As he recounts these crises, he follows the classic pattern of infatuation, and once the emotion reaches a climax, the object becomes so indifferent to him as to be seldom thereafter mentioned. In the autumn of 1856 he suddenly becomes obsessed by the "dear wholesome color of shrub oak leaves, so clean and firm," just as another man might find himself surprised by an irresistible desire for a neighbor's wife. One divines something of the libertine whom Thoreau hid behind what Emerson miscalled his "Stoic" exterior as he perceives that Thoreau was conscious of what these surges meant, that he indulged himself in them: "I love and could embrace the shrub oak with its scanty garment of leaves rising above the snow, lowly whispering to me, akin to winter thoughts, and sunsets, and to all virtue." Again and again in these spasms the language becomes highly erotic. As he himself says of this occasion, "I fell in love with a shrub oak." [103]

The Journal

Every needle of the white pine trembles distinctly in the breeze, which on the sunny side gives the whole tree a shimmering seething aspect.

I stopped short in the path today to admire how the trees grow up without forethought regardless of the time and circumstances. They do not wait as men do — now is the golden age of the sapling — Earth, air, sun, and rain, are occasion enough — They were no better in primeval centuries. The "winter of their discontent" never comes — Witness the buds of the native poplar, standing gaily out to the frost, on the sides of its bare switches. They express a naked confidence.

With cheerful heart I could be a sojourner in the wilderness if I were sure to find there the catkins of the alder. When I read of them in the accounts of northern adventurers, by Baffin's bay or Mackenzie's river, I see how even there too I could dwell. They are my little vegetable redeemer. Methinks my virtue will not flag ere they come again. They are worthy to have had a greater than Neptune or Ceres for their donor — Who was the benignant goddess that bestowed them on mankind? *

I saw a fox run across the pond today on the snow with the carelessness of freedom. As at intervals I traced his course in the sunshine as he trotted along the ridge of a hill on the crust, it seemed as if the sun never shone so proudly, sheer down on the hill side, and the winds and woods were hushed in sympathy. I gave up to him sun and earth, as to their true proprietor. He did not go in the sunshine, but the sunshine

---

* This, combined with the entry above it, is stuck into "Natural History of Massachusetts" (with several "I's" changed to "we's"), much as a cook sticks cloves into a ham.[104]

seemed to follow him. There was a visible sympathy between him and it.*

It would be worth the while to be a wood-chopper, for every sound would echo to heaven. — Virgil says as much.

Jan. 4th 1841.

I know a woman who is as true to me and as incessant with her mild rebuke as the blue sky — When I stand under her cope, and instantly all pretension drops off — & I am swept by her influence as by the wind and rain, to remove all taint. I am fortunate that I can pass and repass before her (as a mirror) each day — and prove my strength in her glances. She is far truer to me than to herself. Her eyes are like the windows of nature, through which I catch glimpses of the native land of the soul and from them comes a light which is not of the sun. (The sun shines for this inner and lower world, but through them gleams a milder and steadier light than his.) His rays are in eclipse when they shine on me. Methinks in these *soular* rays there is no refraction of the light.†

---

* Bits of this entry are combined with another of January 30[105] to make a fox-mosaic in "Natural History of Massachusetts." [106]

. . .

† Though we must always be wary of reading biographical implications into Thoreau's *Journal*, still this curious paragraph (with its still more curious revisions) inevitably poses the question of *who*, if anybody, was this woman. The similarity of the language to that of an Elizabethan conceit is the first obvious fact. The second is that in the *Week*,[107] in the midst of the digression on friendship, is an equally enigmatic passage, which begins in almost the same strain:

> I know a woman who possesses a restless and intelligent mind, interested in her own culture, and earnest to enjoy the highest possible advantages, and I meet her

Tuesday   Jan. 5th 1841.

I grudge to the record that lavish expenditure of love and grace which are due rather to the spoken thought — A man writes because he has no opportunity to speak. — Why should he be the only mute creature, and his speech no part of the melody of the grove? He never gladdens the ear of nature — he ushers in no spring with his lays.

We are more anxious to speak than to be heard.*

---

with pleasure as a natural person who not a little provokes me, and I suppose is stimulated in turn by myself.

But, as he goes on to say, their acquaintance does not attain to that degree of sentiment "which women, which all, in fact, covet." After a typical explanation that incomplete intercourse is better than an "unreserved" one, Thoreau works up to his poem, "My love must be as free/ As is the eagle's wing," which was first printed in *The Dial* in October 1842,[108] and which, whatever else it may be, is in substance a flight from matrimony. Mr. Canby (who had access to volume 3 before it came to the Morgan Library) misquoted this entry as part of his contention that the woman should be read as Lidian Emerson,[109] and then conjectured that the passage in the *Week*, along with the poem, must have had Margaret Fuller "for its subject." [110] On the strength of these absurdities, Mr. Canby surmises that by 1847, when the *Week* was finished, "this tragic correspondence must be presumed to have been consummated."

The hypothesis is patent nonsense; still we suspect that there is some connection, beyond the rhetorical opening, between the *Journal* entry of January 4, 1841, and the oblique paragraph of the *Week*. Whatever this may turn out to be, supposing that some detective will ever solve the puzzle, the essential fact remains that both paragraphs are infinitely more literary hyperboles than intimate confessions.

• • •

* This may, of course, have some bearing on the issue of the previous note, but I suspect it has more relevance to Thoreau's

Wednesday Jan. 6ᵗʰ 1841.

We are apt to imagine that this hubbub of Philosophy —
Literature, and Religion — which is heard in pulpits — Lyceums & parlors — vibrates through the universe — and is as
catholic a sound as the creaking of the earth's axle — But if a
man sleep soundly he will forget it all between sunset and
dawn. It is the three inch swing of some pendulum in a
cubbord. — Which the great pulse of nature vibrates clearly
and through each instant. — When we lift our lids — and
open our ears — it disappears, with smoke and rattle, like the
cars on the railroad.*

Thursday Jan. 7ᵗʰ 1841.

There is no covert in nature but it covers a man — this is
what we mean by the genialness of nature.

There is a total disinterestedness and self-abandonment vein
in fretfulness and despondency, which few attain to. If there
is no personality or selfishness, you may be as fretful as you
please. I congratulate myself on the richness of human nature, which a virtuous and even temper had not wholly exhibited. May it not whine like a kitten or squeak like a squirrel?
Sometimes the weakness of my fellow discovers a new suppleness, which I had not anticipated.

---

secret ambition (his to-be-thwarted ambition) to make a name
and a living from lecturing, as Emerson was already beginning
to do. He and John Thoreau were at this date already scheduled
for the debate with Alcott at the Concord Lyceum which took
place on the 27th, and he seems here to be a little apprehensive.

• • •

* We find this pressed into service as the opening of a paragraph
in "Natural History of Massachusetts," [111] which is a marvelous
mosaic of early *Journal* entities. In print Thoreau's "cubbord"
becomes the orthodox "cupboard," but this is the way he spelled
and pronounced it when left to himself.

We are not inspired to speak, I guess, but to be silent.*

Jan. 8ᵗʰ 1841.

Man finds himself in life, but with no hint for the conduct of an hour. — Conscience only informs that he must *behave*.

Jan. 9ᵗʰ 1841.

Each hearty stroke we deal with these outward hands, slays an inward foe.

Sunday   Jan. 10ᵗʰ 1841.

A perfectly healthy sentence is extremely rare[.] Sometimes I read one which was written while the world went round, while grass grew and water ran.†

The church bell is not a natural sound to the church goer.

---

* I am tempted to call attention here to how much Thoreau has learned about writing — about compression and epigram — since July.

• • •

† This becomes, in part, an element in an elaborate mosaic of the *Week*.[112] That section ends with a paragraph which is a significant refashioning of a *Journal* entry for June 23, 1840,[113] just before our volume begins; in the *Week* it reads:

> There is no doubt that the loftiest written wisdom is either rhymed or in some way musically measured, — is, in form as well as substance, poetry; and a volume which should contain the condensed wisdom of mankind need not have one rhythmless line.

Since we know how Thoreau treasured every entry he put into his *Journal*, we may conceive how this came back to him when he read, and still more, when he confronted, Walt Whitman:[114] "He may turn out the least of a braggart of all, having a better right to be confident."

Who hears the parson
Will not hear the bell,
But if he deafly pass on
He will hear of hell.

I' faith the people go to church
To leave the devil in the lurch,
But since they've carpeted the pews
To squat with hymn book he doth use[.]

The first beams of the sun are a sovereign remedy for wrinkles.

He seems to come rolling his car over the slopes with the faint clashing or swinging sound of cymbals.

I don't like people who are too good for this world. Let a man reserve a good appetite for his peck of dirt, and expect his chief wealth in unwashed diamonds. To know nature and ourselves well, we must have acquired a certain hardness and habitual equanimity.

The virtue of some is only an excessive refinement. — In comparison with theirs[,] the sternness and rigidity of the Hebrew faith is refreshing.

Only the tender sex, and their hangers on, will mind such a last trump as I have heard foretold, but men of true mettle will prefer to buffet it here a spell longer.

Monday   Jan. 11th 1841.

"In the 'human face divine,' portrait painters affirm that the two sides never correspond; and even when the external form of an animal exhibits an appearance of bilateral or radiate symmetry, nature departs from it in her arrangement of the internal structure."

H. E. Strickland "on the Natural System" — in "The Annals and Magazine of Natural History" — No 36 for Nov. 1840. London.[115]

My friends know me pretty well — that is they have got a correct total impression — but yet they do not know my right side from my left. If I should stand on my head they would perceive the difference but if my right side should be exchanged for my left they would not[.] *

Wednesday Jan. 13th 1841.

We should offer up our *perfect* thoughts to the gods daily — our writing should be hymns and psalms. Who keeps a journal is purveyor for the Gods. There are two sides to every sentence; the one is contiguous to me, but the other faces the gods, and no man ever fronted it. When I utter a thought I launch a vessel which never sails in my haven more, but goes sheer off into the deep. Consequently it demands a godlike insight — a fronting view, to read what was greatly written.

Jan. 14th 1841.

As for public speaking, diffidence may prompt us to excessive circumspection, and to hold ourselves in our own hands, and over see our own conduct in the debate, or we may throw ourselves on the occasion, and the sympathies of the audience. In the former case we are quite defenceless because prepared but for one thing, and may be discomfitted by any simple and natural accident, in the latter this will help us, and furnish an argument for the truth we are asserting.†

Friday Jan. 15th 1841.

When men die they do not leave their works behind them — but they will find rather that they have gone before them.

---

* This, in a penciled interlineation, is apparently an afterthought to the previous entry in ink.

• • •

† Obviously, Henry is nervous about his performance, scheduled for, and delivered on, the 27th. This sort of anxiety was to prevent him, in spite of many efforts, from becoming a successful lecturer.

The Journal

Saturday   Jan. 16th 1841.

"Sic Vita" — in the Dial.*

Sunday   Jan. 17th 1841.

A true happiness never happened, but rather is proof against all haps. I would not be a happy, that is, a lucky man, but rather a necessitated and doomed one.

After so many years of study I have not learned my duty for one hour. I am stranded at each reflux of the tide — and I who sailed as boyantly on the middle deep as a ship, am as helpless as a muscle on the rock. I cannot account to myself for the hour I live. Here time has given me a dull prosaic evening, not of kin to Vesper or Cynthia — a dead lapse — where time's stream seems settling into a pool — a stillness not as if nature's breath were held but expired. But let me know that such hours as this are the wealthiest in time's gift — It is the insufficiency of the hour, which if we but feel and understand, we shall reassert our independence then.†

---

* This, like the reference to "Friendship" at the beginning of January, is enigmatic, since the poem "Sic Vita" was printed in The Dial for July 1841.[116] We know it was in Emerson's hands in April;[117] my guess is that Thoreau, in this January, submitted his two poems, and was simply convinced, beyond argument, that while Emerson and Margaret Fuller might object to his prose, they would have to print his verse.

•   •   •

† Here, the analyst may observe, we have the definite onset of that Transcendentalized *ubi-sunt* motif which is increasingly to haunt Thoreau's *Journal*, as it does all the recollections of the fervent fellowship, until Emerson tries to call a halt with "Terminus." All of them — Parker and Orestes Brownson, no less than Emerson, Thoreau, and Margaret Fuller — had the temerity to stake their fate upon the insights of youth; those who survived the Civil War found themselves in a world they never intended to make, and only Alcott remained impervious.

Monday   Jan. 18th 1841.

We must expect no income beside our outgoes — we must succeed now, and we shall not fail hereafter. So soon as we begin to count the cost the cost begins.

If our scheme is well built within, any mishap to the out-building will not be fatal.

The capital wanted is an entire independence upon all capital, but a clear conscience, and a resolute will.

When we are so poor that the howling of the wind shall have a music in it, and not declare war against our property — the proprietors may well envy us. We have been seeking riches not by a true industry or building within, but by mere accumulation, putting together what was without[,] till it rose a heap beside us. — We should rather acquire them by the utter renunciation of them. If I hold a house and land as property, am I not disinherited of sun, wind, rain, and all good beside? The richest are only some degrees poorer than nature.

It is impossible to have more property than we dispense — Genius is only as rich as it is generous, if it hoards it impoverishes itself. — What the banker sighs for the meanest clown may have, leisure and a quiet mind.

Tuesday   Jan. 19th 1841.

The mind which first contemplated the present order of things at some remote era — must have been visionary and Utopian.

Coleridge, speaking of the love of God, says — "He that loves, may be sure he was loved first." The love wherewith we are loved is already declared, and afloat in the atmosphere, and our love is only the inlet to it. It is an inexhaustible harvest — always ripe and ready for the sickle. It grows on every bush, and let not them complain of their fates who will not pluck it. We need make no beggarly demand for it, but pay the price, and depart. No transaction can be simpler —

Love[']s accounts are kept by single-entry. When we are amiable, then is love in the gale, and in sun and shade, and day and night, and to sigh under the cold cold moon for a love unrequited, is to put a slight upon nature; the natural remedy would be to fall in love with the moon and the night, and find our love requited.*

I anticipate a more thorough sympathy with nature when my thigh-bones shall strew the ground like the boughs which the wind has scattered. — Thus troublesome humors will flower into early anemonies, and perhaps in the very lachrymal sinus, nourished by its juices, some young pine or oak will strike root.

What I call pain when I speak in the spirit of a partisan, and not as a citizen of the body, would be serene being if our interests were one. Sickness is civil war — We have no external foes — even death will take place when I make peace with my body — and set my seal to that treaty which transcendent justice has so long required. I shall at length join interest with it.†

The mind never makes so great effort, without a corresponding energy of the body — when great resolves are entertained its nerves are not relaxed, nor its limbs reclined.

---

* This, in short, was the "natural" remedy Thoreau administered to himself: Was his love "requited"?

· · ·

† Here in little is a prefiguration of the stratagem by which Thoreau, up to his deathbed — and all the other Transcendentalists straggling behind him — prepared himself to cope with the one brute fact even they could not deny. Because they loved life so intensely — beyond most Americans of their epoch — they sought ways, in anticipation, to humanize death. Hence the icy impersonality of their mortuary poetry.

Wednesday Jan. 20th 1841.

Disappointment will make us conversant with the nobler part of our nature, it will chasten us, and prepare us to meet accident on higher ground the next time — As Hannibal taught the Romans the art of war. So is all misfortune only a stepping-stone to fortune.

The desultory moments — which are the grimmest features of misfortune — are a step before me on which I should set foot, and not stumbling blocks in the path. — To extract its whole good I must be disappointed with the best fortune, and not be bribed by sunshine nor health.

Oh Happiness — what is the stuff thou art made of? Is it not gossamer and floating spider's webs? — a crumpled sunbeam — a coiled dew-line settling on some flower? What moments will most supply the reel from which thou may'st be wound off? — Thou art as subtle as the pollen of flowers — and the sporules of the fungi.

When I meet a person unlike me, I find myself *wholly* in the unlikeness. In what I am unlike others, in that I am.

When we ask for society — we do not want the double of ourselves — but the complement rather. Society should be additive and helpful, we would be reinforced by its alliance. True friends will know how to use each other in this respect, and never barter or interchange their commonwealths, just as barter is unknown in families. They will not dabble in the general coffers, but each put his finger into the private coffer of the other. They will be most familiar, they will be most unfamiliar, for they will be so one and single that common themes and things will have to be bandied between them, but in silence. They will digest them as one mind; but they will at the same time be so two and double, that each will be to the other as admirable and as inaccessible as a star. When my friend comes I view his orb "through optic glass," "At evening from the top of Fesolé." [118]

After the longest earthly period he will still be in apogee to me.

But we should so meet ourselves as we meet our friends, and still ever seek for us in that which is above us, and unlike us. So only shall we see the light of our own countenances.

Jan. 21st 1841.

We can render men the best assistance, by letting them see how sore a thing it is to need any assistance. I am not in haste to help men more than God is. If they will not help themselves, shall I become their abettor?

If I have unintentionally injured the feelings of any — or prophaned their sacred character, we shall be necessitated to know each other better than before. — I have gained a glorious vantage ground then. And to the other, the shaft which carried the wound, will bear its own remedy with it, for we cannot be prophaned without the consciousness that we have a holy fane for our asylum somewhere.

Would that sincere words might always drive men thus to earth themselves!

Jan. 22^d 1841.

I hear it complained of some modern books of genius, that they are irregular, and have no flow, but we should consider that the flow of thought is more like a tidal wave than a prone river, and is the effect of a celestial influence, or sort of ground swell, it may be, and not of any declivity in its channel, each wave rising higher than the former, and partially subsiding back on it. But the river flows, because it runs down hill, and descends faster, as it flows more rapidly. The one obeys the earthly attraction, the other the heavenly attraction. The one runs smoothly because it gravitates toward the earth alone, the other irregularly because it gravitates toward the heavens as well.

The reader who has been accustomed to expend all his energy in the launching — as if he were to float down stream for the whole voyage — may well complain of nauseating ground swells, and choppings of the sea, when his frail shore craft gets amidst the breakers of the ocean stream — which flows as much to sun and moon, as lesser streams to it. If he would appreciate the true flow that is in these books, he must expect to see it rise from the page like an exhalation — and wash away the brains of most like burr-millstones. They flow not from right to left, or from left to right, but to higher levels, above and behind the reader.*

Though I should front an object for a lifetime[,] I should only see what it concerned me to see.†

What we know we know intimately & centrally not superficially. I know my friend's face though I see but half of it, and yet I do not know which half it is — and if the right side

---

* A highly compressed version of this entry, amalgamated with a similar meditation of March 27, 1842, becomes a self-defensive oration in the *Week*.[119] Readers of 1849, such few as there were, would take the finished utterance as an apology for Carlyle, and to some extent for the style of Emerson. But it must now be clear that Thoreau, either in the *Journal* or in the *Week*, was not pleading for his masters: he was justifying himself.

· · ·

† This is a scribble on the inside of the back cover. Volume 3 of the *Journal* properly ends with the previous dissertation on modern books.

were exchanged for the left — as happens in the glass, I should not perceive it. Yet portrait painters affirm that the two sides of the face are never alike.

We no doubt detect differences as slight between man & man as exist between the two sides of one face. We do not see halves — we retain only total impressions.[120]

Notes

PART I, INTRODUCTION

CHAPTER 1: "A JOURNAL, OF NO VERY WIDE CIRCULATION"

1. *Walden*, p. 19.

CHAPTER 2: THE BIOGRAPHICAL PROVENIENCE

1. Thoreau, *Familiar Letters*, p. 9.
2. Emerson, *Journals*, IV, 395.
3. Emerson, *Letters*, II, 225.
4. *Ibid.*, p. 259.
5. *Ibid.*, pp. 280–281.
6. *Ibid.*, p. 287.
7. *Ibid.*, p. 291.
8. *Ibid.*, p. 293.
9. *Ibid.*, p. 317.
10. *Ibid.*, p. 320.
11. *Ibid.*, p. 322.
12. *Ibid.*, pp. 323–324.
13. *Week*, pp. 327–333.
14. Emerson, *Letters*, II, 310.
15. *Ibid.*, p. 369.
16. Walter Harding, "A Check List of Thoreau's Lectures," *Bulletin of the New York Public Library* (February 1948), p. 2.
17. Emerson, *Letters*, II, 344.
18. *J*, III, 41.
19. *J*, I, 432.
20. F. B. Sanborn and W. T. Harris, A. *Bronson Alcott* (Boston, 1893), I, 308.

21. *Ibid.*, p. 323.
22. *Ibid.*, p. 343.
23. Henry Seidel Canby, *Thoreau: A Biography* (Boston, 1939), p. 157.
24. J, I, 319.
25. J, V, 459.

Chapter 3: The Method

1. The latter is probably the same folio journal, covering August 31, 1839, to March 13, 1846, now in the Pierpont Morgan Library, though this may be a culling from still earlier manuscripts.
2. F. B. Sanborn, *The First and Last Journeys of Thoreau* (Boston, 1905), I, 64.
3. *Walden*, p. 328.
4. J, I, 413.
5. J, X, 115.
6. J, II, 376.
7. J, I, 207.
8. J, I, 182.
9. J, VIII, 134.
10. J, I, 138.
11. J, I, 188 (January 31, 1841).
12. J, II, 419.
13. J, I, 342.
14. J, I, 143.
15. J, IX, 306.
16. J, III, 99.
17. J, II, 341.
18. J, III, 390.
19. J, II, 383–388.

CHAPTER 4: CONSCIOUSNESS

1. *J*, III, 239.
2. *J*, III, 217.
3. See Leo Stoller, "A Note on Thoreau's Place in the History of Phenology," *Isis*, XLVII (June 1956), 172–181.
4. *J*, I, 327.
5. *J*, I, 53–54.
6. Emerson, *Letters*, III, 335–336.
7. Harvard College Papers, Second Series, XVII (1849–1850), 88.
8. *Walden*, p. 45.

CHAPTER 5: CONSCIOUSNESS AT HARVARD

1. F. B. Sanborn, *The Life of Henry David Thoreau* (Boston, 1917), p. 187.
2. *Ibid.*, p. 188.
3. Carl Bode, "A New College Manuscript of Thoreau's," *American Literature*, XXI (November 1949), 311–318.
4. Sanborn, *Life*, p. 86.
5. *Ibid.*, pp. 90–92.
6. *Ibid.*, pp. 171–173.
7. *Ibid.*, p. 182.
8. *Ibid.*, p. 158.
9. *Ibid.*, pp. 131–133.
10. Wendell Glick, "Three Early Manuscripts by Thoreau," *The Huntington Library Quarterly*, XV (November 1951), 59–71.
11. Thoreau, *Familiar Letters*, p. 345.
12. Sanborn, *Life*, pp. 73–74.
13. *Ibid.*, p. 74.
14. *Walden*, p. 3.
15. *The Dial*, IV, 180.
16. *J*, I, 62.
17. Because Carlyle and Emerson so advertised the standard pattern of Transcendentalist growth of the spirit — "Shut thy

Byron, open thy Goethe!" — we forget that the Byronic mood surrounded their youth as densely as it did that of Jeunes-France. In an essay of his senior year Thoreau wrote in the expected affirmative on another of Professor Channing's profundities, "Whether Moral Excellence tend directly to increase Intellectual Power?", but at one point, explaining that only the highest minds can attain this virtue, he developed his argument in a way that may have jolted his "Professor":

> With by far the greater part of mankind, religion is a habit, or rather, habit is religion, their views of things are illiberal and contracted, for the very reason that they possess not intellectual power sufficient to attain to moral excellence. However paradoxical it may seem, it appears to me that to reject Religion is the first step towards moral excellence; at least, no man ever attained to the highest degree by any other road. Byron's character is a favorite argument with those who maintain the opposite opinion; a better for my own purpose I could not have desired. He advanced just far enough on the road to excellence to depart from the religion of the vulgar, nay further; twelve lines, says Constant, (and he quotes them) of his poetry, contain more true religion than was ever possessed by any or all of his calumniators. (Reginald Lansing Cook, *The Concord Saunterer*, Middlebury, Vermont, 1940, pp. 60–61)

It should, however, be pointed out that by 1837 this sort of defense of Byron, as one who sinned out of excess of nobility, had become fairly conventional, which is perhaps one reason why young rebels were beginning to lose interest in him; much more challenging to the religion of the vulgar was the Olympian libertine, Goethe.

18. *Walden*, p. 4.
19. T. W. Higginson, *Margaret Fuller Ossoli* (Boston, 1884), p. 70.
20. Mrs. Samuel Hoar is reported as saying (one imagines with a sniff of scorn), "Henry talks about Nature just as if she'd been born and brought up in Concord" (Mark Van Doren, *Henry David Thoreau*, Boston, 1916, p. 32).

21. *The Service,* p. 26.
22. P. 90 of the Metcalf edition.
23. *Week,* p. 186.
24. *J,* I, 144–145.
25. *J,* III, 240.
26. *J,* II, 285.

CHAPTER 6: THE STRATAGEMS OF CONSCIOUSNESS — DEATH

1. Emerson, *Letters,* III, 180.
2. *J,* I, 321.
3. *J,* I, 324.
4. *J,* II, 130.
5. *J,* VIII, 457 (August 6, 1856).
6. *J,* I, 302.
7. *J,* I, 177.
8. *Week,* p. 314.
9. *Week,* p. 179.
10. This page starts a sentence with, "We believe in a speedy resurrection of the body . . . ," then breaks off. Another sheet shows how Thoreau went on.
11. *Week,* p. 177.
12. *Walden,* p. 367.
13. Among the pages from a manuscript, probably a piece of what I call the "Ur-journal," once in the possession of Mr. George S. Hellman, it appears that Thoreau had already copied out the stanzas from Byron, that he had entered them after a quotation from Coleridge's "Ode to Dejection." That Thoreau should take the pains to transcribe them exhibits how his mind in these years was working. This combination of the two great romantics indicates even more of his always nagging anxiety about approaching senescence. All accounts confirm that, as long as possible, he avoided any mention of John's death, and that on the one time he is known to have spoken of it, at the Ricketsons' in 1854, "he turned pale and was forced to go to the door for air" (Mark Van Doren, *Henry David Thoreau,* pp. 8, 15).

14. Thoreau, *Familiar Letters*, p. 40.
15. *Ibid.*, p. 39.
16. *J*, II, 378.
17. *J*, III, 5.
18. *J*, I, 319.
19. *J*, III, 268 (February 2, 1852).
20. *J*, II, 97.
21. *J*, II, 144.
22. *J*, II, 97 (November 15, 1850).

CHAPTER 7: THE STRATAGEMS OF CONSCIOUSNESS —
WOMAN AND MEN

1. Thoreau, *Familiar Letters*, pp. 138–139.
2. See Walter Harding, "Thoreau's Feminine Foe," *PMLA*, LXIX (March 1954), 110–116.
3. *J*, IV, 280.
4. *J*, IV, 315.
5. Walter Harding, *Thoreau: A Century of Criticism* (Dallas, 1954), pp. 77, 85.
6. T. M. Raysor, "The Love Story of Thoreau," *Studies in Philology*, XXIII (October 1926), 457–463.
7. *Week*, p. 45.
8. *J*, I, 177.
9. *Week*, pp. 119–120.
10. *J*, I, 139–140.
11. *Week*, pp. 44–45.
12. *J*, I, 142.
13. *J*, I, 225.
14. *J*, I, 144.
15. Although recent biographers have been busy with the Ellen Sewall affair, there seems no reason to alter the divination that Mark Van Doren proposed in 1916: the verses "To the Maiden in the East," he hazarded, "cannot be autobiographical so much as expressive of the fastidious ideal of love that Thoreau's melancholy had fashioned out of the egoistic ma-

terials of his temperament" (*Henry David Thoreau*, p. 23).

16. *J*, I, 40.
17. *J*, I, 107.
18. *J*, I, 121.
19. *Week*, pp. 274–307.
20. Emerson, *Essays: First Series*, p. 213.
21. Emerson, *Familiar Letters*, p. 200.
22. *Ibid.*, p. 201.
23. *J*, II, 161–162.
24. *J*, V, 188.
25. *J*, III, 262–265.
26. *J*, III, 253.
27. There must have been something so pontifical in Blake as to call out this tone; Emerson's letters generally convey a sweet informality, which makes them a joy to read, but the moment he addressed Blake, he too became oracular (Emerson, *Letters*, II, 212–213). For some fascinating light on Blake, see Van Wyck Brooks, *Scenes and Portraits* (New York, 1954), pp. 40–46.
28. *J*, XI, 204.
29. Neither of the two (as far as I know) of the serious efforts to explore these issues has yet been printed, but to the credit of *The Thoreau Society Bulletin*, under the gallant editorship of Mr. Walter Harding, a digest of each is available: David Kalman, "A Study of Thoreau," *TSB*, No. 22 (January 1948); Raymond Gozzi, "Tropes and Figures: A Psychological Study of David Henry Thoreau," *TSB*, No. 58 (Winter 1957). The second of these comes from an unpublished dissertation at New York University; it finds the friendship section of the *Week* displaying "an unconscious homoerotic orientation," notes the "sympathetic" oddity of Henry's attack of lockjaw and calls attention to the tantrums in his relationship with Channing. To judge from the digest, it is a careful effort at interpretation. It might also have noted that in later years, when Thoreau's behavior toward Emerson had become petulant, the latter could explode that Thoreau was behaving about Blake as though Blake were his wife.

A large portion of Thoreau's *Familiar Letters* are addressed to Blake. As Ellery Channing slyly remarked of them, they are "abominably didactic." That seems to be what Blake wanted; after Thoreau's death he wrote of them:

> Geniality, versatility, personal familiarity are, of course, agreeable in those about us, and seem necessary in human intercourse, but I did not miss them in Thoreau, who was, while living, and is still in my recollection and in what he has left to us, such an effectual witness to what is highest and most precious in life. As I re-read his letters from time to time, which I never tire of doing, I am apt to find new significance in them, am still warmed and instructed by them, but with more force occasionally than ever before; so that in a sense they are still in the mail, have not altogether reached me yet, and will not probably before I die.

In 1857 Thoreau took Alcott for a visit with Daniel Ricketson; this shrewd sage noted that while Ricketson was a disciple, he could play the "manly" part in defending his independence against "thoroughcraft," wherein, mused Alcott, he was different from Blake, who was the "absolute" disciple: "whose love for his genius partakes of the exceeding tenderness of woman, and is a pure Platonism to fineness and delicacy of the devotees sensibility" (Henry S. Salt, *Henry David Thoreau*, London, 1896, pp. 110, 121). Such is the labyrinth of friendship among Transcendentalists! It was on this visit that Thoreau offended Ricketson by singing and dancing to "Tom Bowline," in which performance Thoreau made a point of treading on the toes of the beaming Alcott, who could never remotely suppose that one friend would wantonly humiliate another.

30. *Week*, p. 281.
31. Emerson, *Journals*, II, 423.
32. *Ibid.*, III, 290.
33. *J*, I, 147–148.
34. *J*, X, 131.
35. *Week*, p. 294.
36. *Week*, p. 295.

37. Emerson, *Letters*, II, 415–416.
38. *Week*, p. 290.
39. Sanborn printed pages from this portion of the manuscript (which I here transcribe from the original in the Huntington Library) in *First and Last Journeys* (I, 105–113), but he rearranged the sequence and suppressed what he found embarrassing.

CHAPTER 8: THE STRATAGEMS OF CONSCIOUSNESS — ANTICIPATION

1. *Walden*, p. 19.
2. Thoreau, *Familiar Letters*, p. 163.
3. *J*, XI, 260.
4. *J*, XI, 301.
5. *J*, XI, 321.
6. *J*, XI, 375.
7. *J*, XI, 286.
8. *J*, XI, 324.
9. *J*, XI, 269–270.
10. *J*, I, 3–4.
11. *Week*, p. 375.
12. Emerson, *Letters*, II, 250.
13. Emerson, *Journals*, V, 451.
14. Emerson, *Letters*, II, 352.
15. Emerson, *Essays: First Series*, pp. 209–211. While I believe that a comparison of his *Journals'* version with the completed form reinforces my point that in printing Emerson's manuscripts the editors were well advised to leave out passages thus taken over, still I think it also testifies to the fecundity and spontaneity of Emerson's mind. "E.H." in the manuscript is undoubtedly Elizabeth Hoar, with whom Emerson could more safely discuss these matters than with Margaret Fuller, though perhaps not so instructively.
16. *J*, I, 279.
17. *J*, I, 277.
18. *J*, I, 330–331.

19. *Week*, p. 156.
20. *J*, I, 207–208.
21. *J*, II, 21–25.
22. *Week*, p. 304.
23. *J*, I, 148.
24. *J*, I, 324.
25. *Walden*, p. 336.
26. *Walden*, p. 339.
27. *Walden*, p. 336.
28. *Walden*, p. 346.

CHAPTER 9: A NOTE ON THE EDITING

1. *J*, I, 56.
2. *J*, I, 94.

PART II, THE JOURNAL

1. *J*, I, 342; *Week*, p. 107.
2. See reworkings of this, p. 151, and my comment, p. 236.
3. See p. 199.
4. See p. 200.
5. *Miscellanies*, p. 458.
6. See the revision of this, p. 151, and my comment, p. 236.
7. *J*, I, 357.
8. *Week*, p. 41.
9. *Week*, p. 45.
10. *J*, IV, 107.
11. *J*, I, 58: *The Service*, p. 4.
12. *The Service*, p. x.
13. *J*, II, 44.
14. *The Service*, pp. 17–18.

15. *The Service,* p. 19.
16. This is exactly as in "The Service"; *The Service,* p. 5.
17. *The Service,* p. 1.
18. *The Service,* pp. 1–2.
19. *The Service,* p. 3.
20. *Walden,* p. 358.
21. With a reordering of the sentences, in *The Service,* p. 21.
22. Verbatim, *loc. cit.*
23. *The Service,* p. 22.
24. *The Service,* p. 25.
25. *The Service,* p. 26.
26. *Sir Walter Raleigh,* p. 90.
27. *Week,* p. 186.
28. *Week,* p. 78.
29. *The Dial,* III, 19–40.
30. *Excursions,* p. 106.
31. *Week,* p. 124.
32. *J,* I, 12.
33. See Joseph Slater, "Music at Col. Grangerford's," *American Literature,* XXI (March 1949), 108–111.
34. Canby, *Thoreau,* p. 116.
35. Sanborn, *First and Last Journeys,* I, 67.
36. *J,* XI, 166.
37. *Week,* p. 271.
38. *Walden,* p. 90.
39. *Week,* p. 350.
40. *Walden,* p. 4.
41. *Week,* p. 323.
42. *Walden,* p. 54.
43. *Week,* p. 183.
44. *Week,* pp. 155–157.
45. See Sanborn, *First and Last Journeys,* I, 20–21.
46. *Raleigh,* p. 33.
47. *Raleigh,* p. 51.
48. *Raleigh,* pp. 21–22.
49. *Raleigh,* pp. 79–80.

50. *Week*, p. 158.
51. *Week*, p. 156; note how it is redesigned there to fit the mosaic. See above, pp. 114–115.
52. Marie Joseph de Gérando, *Histoire Comparée des Systèmes de Philosophie* (Paris, 1804, 1822), was avidly read by all the young Transcendentalists; from it they got most of their elementary ideas about oriental philosophy.
53. *Raleigh*, p. 85.
54. *Excursions*, pp. 131–132.
55. See *J*, I, 18.
56. *Week*, p. 362.
57. *Week*, p. 340.
58. See the *Week*, pp. 339–341.
59. *Week*, pp. 401–402.
60. *Miscellanies*, p. 475.
61. *Week*, p. 362.
62. *Loc. cit.*
63. *Week*, p. 162.
64. *Excursions*, p. 131.
65. *Week*, p. 133.
66. *Excursions*, p. 131.
67. *Week*, p. 65.
68. *J*, I, 33.
69. See *J*, I, 391; 1845?
70. *Week*, p. 402.
71. See the *Week*, p. 283: "Even the utmost good-will and harmony and practical kindness are not sufficient for Friendship, for Friends do not live in harmony merely, as some say, but in melody."
72. *Excursions*, pp. 130–131.
73. Emerson, *Letters*, II, 167.
74. *Ibid.*, p. 404.
75. See below, p. 238.
76. *Week*, p. 386.
77. *J*, II, 406.
78. *J*, III, 378.
79. *J*, V, 4.

80. See the *Week*, p. 331.
81. *The Dial*, IV, 211–218.
82. *Excursions*, pp. xiii, 175.
83. Emerson, *Letters*, II, 423.
84. *Week*, p. 183.
85. *Week*, pp. 338–339.
86. *Excursions*, p. xiii.
87. *Excursions*, p. 175.
88. *Excursions*, p. 176.
89. *Excursions*, p. 119.
90. *Excursions*, p. 178.
91. *Excursions*, pp. 168, 169.
92. *Excursions*, p. 174.
93. *Excursions*, p. 171.
94. *Excursions*, p. xiii.
95. *Walden*, pp. 132, 142, 280, 292.
96. *Week*, p. 339.
97. *J*, I, 300.
98. *The Dial*, II, 204.
99. *Excursions*, p. 167.
100. *The Maine Woods*, pp. 77–79.
101. Wendell Glick, "Three Early Manuscripts by Thoreau," *The Huntington Library Quarterly*, XV (November 1951), 66.
102. *J*, VII, 188.
103. *J*, IX, 145–146.
104. *Excursions*, p. 125.
105. *J*, I, 186–187.
106. *Excursions*, pp. 117–118.
107. *Week*, p. 296.
108. *The Dial*, III, 199.
109. Canby, *Thoreau*, p. 150.
110. *Ibid.*, pp. 263–265.
111. *Excursions*, pp. 106–107.
112. *Week*, pp. 93–94.
113. *J*, I, 151.
114. See Thoreau, *Familiar Letters*, p. 296.
115. Thoreau's annotation; see above, p. 10.

116. *The Dial,* II, 81.
117. Emerson, *Letters,* II, 395.
118. Cf., *Paradise Lost,* I, 288–290.
119. *Week,* pp. 105–106.
120. See "Notes on Textual Variants," following, pp. 235–240.

Notes on Textual Variants

133 "all our days." This and the next four entries are written on
the front cover lining. In this period, and indeed later,
Thoreau tried to keep the "contents" of his formal volumes
clear and finished, a witness of how he fashioned the material in the Ur-journal before transcribing it. But as he read
over his volumes, or possibly while doing the transcribing, he
would jot down inspirations or notes on the linings and fly-
leaves. Generally these are in pencil, though here the second
and fifth are in ink. In a sense these improvisations are not a
part of the *Journal*, which he would admit by his efforts
generally to fix them up and inscribe them at some later time.
134 "others have detected." This and the next four entries,
through "on the ash," are penciled scribblings on the flyleaf
recto, and must be considered improvisations more in the
manner of the Ur-journal than of the volumes we possess.
Even on this page he was reworking his original idea. Above
"Creator" he inserted "an inspired or demonic man." In the
next space he revised this, indicating by an arrow that he
would rather insert "a demon equal or superior to nature."
135 "would have been," "in the meanwhile." Both these are
scribblings on the flyleaf recto, the first pencil, the second
ink. Thoreau numbers the next page "1," and with the verse
beginning "I've heard my neighbor's pump" volume 3 of the
Journal properly begins.
139 "to thee I sing." Here Thoreau undertook to tinker without
coming to a decision — rather a rarity in the early volumes. I
give the entry as originally entered in ink. But of the first line
he crosses out with pencil "if" and "be objected," and above it
writes in: "Let me not because I stand apart from politics &
devote myself to the search after truth be accused," this ap-

parently intended to fasten on to "want of patriotism." He also knocks out "in like case" and "because he had withdrawn from it, and devoted himself to the search after truth"; also eliminated is "he replied" and above this is written "as Anaxagoras in a similar case." What he was trying to do is clear — to get from "us" to "I." As usual, he let nothing go to waste: he transferred the revised paragraph, with the grammar straightened out, to the journal of 1843; evidently it was to be worked into another essay on friendship, but it does not appear in anything he ever printed (Sanborn, *First and Last Journeys*, I, 136).

151 "the works of genius." This and the second passage after it reveal Thoreau at work. The manuscript shows that he first entered in ink one sentence: "Art is that which two may know — It is not lonely as Genius is." I guess that he next played with the idea on the flyleaf recto; he then wrote around his sentence in pencil, clearly incorporating it into the full statement as here given. I find it interesting that in the final form (*Week*, p. 350) he retained the word "demonic" from the flyleaf's draft (where it is "a demon equal or superior to nature"), which he did not use in either of these entries; yet in that final statement he left out any suggestion of the genius being "superior" to nature.

151 "house or *roof*." The phrases "that is," "a *seat* or *residence*" (the first time used), and "a roof or shelter" are later pencil insertions.

151 "originator or creator." This whole passage is in pencil, and would appear to be an effort to restate the already reworked passage two above it. The first writing is "he who performs"; over the verb Thoreau has written "originates."

153 "up in the path." This is the revised version. At first, Thoreau wrote "the prey of a speedy familiarity," changed it to "soon run over." Originally, "my mind" and "as near as Cathay, and as far too." Originally, "I can make," changed to "We."

155 "thoughts were dreams." Several interesting revisions: original second sentence, "The sun vaulted with elastic step"; "blue" inserted before "artery"; "the morning was as the eve of a deep

blue night" instead of "celestial day"; the sun "shone" instead of "seemed to shine"; "We floated noislessly" becomes "We flowed," and at first "through" the veins instead of "in."

156 "no one calculates." Thoreau first wrote "momentous," substituted "important."

161 "subject of instruction." This begins "Out of man's," which is then crossed out.

165 "in all these." Original has last sentence of first paragraph end with period after "experience"; "of the dumb members" is added.

168 "not at hand." The original, five sentences from the end, is "How clear the morning air is even at this day." Above it the revision inserts in pencil, "The world is well kept no rubbish accumulates," and below it "No dust has settled upon the grass." The sentence is then adjusted by a cancellation of "How clear" and the insertion of "clear" before "even at this day." This is an interesting revision because of the entire entry this segment was the one part he could salvage (*Week*, p. 340).

169 "the latest fashion." Original ending reads "latest Parisian fashion," with "Parisian" crossed out.

169 "bird of paradise." The original begins "To the finest talent or genius," revision substitutes "rarest" and indicates transposition of "genius" and "talent." The script at the beginning of next sentence is obscure; it seems to run: "Talent is the worst of lumber when not the best utensil." This is revised as here shown; when the passage goes into the *Week* (p. 362), the subject of the second sentence definitely becomes "Genius," to suit the revision of the last clause.

170 "can never reach." As revised here in pencil the paragraph goes with hardly any change into the *Week* (p. 362); original of first sentence is: "He is the best sailor who can steer within the fewest points of the wind, and makes the least occasion fill his sails longer." Minor revisions thereafter adjust to the cutting out of the last clause; "within the tropics" is moved from after "compass" to its present position.

174 "polishing the pyramids." "Our etiquette is for little men"

written with pencil. Original is "Think you if Socrates," with "Zoroaster or Homer or" inserted, and the following "he" changed to "they"; "of introduction" is pencil insertion after "letters." In the second paragraph, after "naturally" is inserted "from the roots upwards."

178 "not virtue's face." This entry is so inconclusively reworked that it is difficult to determine the intended final form. In first sentence of original, it goes "but certainly all he is." At beginning of second sentence, "Just as" is knocked out. The parentheses seem to indicate planned omissions. The second sentence of the second paragraph originally reads, "In his aspirations virtue is but a superficies and I know not . . ." Before "the features" a "but" is crossed out, and "whatever they are" is inserted above the line.

182 "of weights and measures." In the second paragraph, above "humanity," is an unfinished insertion: "and so is math — applied Arithmetick." The end of the third paragraph is originally written:

> Men demand that the truth be clothed in the warm colors of life and wear a flesh and blood dress. They do not love the absolute truth, but the partial, because it fits and measures them and their commodities best — but let them remember that notwithstanding these delinquencies in practice — Science still exists as the sealer of weights and measures.

188 "is the forest." Originally Thoreau writes "a much more agreeable fact," inserts "refreshing fact" above this without canceling.

191 "to hear — &c." Original in first sentence of last paragraph: "all the senses are indulged."

192 "wind, and rain." In first sentence, "at this season" is added in pencil. Next two sentences originally read: "A pine or two, with a dash of vapor in the sky — and an elysium is made. — Each tree takes my own attitude sometime."

199 "melts the *great snow*." In first sentence, "your voice rings"

is changed to "our voices ring." After "chamber," "&" is substituted for the dash. The first paragraph ends with a canceled sentence: "All sound in the woods is private and domestic still, though never so loud." The second paragraph originally begins: "I have observed of a clear winter's morning that . . ." In original, after "the shrub oak on the hill side" a phrase is struck out: "— and the green pine needles." The sentence, "The oaks have more heat than the pines, green is a cold color," is written in the margin, with line indicating the point of insertion.

200 "from Pluto's barn-yard." Original ends, "from over the styx."

207 "refraction of the light." This paragraph is so obviously struggled with that a minute chronicle of the corrections seems especially in order.

After "blue sky," above the dash, "when" is inserted. The "and" after "cope" then becomes superfluous, but is not crossed out. After "drops off," with a dash, the original reads, "for she plys me like wind and rain"; this being crossed out, Thoreau inserts as quoted. The parentheses remain as indicated. The original continues, "Her eyes are such bottomless and inexhaustible depths as if they were like the windows . . ." The "catch" in the following clause is originally "caught." In the original, "the native land of the soul" is followed by a period, but between the lines is written in pencil, "and from them comes a light which is not of the sun." As indicated, *"soular"* is underscored. It is one among many of his lamentable puns: he could not resist them!

209 "on the railroad." Originally Thoreau writes, "But if a man may forget it all," corrects this to, "But if a man sleep soundly he will forget it all . . ."

219 "are never alike." This entry is written on the back cover lining. It would seem that on this page, and on the blank page opposite it, Thoreau is worrying still further the idea he broached on January 11, that the face of genius may present contradictory profiles (above, p. 211). We are forced to assume that he, along with others, was noting this presentation

in Emerson. On the page opposite the back cover there are some penciled notes, the sum of which I can not decipher; to the extent that I am able to read them, they go:

> How much of those whom we know lack the knowledge not superficially but centrally vital to the case. Men distinguish only so much of our face as its necessary to see. I know my friends face though I see left half of it & yet I do not know the right side from the left & If ever he stand upon his head I should perceive the difference but if his right side were exchanged for his left I should not know it & yet portrait painters affirm that the two sides of the face are never alike.

In the ink passage on the back cover, which is clearly an effort to simplify and parse the above, Thoreau originally writes, "Yet I do not know the right side from the left — and if the right side were exchanged for the other," and revises this to read as here printed. In the last phrase he originally writes "we remember only total impressions," then changes "remember" to "retain."

219 "total impressions." On this back cover lining he also makes, as he does on every volume of the manuscript *Journal*, his index. This is interesting if only because it reveals what topics he conceived himself dealing with. I list his notations with an indication of those passages, within my pagination, he thus formulated:

No courage but hope, p. 144
The pathless regions of thought, p. 153
Cannot wheedle a Genius, p. 167
The bird of paradise flies against the wind, p. 169
Sincerity deeply laid like stone walls, p. 172
Etiquette for little men, p. 174
Every maggot lives downtown, p. 175
Show the Amatics [*sic*], p. 182

Index

Adams, Henry, 4, 43–44, 104
Alcott, Bronson, 38, 56–58, 62, 63, 74, 213; presence in Concord,
    14–16, 41, 133, 154–155, 173
Allen, Francis H., 3, 4, 6, 19, 109, 129

Blake, Harrison Gray Otis, 6–7, 32–33, 58, 89–90, 94, 106, 107, 128
Byron, 22, 34, 35, 50–54, 72, 74–75, 79, 88, 101, 103

Channing, Professor Edward Tyrrell, 39–47, 78
Channing, William Ellery, 16, 43
Channing, William Ellery (the younger), 6, 25–26, 39, 48–49, 55, 95,
    117

Dickinson, Emily, 4, 67, 117

Emerson, Ralph Waldo, 4, 14, 15, 35–36, 39, 55, 58, 65–66, 71, 104,
    117, 180, 209; relations with Thoreau, 9–10, 11–13, 33, 40, 41, 46,
    62, 76, 77, 81, 92, 95, 101, 129, 133, 137, 199, 213; editor of *Dial*,
    11–13, 17, 49–50, 157, 186, 195; and friendship, 87, 88–90, 99–100,
    11–11, 186
    Nature, 41, 42, 56–57
    Journals, 4, 22, 28, 29, 32, 110–114
Everett, Edward, 37, 43

Fuller, Margaret, 15, 49, 53, 56, 88, 89, 99–100, 105, 110–111, 116;
    attitude toward Thoreau, 11–12, 13, 39, 52, 109, 134, 137–138,
    142–143, 213

Gibbon, Edward, 193–194
Goethe, 28, 34, 50, 52
Goodwin, John, 29, 38

James, Henry, 4, 28

Joyce, James, 30–31, 93

Lowell, James Russell, 35, 45, 78, 81

Melville, Herman, 29, 45, 79, 96, 107, 117
Milton, John, 44, 217
Minott, George, 14, 15, 29, 154–155

Parker, Theodore, 12–13, 57, 58, 118, 213

Ripley, George, 14, 41

Sanborn, Franklin B., 6, 19, 23, 40, 43, 48, 83, 95, 101, 120, 140, 141
Sewall, Edmund, 10, 95
Sewall, Ellen Devereaux, 10, 82–86, 90, 95, 100, 101, 111, 136, 148, 161
Shakespeare, 28, 44, 96–99, 138
Sparks, Jared, 36–37, 38
Stevenson, Robert Louis, 77, 81, 94

Thoreau, Helen, 8, 101–102
Thoreau, Henry, early life, 8; relations with Harvard College, 9, 36–37, 40–48, 77, 102, 118; relations with Emerson, 9–10, 11–14, 46, 62, 64–65, 76, 77, 81, 92, 101; connection with *Dial*, 11–13; relations with Alcott, 14–16; correspondence with Williams, 56–75, 102, 105; attitude toward death, 66–74, 79, 105, 133, 188–190, 215; relations with Ellen Sewall, 82–87, 100, 101; on friendship, 87, 88–90, 96, 98–99, 100, 121–122, 176, 177–178, 202–204; on Shakespeare, 97; sets woods afire, 119–121
  "Aulus Persius Flaccus," 11–13, 17, 52
  "Friendship," 13, 202
  Journal, history of volume 3, 3–7, 18; method of composition, 20–27, 108–111; character of later sections, 29–34, 106–107, 204–205; Thoreau's conception of, 47–48, 51–54; relation to the *Week*, 67, 85–86, 110, 114–116, 121–125, 136, 145, 151–152, 167
  "The Landlord," 17
  "Natural History of Massachusetts," 17, 144–145, 166–167, 171, 172, 178–179, 197, 206, 207
  "Paradise (To Be) Regained," 17

Index

"The Service," 11–12, 15, 52–53, 136–144, 146

"Sic Vita," 13, 213

"Sir Walter Raleigh," 11, 21, 52, 53, 134, 143, 144, 156–159, 164–165

"Sympathy," 10, 95

Walden, 3, 4–5, 18, 20, 21, 29, 31, 54, 70–71, 75, 78, 79, 104, 106, 107, 116, 126–127, 151, 153, 199

"Walking," 79

"A Walk to Wachusett," 17

A Week on the Concord and Merrimack Rivers, 3, 4, 13, 21, 29, 54, 95, 207–208; method of composition, 17, 53, 67–69, 85–86, 109, 110, 114–116, 143, 144, 150, 154, 167, 169–170, 172–173, 174, 181–184, 187, 193, 199, 210, 218

"A Winter Walk," 186, 195, 197, 198, 199, 204

Thoreau, John, 8, 9, 10, 14, 16, 62, 84, 209; death of, 17, 33–34, 65, 67, 68, 71–72, 102

Thoreau, Sophia, 6, 8, 40

Torrey, Bradford, 3, 6, 19, 24, 29, 33, 109, 128–129

Washington, George, 196–197

Whitman, Walt, 44, 79, 107, 117

Williams, Isaiah Thornton, 55–66, 71–76, 80, 89, 102, 105

"Young America," in New York, 45–46, 77